Real-Resumes For Real Estate & Property Management Jobs

...including real resumes used to change careers
and resumes used to gain federal employment

Anne McKinney, Editor

PREP PUBLISHING

FAYETTEVILLE, NC

PREP Publishing

1110 ½ Hay Street

Fayetteville, NC 28305

(910) 483-6611

Library of Congress Cataloging-in-Publication Data

Real-resumes for real estate & property management jobs : ...including resumes used to change careers and resumes used to gain federal employment / Anne McKinney.
     p. cm. -- (Real-resumes series)
  ISBN 978-1475099881; 1475099886 (trade paper)
  1. Resumes (Employment) 2. Real estate business. I. McKinney, Anne, 1948- II. Series.

  HF5383.R395885 2006
  650.14'2'0243333--dc22   2006053534

Printed in the United States of America

Contents

Real-Resumes For Real Estate
& Property Management Jobs

Anne McKinney, Editor

A WORD FROM THE EDITOR:
ABOUT THE REAL-RESUMES SERIES

Welcome to the Real-Resumes Series. The Real-Resumes Series is a series of books which have been developed based on the experiences of real job hunters and which target specialized fields or types of resumes. As the editor of the series, I have carefully selected resumes and cover letters (with names and other key data disguised, of course) which have been used successfully in real job hunts. That's what we mean by "Real-Resumes." What you see in this book are *real* resumes and cover letters which helped real people get ahead in their careers.

We hope the superior samples will help you manage your current job campaign and your career so that you will find work aligned to your career interests.

The Real-Resumes Series is based on the work of the country's oldest resume-preparation company known as PREP Resumes. If you would like a free information packet describing the company's resume preparation services, call 910-483-6611 or write to PREP at 1110½ Hay Street, Fayetteville, NC 28305. If you have a job hunting experience you would like to share with our staff at the Real-Resumes Series, please contact us at preppub@aol.com or visit our website at www.prep-pub.com.

The resumes and cover letters in this book are designed to be of most value to people already in a job hunt or contemplating a career change. If we could give you one word of advice about your career, here's what we would say: Manage your career and don't stumble from job to job in an incoherent pattern. Try to find work that interests you, and then identify prosperous industries which need work performed of the type you want to do. Learn early in your working life that a great resume and cover letter can blow doors open for you and help you maximize your salary.

As the editor of this book, I would like to give you some tips on how to make the best use of the information you will find here. Because you are considering a career change, you already understand the concept of managing your career for maximum enjoyment and self-fulfillment. The purpose of this book is to provide expert tools and advice so that you *can* manage your career. Inside these pages you will find resumes and cover letters that will help you find not just a job but the type of work you want to do.

Overview of the Book

Every resume and cover letter in this book actually worked. And most of the resumes and cover letters have common features: most are one-page, most are in the chronological format, and most resumes are accompanied by a companion cover letter. In this section you will find helpful advice about job hunting. Step One begins with a discussion of why employers prefer the one-page, chronological resume. In Step Two you are introduced to the direct approach and to the proper format for a cover letter. In Step Three you learn the 14 main reasons why job hunters are not offered the jobs they want, and you learn the six key areas employers focus on when they interview you. Step Four gives nuts-and-bolts advice on how to handle the interview, send a follow-up letter after an interview, and negotiate your salary.

The cover letter plays such a critical role in a career change. You will learn from the experts how to format your cover letters and you will see suggested language to use in particular career-change situations. It has been said that "A picture is worth a thousand words" and, for that reason, you will see numerous examples of effective cover letters used by real individuals to change fields, functions, and industries.

The most important part of the book is the Real-Resumes section. Some of the individuals whose resumes and cover letters you see spent a lengthy career in an industry they loved. Then there are resumes and cover letters of people who wanted a change but who probably wanted to remain in their industry. Many of you will be especially interested by the resumes and cover letters of individuals who knew they definitely wanted a career change but had no idea what they wanted to do next. Other resumes and cover letters show individuals who knew they wanted to change fields and had a pretty good idea of what they wanted to do next.

Whatever your field, and whatever your circumstances, you'll find resumes and cover letters that will "show you the ropes" in terms of successfully changing jobs and switching careers.

Before you proceed further, think about why you picked up this book.
- Are you dissatisfied with the type of work you are now doing?
- Would you like to change careers, change companies, or change industries?
- Are you satisfied with your industry but not with your niche or function within it?
- Do you want to transfer your skills to a new product or service?
- Even if you have excelled in your field, have you "had enough"? Would you like the stimulation of a new challenge?
- Are you aware of the importance of a great cover letter but unsure of how to write one?
- Are you preparing to launch a second career after retirement?
- Have you been downsized, or do you anticipate becoming a victim of downsizing?
- Do you need expert advice on how to plan and implement a job campaign that will open the maximum number of doors?
- Do you want to make sure you handle an interview to your maximum advantage?

Introduction:
The Art of
Changing
Jobs...
and Finding
New Careers

- Would you like to master the techniques of negotiating salary and benefits?
- Do you want to learn the secrets and shortcuts of professional resume writers?

Using the Direct Approach

As you consider the possibility of a job hunt or career change, you need to be aware that most people end up having at least three distinctly different careers in their working lifetimes, and often those careers are different from each other. Yet people usually stumble through each job campaign, unsure of what they should be doing. Whether you find yourself voluntarily or unexpectedly in a job hunt, the direct approach is the job hunting strategy most likely to yield a full-time permanent job. The direct approach is an active, take-the-initiative style of job hunting in which you choose your next employer rather than relying on responding to ads, using employment agencies, or depending on other methods of finding jobs. You will learn how to use the direct approach in this book, and you will see that an effective cover letter is a critical ingredient in using the direct approach.

The "direct approach" is the style of job hunting most likely to yield the maximum number of job interviews.

Lack of Industry Experience Not a Major Barrier to Entering New Field

"Lack of experience" is often the last reason people are not offered jobs, according to the companies who do the hiring. If you are changing careers, you will be glad to learn that experienced professionals often are selling "potential" rather than experience in a job hunt. Companies look for personal qualities that they know tend to be present in their most effective professionals, such as communication skills, initiative, persistence, organizational and time management skills, and creativity. Frequently companies are trying to discover "personality type," "talent," "ability," "aptitude," and "potential" rather than seeking actual hands-on experience, so your resume should be designed to aggressively present your accomplishments. Attitude, enthusiasm, personality, and a track record of achievements in any type of work are the primary "indicators of success" which employers are seeking, and you will see numerous examples in this book of resumes written in an all-purpose fashion so that the professional can approach various industries and companies.

Using references in a skillful fashion in your job hunt will inspire confidence in prospective employers and help you "close the sale" after interviews.

The Art of Using References in a Job Hunt

You probably already know that you need to provide references during a job hunt, but you may not be sure of how and when to use references for maximum advantage. You can use references very creatively during a job hunt to call attention to your strengths and make yourself "stand out." Your references will rarely get you a job, no matter how impressive the names, but the way you use references can boost the employer's confidence in you and lead to a job offer in the least time.

You should ask from three to five people, including people who have supervised you, if you can use them as a reference during your job hunt. You may not be able to ask your current boss since your job hunt is probably confidential.

A common question in resume preparation is: "Do I need to put my references on my resume?" No, you don't. Even if you create a references page at the same time you prepare your resume, you don't need to mail, e-mail, or fax your references page with the resume and cover letter. Usually the potential employer is not interested in references until he meets you, so the earliest you need to have references ready is at the first interview. Obviously there are exceptions to this standard rule of thumb; sometimes an ad will ask you to send references with your first response. Wait until the employer requests references before providing them.

An excellent attention-getting technique is to take to the first interview not just a page of references (giving names, addresses, and telephone numbers) but an actual letter of reference written by someone who knows you well and who preferably has supervised or employed you. A professional way to close the first interview is to thank the interviewer, shake his or her hand, and then say you'd like to give him or her a copy of a letter of reference from a previous employer. Hopefully you already made a good impression during the interview, but you'll "close the sale" in a dynamic fashion if you leave a letter praising you and your accomplishments. For that reason, it's a good idea to ask supervisors during your final weeks in a job if they will provide you with a written letter of recommendation which you can use in future job hunts. Most employers will oblige, and you will have a letter that has a useful "shelf life" of many years. Such a letter often gives the prospective employer enough confidence in his opinion of you that he may forego checking out other references and decide to offer you the job on the spot or in the next few days.

Whom should you ask to serve as references? References should be people who have known or supervised you in a professional, academic, or work situation. References with big titles, like school superintendent or congressman, are fine, but remind busy people when you get to the interview stage that they may be contacted soon. Make sure the busy official recognizes your name and has instant positive recall of you! If you're asked to provide references on a formal company application, you can simply transcribe names from your references list. In summary, follow this rule in using references: If you've got them, flaunt them! If you've obtained well-written letters of reference, make sure you find a polite way to push those references under the nose of the interviewer so he or she can hear someone other than you describing your strengths. Your references probably won't ever get you a job, but glowing letters of reference can give you credibility and visibility that can make you stand out among candidates with similar credentials and potential!

The approach taken by this book is to (1) help you master the proven best techniques of conducting a job hunt and (2) show you how to stand out in a job hunt through your resume, cover letter, interviewing skills, as well as the way in which you present your references and follow up on interviews. Now, the best way to "get in the mood" for writing your own resume and cover letter is to select samples from the Table of Contents that interest you and then read them. A great resume is a "photograph," usually on one page, of an individual. If you wish to seek professional advice in preparing your resume, you may contact one of the professional writers at Professional Resume & Employment Publishing (PREP) for a brief free consultation by calling 1-910-483-6611.

With regard to references, it's best to provide the names and addresses of people who have supervised you or observed you in a work situation.

Part One: Some Advice About Your Job Hunt

What if you don't know what you want to do?

Your job hunt will be more comfortable if you can figure out what type of work you want to do. But you are not alone if you have no idea what you want to do next! You may have knowledge and skills in certain areas but want to get into another type of work. What *The Wall Street Journal* has discovered in its research on careers is that most of us end up having at least three distinctly different careers in our working lives; it seems that, even if we really like a particular kind of activity, twenty years of doing it is enough for most of us and we want to move on to something else!

That's why we strongly believe that you need to spend some time figuring out ***what interests you*** rather than taking an inventory of the skills you have. You may have skills that you simply don't want to use, but if you can build your career on the things that interest you, you will be more likely to be happy and satisfied in your job. Realize, too, that interests can change over time; the activities that interest you now may not be the ones that interested you years ago. For example, some professionals may decide that they've had enough of retail sales and want a job selling another product or service, even though they have earned a reputation for being an excellent retail manager. We strongly believe that interests rather than skills should be the determining factor in deciding what types of jobs you want to apply for and what directions you explore in your job hunt. Obviously one cannot be a lawyer without a law degree or a secretary without secretarial skills; but a professional can embark on a next career as a financial consultant, property manager, plant manager, production supervisor, retail manager, or other occupation if he/she has a strong interest in that type of work and can provide a resume that clearly demonstrates past excellent performance in *any* field and *potential* to excel in another field. As you will see later in this book, "lack of exact experience" is the last reason why people are turned down for the jobs they apply for.

How can you have a resume prepared if you don't know what you want to do?

You may be wondering how you can have a resume prepared if you don't know what you want to do next. The approach to resume writing which PREP, the country's oldest resume-preparation company, has used successfully for many years is to develop an "all-purpose" resume that translates your skills, experience, and accomplishments into language employers can understand. What most people need in a job hunt is a versatile resume that will allow them to apply for numerous types of jobs. For example, you may want to apply for a job in pharmaceutical sales but you may also want to have a resume that will be versatile enough for you to apply for jobs in the construction, financial services, or automotive industries.

Based on more than 20 years of serving job hunters, we at PREP have found that your best approach to job hunting is **an all-purpose resume** and **specific cover letters tailored to specific fields** rather than using the approach of trying to create different resumes for every job. If you are remaining in your field, you may not even need more than one "all-purpose" cover letter, although the cover letter rather than the resume is the place to communicate your interest in a narrow or specific field. An all-purpose resume and cover letter that translate your experience and accomplishments into plain English are the tools that will maximize the number of doors which open for you while permitting you to "fish" in the widest range of job areas.

Figure out what interests you and you will hold the key to a successful job hunt and working career. (And be prepared for your interests to change over time!)

"Lack of exact experience" is the last reason people are turned down for the jobs for which they apply.

Your resume will provide the script for your job interview.
When you get down to it, your resume has a simple job to do: Its purpose is to blow as many doors open as possible and to make as many people as possible want to meet you. So a well-written resume that really "sells" you is a key that will create opportunities for you in a job hunt.

This statistic explains why: The typical newspaper advertisement for a job opening receives more than 245 replies. And normally only 10 or 12 will be invited to an interview.

But here's another purpose of the resume: it provides the "script" the employer uses when he interviews you. If your resume has been written in such a way that your strengths and achievements are revealed, that's what you'll end up talking about at the job interview. Since the resume will govern what you get asked about at your interviews, you can't overestimate the importance of making sure your resume makes you look and sound as good as you are.

Your resume is the "script" for your job interviews. Make sure you put on your resume what you want to talk about or be asked about at the job interview.

So what is a "good" resume?
Very literally, your resume should motivate the person reading it to dial the phone number or e-mail the screen name you have put on the resume. When you are relocating, you should put a local phone number on your resume if your physical address is several states away; employers are more likely to dial a local telephone number than a long-distance number when they're looking for potential employees.

If you have a resume already, look at it objectively. Is it a limp, colorless "laundry list" of your job titles and duties? Or does it "paint a picture" of your skills, abilities, and accomplishments in a way that would make someone want to meet you? Can people understand what you're saying? If you are attempting to change fields or industries, can potential employers see that your skills and knowledge are transferable to other environments? For example, have you described accomplishments which reveal your problem-solving abilities or communication skills?

The one-page resume in chronological format is the format preferred by most employers.

How long should your resume be?
One page, maybe two. Usually only people in the academic community have a resume (which they usually call a *curriculum vitae*) longer than one or two pages. Remember that your resume is almost always accompanied by a cover letter, and a potential employer does not want to read more than two or three pages about a total stranger in order to decide if he wants to meet that person! Besides, don't forget that the more you tell someone about yourself, the more opportunity you are providing for the employer to screen you out at the "first-cut" stage. A resume should be concise and exciting and designed to make the reader want to meet you in person!

Should resumes be functional or chronological?
Employers almost always prefer a chronological resume; in other words, an employer will find a resume easier to read if it is immediately apparent what your current or most recent job is, what you did before that, and so forth, in reverse chronological order. A resume that goes back in detail for the last ten years of employment will generally satisfy the employer's curiosity about your background. Employment more than ten years old can be shown even more briefly in an "Other Experience" section at the end of your "Experience" section. Remember that your intention is not to tell everything you've done but to "hit the high points" and especially impress the employer with what you learned, contributed, or accomplished in each job you describe.

Once you get your resume, what do you do with it?

You will be using your resume to answer ads, as a tool to use in talking with friends and relatives about your job search, and, most importantly, in using the "direct approach" described in this book.

When you e-mail, fax, or mail your resume, always send a "cover letter."

A "cover letter," sometimes called a "resume letter" or "letter of interest," is a letter that accompanies and introduces your resume. Your cover letter is a way of personalizing the resume by sending it to the specific person you think you might want to work for at each company. Your cover letter should contain a few highlights from your resume—just enough to make someone want to meet you. Cover letters should always be typed or word processed on a computer—never handwritten.

Never e-mail, mail, or fax your resume without a cover letter.

1. Learn the art of answering ads.

There is an "art," part of which can be learned, in using your "bestselling" resume to reply to advertisements.

Sometimes an exciting job lurks behind a boring ad that someone dictated in a hurry, so reply to any ad that interests you. Don't worry that you aren't "25 years old with an MBA" like the ad asks for. Employers will always make compromises in their requirements if they think you're the "best fit" overall.

What about ads that ask for "salary requirements?"

What if the ad you're answering asks for "salary requirements?" The first rule is to avoid committing yourself in writing at that point to a specific salary. You don't want to "lock yourself in."

There are two ways to handle the ad that asks for "salary requirements."

What if the ad asks for your "salary requirements?"

First, you can ignore that part of the ad and accompany your resume with a cover letter that focuses on "selling" you, your abilities, and even some of your philosophy about work or your field. You may include a sentence in your cover letter like this: "I can provide excellent personal and professional references at your request, and I would be delighted to share the private details of my salary history with you in person."

Second, if you feel you must give some kind of number, just state a range in your cover letter that includes your medical, dental, other benefits, and expected bonuses. You might state, for example, "My current compensation, including benefits and bonuses, is in the range of $30,000-$40,000."

Analyze the ad and "tailor" yourself to it.

When you're replying to ads, a finely tailored cover letter is an important tool in getting your resume noticed and read. On the next page is a cover letter which has been "tailored to fit" a specific ad. Notice the "art" used by PREP writers of analyzing the ad's main requirements and then writing the letter so that the person's background, work habits, and interests seem "tailor-made" to the company's needs. Use this cover letter as a model when you prepare your own reply to ads.

Date

Exact Name of Person
Exact Title
Exact Name of Company
Address
City, State, Zip

Dear Exact Name of Person (or Dear Sir or Madam if answering a blind ad):

With the enclosed resume, I would like to express my interest in exploring employment opportunities with your organization.

As you will see from my resume, I have excelled in a track record of promotion with a company involved in property management. I have earned a reputation as a gifted problem solver while managing up to 350 units. Before I took over the management of Meadow Brooks Apartments, the complex was in disrepair and had a poor reputation. With the blessing of the owners, I brought overdue maintenance projects up-to-date and managed inexpensive landscaping projects that gave the complex a glamorous new look. The complex now has an outstanding reputation, and there is a waiting list for apartments, which are now 100% occupied.

I can provide outstanding references from my employer, who recently sold Meadow Brooks Apartments to an out-of-state company. Although I was offered a senior management position by the new owners, I have decided to selectively explore opportunities in other property management organizations. I would appreciate your holding my interest in your company in confidence at this time.

I believe that my success in the property management field thus far has been due to my ability to look at each problem I encounter with a creative yet practical problem-solving approach. To use the vernacular, I am able to "think outside the box." I take pride in the contributions I have made to my employer's bottom line through maximizing occupancy and boosting customer satisfaction to record levels. I offer an ability to work effectively with others at all organizational levels.

I hope you will call or write me soon to suggest a time convenient for us to meet to discuss your current and future needs and how I might serve them. Thank you in advance for your time.

Sincerely,

Jared Coolidge

Alternate last paragraph:
I hope you will welcome my call soon to arrange a brief meeting to discuss your current and future needs and how I might serve them. Thank you in advance for your time.

Employers are trying to identify the individual who wants the job they are filling. Don't be afraid to express your enthusiasm in the cover letter!

2. Talk to friends and relatives.

Don't be shy about telling your friends and relatives the kind of job you're looking for. Looking for the job you want involves using your network of contacts, so tell people what you're looking for. They may be able to make introductions and help set up interviews.

About 25% of all interviews are set up through "who you know," so don't ignore this approach.

3. Finally, and most importantly, use the "direct approach."

The "direct approach" is a strategy in which you choose your next employer.

More than 50% of all job interviews are set up by the "direct approach." That means you actually mail, e-mail, or fax a resume and a cover letter to a company you think might be interesting to work for.

To whom do you write?

In general, you should write directly to the *exact name* of the person who would be hiring you: say, the vice-president of marketing or data processing. If you're in doubt about to whom to address the letter, address it to the president by name and he or she will make sure it gets forwarded to the right person within the company who has hiring authority in your area.

How do you find the names of potential employers?

You're not alone if you feel that the biggest problem in your job search is finding the right names at the companies you want to contact. But you can usually figure out the names of companies you want to approach by deciding first if your job hunt is primarily geography-driven or industry-driven.

In a **geography-driven job hunt,** you could select a list of, say, 50 companies you want to contact **by location** from the lists that the U.S. Chambers of Commerce publish yearly of their "major area employers." There are hundreds of local Chambers of Commerce across America, and most of them will have an 800 number which you can find through 1-800-555-1212. If you and your family think Atlanta, Dallas, Ft. Lauderdale, and Virginia Beach might be nice places to live, for example, you could contact the Chamber of Commerce in those cities and ask how you can obtain a copy of their list of major employers. Your nearest library will have the book which lists the addresses of all chambers.

In an **industry-driven job hunt,** and if you are willing to relocate, you will be identifying the companies which you find most attractive in the industry in which you want to work. When you select a list of companies to contact **by industry,** you can find the right person to write and the address of firms by industrial category in *Standard and Poor's, Moody's,* and other excellent books in public libraries. Many Web sites also provide contact information.

Many people feel it's a good investment to actually call the company to either find out or double-check the name of the person to whom they want to send a resume and cover letter. It's important to do as much as you feasibly can to assure that the letter gets to the right person in the company.

On-line research will be the best way for many people to locate organizations to which they wish to send their resume. It is outside the scope of this book to teach Internet research skills, but librarians are often useful in this area.

What's the correct way to follow up on a resume you send?

There is a polite way to be aggressively interested in a company during your job hunt. It is ideal to end the cover letter accompanying your resume by saying, "I hope you'll welcome my call next week when I try to arrange a brief meeting at your convenience to discuss your current and future needs and how I might serve them." Keep it low key, and just ask for a "brief meeting," not an interview. Employers want people who show a determined interest in working with them, so don't be shy about following up on the resume and cover letter you've mailed.

> It pays to be aware of the 14 most common pitfalls for job hunters.

STEP THREE: Preparing for Interviews

But a resume and cover letter by themselves can't get you the job you want. You need to "prep" yourself before the interview. Step Three in your job campaign is "Preparing for Interviews." First, let's look at interviewing from the hiring organization's point of view.

What are the biggest "turnoffs" for potential employers?

One of the ways to help yourself perform well at an interview is to look at the main reasons why organizations *don't* hire the people they interview, according to those who do the interviewing.

Notice that "lack of appropriate background" (or lack of experience) is the *last* reason for not being offered the job.

The 14 Most Common Reasons Job Hunters Are Not Offered Jobs (according to the companies who do the interviewing and hiring):

1. Low level of accomplishment
2. Poor attitude, lack of self-confidence
3. Lack of goals/objectives
4. Lack of enthusiasm
5. Lack of interest in the company's business
6. Inability to sell or express yourself
7. Unrealistic salary demands
8. Poor appearance
9. Lack of maturity, no leadership potential
10. Lack of extracurricular activities
11. Lack of preparation for the interview, no knowledge about company
12. Objecting to travel
13. Excessive interest in security and benefits
14. Inappropriate background

Department of Labor studies have proven that smart, "prepared" job hunters can increase their beginning salary while getting a job in *half* the time it normally takes. (4½ months is the average national length of a job search.) Here, from PREP, are some questions that can prepare you to find a job faster.

Are you in the "right" frame of mind?

It seems unfair that we have to look for a job just when we're lowest in morale. Don't worry *too* much if you're nervous before interviews. You're supposed to be a little nervous, especially if the job means a lot to you. But the best way to kill unnecessary fears about job hunting is through 1) making sure you have a great resume and 2) preparing yourself for the interview. Here are three main areas you need to think about before each interview.

Do you know what the company does?

Don't walk into an interview giving the impression that, "If this is Tuesday, this must be General Motors."

Research the company before you go to interviews.

Find out before the interview what the company's main product or service is. Where is the company heading? Is it in a "growth" or declining industry? (Answers to these questions may influence whether or not you want to work there!)

Information about what the company does is in annual reports, in newspaper and magazine articles, and on the Internet. If you're not yet skilled at Internet research, just visit your nearest library and ask the reference librarian to guide you to printed materials on the company.

Do you know what you want to do for the company?

Before the interview, try to decide how you see yourself fitting into the company. Remember, "lack of exact background" the company wants is usually the last reason people are not offered jobs.

Understand before you go to each interview that the burden will be on you to "sell" the interviewer on why you're the best person for the job and the company.

How will you answer the critical interview questions?

Anticipate the questions you will be asked at the interview, and prepare your responses in advance.

Put yourself in the interviewer's position and think about the questions you're most likely to be asked. Here are some of the most commonly asked interview questions:

Q: "What are your greatest strengths?"

A: Don't say you've never thought about it! Go into an interview knowing the three main impressions you want to leave about yourself, such as "I'm hard-working, loyal, and an imaginative cost-cutter."

Q: "What are your greatest weaknesses?"

A: Don't confess that you're lazy or have trouble meeting deadlines! Confessing that you tend to be a "workaholic" or "tend to be a perfectionist and sometimes get frustrated when others don't share my high standards" will make your prospective employer see a "weakness" that he likes. Name a weakness that your interviewer will perceive as a strength.

Q: "What are your long-range goals?"

A: If you're interviewing with Microsoft, don't say you want to work for IBM in five years! Say your long-range goal is to be *with* the company, contributing to its goals and success.

Q: "What motivates you to do your best work?"

A: Don't get dollar signs in your eyes here! "A challenge" is not a bad answer, but it's a little cliched. Saying something like "troubleshooting" or "solving a tough problem" is more interesting and specific. Give an example if you can.

Q: "What do you know about this organization?"

A: Don't say you never heard of it until they asked you to the interview! Name an interesting, positive thing you learned about the company recently from your research. Remember, company executives can sometimes feel rather "maternal" about the company they serve. Don't get onto a negative area of the company if you can think of positive facts you can bring up. Of course, if you learned in your research that the company's sales seem to be taking a nose-dive, or that the company president is being prosecuted for taking bribes, you might politely ask your interviewer to tell you something that could help you better understand what you've been reading. Those are the kinds of company facts that can help you determine whether or not you want to work there.

Go to an interview prepared to tell the company why it should hire you.

Q: "Why should I hire you?"

A: "I'm unemployed and available" is the wrong answer here! Get back to your strengths and say that you believe the organization could benefit by a loyal, hard-working cost-cutter like yourself.

In conclusion, you should decide in advance, before you go to the interview, how you will answer each of these commonly asked questions. Have some practice interviews with a friend to role-play and build your confidence.

STEP FOUR: Handling the Interview and Negotiating Salary

Now you're ready for Step Four: actually handling the interview successfully and effectively. Remember, the purpose of an interview is to get a job offer.

A smile at an interview makes the employer perceive of you as intelligent!

Eight "do's" for the interview

According to leading U.S. companies, there are eight key areas in interviewing success. You can fail at an interview if you mishandle just one area.

1. **Do wear appropriate clothes.**

You can never go wrong by wearing a suit to an interview.

2. **Do be well groomed.**

Don't overlook the obvious things like having clean hair, clothes, and fingernails for the interview.

3. **Do give a firm handshake.**

You'll have to shake hands twice in most interviews: first, before you sit down, and second, when you leave the interview. Limp handshakes turn most people off.

4. **Do smile and show a sense of humor.**

Interviewers are looking for people who would be nice to work with, so don't be so somber that you don't smile. In fact, research shows that people who smile at interviews are perceived as more intelligent. So, smile!

5. **Do be enthusiastic.**

Employers say they are "turned off" by lifeless, unenthusiastic job hunters who show no special interest in that company. The best way to show some enthusiasm for the employer's operation is to find out about the business beforehand.

6. Do show you are flexible and adaptable.

An employer is looking for someone who can contribute to his organization in a flexible, adaptable way. No matter what skills and training you have, employers know every new employee must go through initiation and training on the company's turf. Certainly show pride in your past accomplishments in a specific, factual way ("I saved my last employer $50.00 a week by a new cost-cutting measure I developed"). But don't come across as though there's nothing about the job you couldn't easily handle.

7. Do ask intelligent questions about the employer's business.

An employer is hiring someone because of certain business needs. Show interest in those needs. Asking questions to get a better idea of the employer's needs will help you "stand out" from other candidates interviewing for the job.

8. Do "take charge" when the interviewer "falls down" on the job.

Go into every interview knowing the three or four points about yourself you want the interviewer to remember. And be prepared to take an active part in leading the discussion if the interviewer's "canned approach" does not permit you to display your "strong suit." You can't always depend on the interviewer's asking you the "right" questions so you can stress your strengths and accomplishments.

Employers are seeking people with good attitudes whom they can train and coach to do things their way.

An important "don't": Don't ask questions about salary or benefits at the first interview. Employers don't take warmly to people who look at their organization as just a place to satisfy salary and benefit needs. Don't risk making a negative impression by appearing greedy or self-serving. The place to discuss salary and benefits is normally at the second interview, and the employer will bring it up. Then you can ask questions without appearing excessively interested in what the organization can do for you.

Now…negotiating your salary

Even if an ad requests that you communicate your "salary requirement" or "salary history," you should avoid providing those numbers in your initial cover letter. You can usually say something like this: "I would be delighted to discuss the private details of my salary history with you in person."

Once you're at the interview, you must avoid even appearing *interested* in salary before you are offered the job. Make sure you've "sold" yourself before talking salary. First show you're the "best fit" for the employer and then you'll be in a stronger position from which to negotiate salary. **Never** bring up the subject of salary yourself. Employers say there's no way you can avoid looking greedy if you bring up the issue of salary and benefits before the company has identified you as its "best fit."

Don't appear excessively interested in salary and benefits at the interview.

Interviewers sometimes throw out a salary figure at the first interview to see if you'll accept it. You may not want to commit yourself if you think you will be able to negotiate a better deal later on. Get back to finding out more about the job. This lets the interviewer know you're interested primarily in the job and not the salary.

When the organization brings up salary, it may say something like this: "Well, Mary, we think you'd make a good candidate for this job. What kind of salary are we talking about?" You may not want to name a number here, either. Give the ball back to the interviewer. Act as though you hadn't given the subject of salary much thought and respond something like this: "Ah, Mr. Jones, I wonder if you'd be kind enough to tell me what salary you had in mind when you advertised the job?" Or … "What is the range you have in mind?"

Don't worry, if the interviewer names a figure that you think is too low, you can say so without turning down the job or locking yourself into a rigid position. The point here is to negotiate for yourself as well as you can. You might reply to a number named by the interviewer that you think is low by saying something like this: "Well, Mr. Lee, the job interests me very much, and I think I'd certainly enjoy working with you. But, frankly, I was thinking of something a little higher than that." That leaves the ball in your interviewer's court again, and you haven't turned down the job either, in case it turns out that the interviewer can't increase the offer and you still want the job.

<aside>Salary negotiation can be tricky.</aside>

Last, send a follow-up letter.

Mail, e-mail, or fax a letter right after the interview telling your interviewer you enjoyed the meeting and are certain (if you are) that you are the "best fit" for the job. The people interviewing you will probably have an attitude described as either "professionally loyal" to their companies, or "maternal and proprietary" if the interviewer also owns the company. In either case, they are looking for people who want to work for *that* company in particular. The follow-up letter you send might be just the deciding factor in your favor if the employer is trying to choose between you and someone else. You will see an example of a follow-up letter on page 16.

<aside>A follow-up letter can help the employer choose between you and another qualified candidate.</aside>

A cover letter is an essential part of a job hunt or career change.

Many people are aware of the importance of having a great resume, but most people in a job hunt don't realize just how important a cover letter can be. The purpose of the cover letter, sometimes called a **"letter of interest,"** is to introduce your resume to prospective employers. The cover letter is often the critical ingredient in a job hunt because the cover letter allows you to say a lot of things that just don't "fit" on the resume. For example, you can emphasize your commitment to a new field and stress your related talents. The cover letter also gives you a chance to stress outstanding character and personal values. On the next two pages you will see examples of very effective cover letters.

<aside>**A cover letter is an essential part of a career change.**

Please do not attempt to implement a career change without a cover letter. A cover letter is the first impression of you, and you can influence the way an employer views you by the language and style of your letter.</aside>

Special help for those in career change

We want to emphasize again that, especially in a career change, the cover letter is very important and can help you "build a bridge" to a new career. A creative and appealing cover letter can begin the process of encouraging the potential employer to imagine you in an industry other than the one in which you have worked.

As a special help to those in career change, there are resumes and cover letters included in this book which show valuable techniques and tips you should use when changing fields or industries. The resumes and cover letters of career changers are identified in the table of contents as "Career Change" and you will see the "Career Change" label on cover letters in Part Two where the individuals are changing careers.

Date

**Addressing the Cover
Letter:** Get the exact
name of the person to
whom you are writing. This
makes your approach
personal.

Exact Name of Person
Title or Position
Name of Company
Address
City, State, Zip

Dear Exact Name of Person (or Dear Sir or Madam if answering a blind ad):

First Paragraph: This
explains why you are
writing.

With the enclosed resume, I would like to make you aware of my interest in exploring employment opportunities with your organization and introduce you to my background.

Second Paragraph: You
have a chance to talk
about whatever you feel is
your most distinguishing
feature.

As you will see from my resume, I graduated from Troy State University at Montgomery, AL, where I pursued a major emphasizing sales, marketing, communications, and customer service. After graduation, I accepted two positions in two different companies, and I have become a master at "juggling" my time for maximum efficiency while excelling in jobs in two industries. As a Property Manager for apartment units in AL and GA, I oversee all aspects of bookkeeping while also managing small crews performing repairs and maintenance. As a Marketing Consultant with an insurance company, I have increased sales 5% in six months, and the company projects a 15% annual increase. I am an extremely hardworking and ambitious individual with strong communication and problem-solving skills, and I have learned a great deal by working simultaneously in the insurance business and property management industry.

Third Paragraph: You
bring up your next most
distinguishing qualities and
try to
sell yourself.

While earning my degree at TSU, I worked as a Commissioned Sales Associate, and I played a key role in boosting overall appliance department sales by 15%. Even before my sales experience with Home Depot, I was accustomed to influencing others through my strong communication skills and leadership ability. In high school, I was elected Captain of my varsity soccer team and President of the French Club. I am a highly motivated individual to whom others naturally turn for leadership and direction.

Fourth Paragraph: Here
you have another
opportunity to reveal
qualities or achievements
which will impress your
future employer.

I have decided that I wish to make a permanent career in real estate sales, and I am confident I could make major contributions to the bottom line of an organization that appreciates persistent hard chargers with intellect and charisma. I offer a proven ability to focus my energies in order to maximize profitability and customer satisfaction.

Final Paragraph: He asks
the employer to contact
him. Make sure your
reader knows what the
"next step" is.

If my background and skills interest you, I hope you will contact me to suggest a time when we could meet in person to discuss your needs. Thank you.

Sincerely,

Aaron Friedman

**Alternate Final
Paragraph:** It's more
aggressive (but not too
aggressive) to let the
employer know that you
will be calling him or her.
Don't be afraid to be
persistent. Employers are
looking for people who
know what they want to
do.

Alternate final paragraph: I would enjoy the opportunity to talk with you briefly to see if my background interests you, and I hope you will welcome my call. Thank you in advance for your courtesies.

Date

Exact Name of Person
Title of Person
Name of Company
Address
City, State, Zip

Dear Exact Name of Person: (or Sir or Madam if answering a blind ad.)

Can you use an enthusiastic, results-oriented sales manager who offers outstanding communication skills, a talent for reading people, and a reputation for determination and persistence in reaching goals? I am responding to your online ad for a Property Manager.

With a proven background of success in sales, I have displayed my versatility while selling and marketing a wide variety of products and services including residential real estate and land, new and used automobiles, and financial products/ investment services. In one job I trained and supervised a successful team of mutual fund and insurance sales agents. Most recently as a Real Estate Broker and General Manager of a real estate firm, I achieved the $3 million mark in sales while training and developing junior associates who have become top producers. While excelling in all aspects of the business, I have used my experience to create marketing strategies which reached large audiences and generated much business.

Earlier experience gave me an opportunity to refine my sales and communication abilities as well as gain familiarity with business management including finance and collections, inventory control, personnel administration, and customer service. Prior to owning and managing a business which bought, reconditioned, and marketed automobiles, I was one of Houston Buick's most successful sales professionals, earning the distinction of "Salesman of the Month" for 13 consecutive months and "Salesman of the Year."

If you can use a seasoned professional with the ability to solve tough business problems, maximize profitability, and increase market share under highly competitive conditions, I would enjoy an opportunity to meet with you to discuss your needs and how I might serve them. I can provide outstanding references.

I hope you will welcome my call soon to arrange a brief meeting at your convenience. Thank you in advance for your time.

Sincerely,

Keith Toomey

This accomplished professional is responding to an advertisement. He analyzed the job vacancy opening very closely and he has made sure that he has tailored his letter of interest to the areas mentioned in the vacancy announcement.

Date

Exact Name of Person
Title or Position
Name of Company
Address (number and street)
Address (city, state, and zip)

Follow-up Letter

A great follow-up letter
can motivate the
employer
to make the job offer,
and the salary offer may
be influenced by the
style and tone of your
follow-up
letter, too!

Dear Exact Name:

I am writing to express my appreciation for the time you spent with me on December 9, and I want to let you know that I am sincerely interested in the position of Senior Property Manager which we discussed.

I feel confident that I could skillfully interact with your staff, and I would cheerfully relocate to Tennessee, as we discussed.

As you described to me what you are looking for in the person who fills this position, I had a sense of "déjà vu" because my current employer was in a similar position when I went to work for them. The general manager needed someone to come in and be his "right arm" and take on an increasing amount of his management responsibilities so that he could be freed up to do other things. I have played a key role in the growth and success of the organization, and my supervisor has come to depend on my sound advice as much as well as my proven ability to "cut through" huge volumes of work efficiently and accurately. Since this is one of the busiest times of the year for my employer, I feel that I could not leave during that time. I could certainly make myself available by mid-January.

It would be a pleasure to work for your organization, and I am confident that I could contribute significantly through my strong qualities of loyalty, reliability, and trustworthiness. I am confident that I could quickly learn your style and procedures, and I would welcome being trained to do things your way.

Yours sincerely,

Jacob Evangelisto

PART TWO:
Real-Resumes for Real Estate
& Property Management Jobs

In this section, you will find resumes and cover letters of professionals seeking employment, or already employed, in the real estate world. How do these individuals differ from other job hunters? Why should there be a book dedicated to people seeking jobs in related to real estate and property management? Based on more than 20 years of experience in working with job hunters, this editor is convinced that resumes and cover letters which "speak the lingo" of the field you wish to enter will communicate more effectively than language which is not industry-specific. This book is designed to help people (1) who are seeking to prepare their own resumes and (2) who wish to use as models "real" resumes of individuals who have successfully launched careers in real estate organizations or advanced in those organizations. You will see a wide range of experience levels reflected in the resumes in this book. Some of the resumes and cover letters were used by individuals seeking to enter the field; others were used successfully by senior professionals to advance in the field.

Newcomers to an industry sometimes have advantages over more experienced professionals. In a job hunt, junior professionals can have an advantage over their more experienced counterparts. Prospective employers often view the less experienced workers as "more trainable" and "more coachable" than their seniors. This means that the mature professional who has already excelled in a first career can, with credibility, "change careers" and transfer skills to other industries.

Newcomers to the field may have disadvantages compared to their seniors. Almost by definition, the inexperienced professional—the young person who has recently entered the job market, or the individual who has recently received respected certifications—is less tested and less experienced than senior managers, so the resume and cover letter of the inexperienced professional may often have to "sell" his or her potential to do something he or she has never done before. Lack of experience in the field she wants to enter can be a stumbling block to the junior employee, but remember that many employers believe that someone who has excelled in anything—academics, for example—can excel in many other fields.

Some advice to inexperienced professionals...
If senior professionals could give junior professionals a piece of advice about careers, here's what they would say: Manage your career and don't stumble from job to job in an incoherent pattern. Try to find work that interests you, and then identify prosperous industries which need work performed of the type you want to do. Learn early in your working life that a great resume and cover letter can blow doors open for you and help you maximize your salary.

Special help for career changers...
For those changing careers, you will find useful the resumes and cover letters marked "Career Change" on the following pages. Consult the Table of Contents for page numbers showing career changers.

Date

Exact Name of Person
Title or Position
Name of Company
Address
City, State, Zip

APARTMENT COMPLEX MANAGER

Dear Exact Name of Person: (or Dear Sir or Madam if answering a blind ad)

With the enclosed resume, I would like to indicate my interest in your organization and my desire to explore employment opportunities. I am in the process of relocating permanently to the Ashland area, where my family lives, and I can provide outstanding references from my current employer.

As you will see from my enclosed resume, I offer extensive experience in all aspects of apartment rentals management. On my own initiative, I directed the set-up of 35 corporate apartments and personally marketed the concept to area businesses. This concept has been so successful that the owners of the complex have decided to double the number of corporate rentals by next year.

In previous experience, I was employed for six years by a property management corporation in Oregon, where I was promoted from Leasing Manager to Marketing Manager, a newly created position. In every job I have held, employers have praised my strong personal initiative and resourcefulness. In that job, for example, I was credited with decreasing the number of delinquent accounts through my determination and persistence.

I hope you will welcome my call soon to arrange a brief meeting at your convenience to discuss your current and future needs and how I might serve them. Thank you in advance for your time.

Sincerely yours.

Annette Chase

ANNETTE CHASE

1110½ Hay Street, Fayetteville, NC 28305 • preppub@aol.com • (910) 483-6611

OBJECTIVE

To benefit an organization that can use an articulate, motivated professional with exceptional communication, organizational, and negotiation skills who offers experience in accounts payable, accounts receivable, and office management.

EXPERIENCE

APARTMENT COMPLEX MANAGER. Grant's Village, Portland, OR (2001-present). Supervise all aspects of the operation of an exclusive 200-unit apartment complex, including overseeing leasing and maintenance as well as coordinating the fitness center and landscaping efforts.

- Process accounts payable, making disbursements for corporate utility bills; maintenance and other upkeep; advertising and promotions; and other expenses.
- Manage accounts receivable, taking in monthly lease payments from existing residents and security deposits from new residents, as well as other payments.
- Develop and maintain excellent relationships with local vendors, setting up new accounts and preserving connections with existing suppliers.
- Supervise one office employee and a three-person maintenance crew.
- Direct the rental and set-up of 35 corporate apartments.
- Inspect units being vacated; schedule cleaning and maintenance to ensure apartments are prepared for incoming residents.

Excelled in the following track record of advancement to increasing responsibilities with UDC of Oregon (1995-01).

MARKETING ASSOCIATE. The Village at Smithfield, Portland, OR (1996-01). Was promoted by UDC to a newly created position with this 356-unit complex; was subsequently credited with decreasing the number of delinquent accounts through my collections skill and knowledge in handling cases through Small Claims Court.

- Performed accounts payable and receivable, processing bills from vendors and utility companies for property and receiving lease payments and security deposits from residents.
- Processed lease applications and familiarized new residents with our lease and policies; conducted move-in and move-out inspections.
- Supervised and trained one employee; processed weekly reports promptly.
- Oversaw two corporate accounts.

LEASING MANAGER/ASSISTANT MANAGER. Morganton & Associates, Portland, OR (1995-96). Began with the company as a floating leasing agent and was assigned for two months to the 253-unit Cumberland Trace Apartments complex and then to The Village at Cliffdale before being promoted to Assistant Manager of the 280-unit Morganton Place Apartments.

- Collected accounts receivable and disbursed accounts payable for the property.
- Leased apartments and processed applications; handled lease signings; conducted move-in and move-out inspections; processed weekly reports; wrote a monthly newsletter.

AFFILIATION

Received NALP designation, Portland County Apartment Association.

COMPUTERS

Experienced with Rent Roll and Prentice Hall property management programs.

PERSONAL

Excellent references upon request. Known for my strong work ethic. Am single (never married). Have family in the Ashland area, which I consider home.

Date

Exact Name of Person
Title or Position
Name of Company
Address
City, State, Zip

Dear Exact Name of Person: (or Dear Sir or Madam if answering a blind ad.)

Can you use a mature professional who offers a recent B.A. in Business Management and experience in real property appraisal along with outstanding written and oral communication abilities and a broad background including real estate sales, budgeting, and management?

As you will see from my resume, I am licensed as a Real Estate Salesman in both Arkansas and Louisiana and am presently taking the Appraiser Course at University of Arkansas at Little Rock.

In addition to my technical customer support and hardware installation abilities, I offer "hands-on" computer skills with numerous popular software programs. A fast learner, I am proficient with software including Microsoft Word, Excel, and other specialized software used in the real estate industry. I developed my computer expertise while serving in the U.S. Navy as a Data Systems Technician involved in installing and maintaining computer networks. I have discovered that my strong computer background is a valuable asset in the real estate industry, and recently I made significant contributions to the local area network used by Coldwell Banker.

In addition to my knowledge related to real estate appraisal, sales, financing, and banking, I offer experience in budgeting and inventory control. I offer a proven talent for establishing programs and services which increase efficiency and productivity.

I hope you will welcome my call soon to arrange a brief meeting at your convenience to discuss your current and future needs and how I might serve them. Thank you in advance for your time.

Sincerely yours,

Wayne Coulter

Alternate last paragraph:
I hope you will call or write soon to suggest a time convenient for us to meet and discuss your current and future needs and how I might serve them. Thank you in advance for your time.

WAYNE COULTER

1110½ Hay Street, Fayetteville, NC 28305 • preppub@aol.com • (910) 483-6611

OBJECTIVE

To contribute to an organization through my attention to detail, my problem-solving, customer service, and analytical skills, as well as my talent for establishing and reorganizing programs for increased productivity and efficiency.

EDUCATION & TRAINING

B.A., Business Management, Tulane University, New Orleans, LA, 2004.
A.A., Business Management, Xavier University of Louisiana, New Orleans, LA, 2000.
Currently enrolled in Appraisal Course and have completed course work in banking and funding, University of Arkansas at Little Rock, AR.
Excelled in numerous company-sponsored training programs in banking and finance, management, computer technology, security, and electronics.

LICENSES

Licensed in Real Estate Sales in Arkansas and Louisiana. Hold "General B" Construction license.

EXPERIENCE

APPRAISER and **SALES AGENT.** Coldwell Banker Myrick and Prudential Real Estate, Little Rock, AR (2005-present). Gained experience in appraising, listing, and selling residential properties with Prudential and am growing professionally with Coldwell Banker.
- On my own initiative, have applied my computer networking skills to make the local area network at Coldwell Banker work more efficiently. Have also made contributions to the design of the website.

SALES ASSOCIATE. Jefferson Realty, Inc., New Orleans, LA (2002-04). Refined my time management skills in the process of attending college full time while managing commercial leases and conducting residential real estate sales. Completed new agent training.
- Increased my knowledge of financing, funding, and purchasing procedures in both commercial and residential transactions. Established a 10-point program covering appraisal training, economic trends, and self-training guidelines.

STUDENT. Tulane University, New Orleans, LA (2000-03). Concentrated my studies in Small Business Management and held leadership roles in campus organizations including Student Council Vice President.
- Received two academic scholarships in Accounting.
- Obtained my Louisiana Real Estate and "General B" Construction licenses.

PRODUCT SUPPORT ENGINEER. Nationwide Technologies, Metairie, LA (1996-00). Participated in sales presentations, installed and serviced computer systems, and provided training for individuals and corporate users. Redesigned and reorganized a computer site, thereby preventing the company from losing a major sale.

Highlights of other experience:
- Established a computer service facility and team which is now a profitable full-service operation providing bank in-house/time-sharing support. Provided customer service support to computer sites by coordinating switchboard and user terminal connections.
- Maintained mainframe computers to a 98% "uptime" rate as a U.S. Navy Data Systems Technician supervising five people and providing security.
- Gained experience as a Property Manager and Residential Repair Manager.

PERSONAL

Entrusted with a Secret security clearance while in the U.S. Navy. Am familiar with software used in the real estate industry. Work well under pressure. Will relocate.

Date

Exact Name of Person
Exact Title
Exact Name of Company
Address
City, State, Zip

ARCHITECT IN TRAINING

with an interest in property management. This young professional used this resume and cover letter to land a job in a prominent architectural and property management firm in Florida.

Dear Exact Name of Person: (or Dear Sir or Madam if answering a blind ad):

With the enclosed resume, I would like to make you aware of my interest in pursuing employment opportunities with your firm.

I am in the process of launching my career as an architect and property manager, and I feel that I have much to offer. After growing up in Florida and attending the University of Florida in Gainesville for two years, I transferred to the University of North Carolina at Charlotte, where I earned both my Bachelor of Science in Architecture as well as my Bachelor of Architecture.

From 2002-2006, in the process of earning my college degrees, I worked for a prominent architectural firm in Charlotte. After beginning in a part-time position, I was asked to work full-time, and I advanced to handle the responsibility of managing projects and dealing with clients under the close supervision of the in-house architect. In addition to gaining experience in managing the development of office buildings, I gained experience in the design and production of mixed use development and food service facilities, the design of multifamily high-density housing, and the design and management of up-fittings.

The founder of XYZ Architecture has consistently praised my ability to use my outgoing personality and "southern charm" to establish strong working relationships with clients and others. Although I have been invited to assume a full-time position with XYZ Architecture after graduating with my Bachelor of Architecture, I have decided that I will return to Florida, where I grew up. I have enjoyed living and going to school in the Carolinas, but Florida is home to me, and that is where I wish to establish my career as an architect.

If you can use an articulate communicator, skilled designer, and effective manager, I hope you will contact me to suggest a time when we might talk to discuss your needs. Thank you in advance for your time and professional courtesies.

Sincerely,

Lane Williams

LANE WILLIAMS

1110½ Hay Street, Fayetteville, NC 28305   •   preppub@aol.com   •   (910) 483-6611

OBJECTIVE   I want to contribute to an organization that can use a highly motivated and creative young professional who offers proven leadership, initiative, and practical problem-solving skills.

EDUCATION   **Bachelor of Architecture,** University of North Carolina at Charlotte (UNCC), Charlotte, NC, 2006.
- **Thesis:** My thesis investigated how a basketball arena fits within the dense core of a city to create a positive social and urban environment. It focused on the basketball arena for the Carolina Panthers, which play in an arena 14 miles from uptown Charlotte. In my thesis I add 300,000 sq. ft. of housing, 20,000 square feet of retail, 60,000 sq. ft. of office space, and 10,000 sq. ft. of homeless housing.

Bachelor of Science degree in Architecture, UNCC, 2003.

EXPERIENCE   **ARCHITECT IN TRAINING.** XYZ Architecture, Charlotte, NC (2002-06). Began working for this company part-time, and rapidly became a valued employee. Advanced to handle the responsibility of managing projects and dealing with the client under the close supervision of the in-house architect. Here are examples of projects with which we were involved:

- **Management and production of office buildings:** Managed the development of the Commons Office Building—20,000 sq. ft. of general office space in Charlotte. Was involved in the production phase of Gilead Road Office Building—24,000 sq. ft. of general office space in Cornelius, NC. Was involved in the production phase of Lake Norman Medical Office Building—180,000 sq. ft. of Class A office space in Cornelius, NC.
- **Design and production of mixed use development:** Was involved in the design and production of a mixed use development in Charlotte which was 4,000 sq. ft. of ground floor retail with 12,000 sq. ft. of housing above. Was involved in the design and production of Village of South End Building C—a mixed use development with 6,000 sq. ft. of ground floor retail with 14,000 sq. ft. of housing above.
- **Design and management of food service facilities:** Designed and managed a project that rehabilitated and up-fitted 9,000 sq. ft. of restaurant space for Riley on the Lake. Designed and managed the renovation of a 6,000 sq. ft. food court at Baptist Hospital. Designed and managed a 1,100 sq. ft. up-fitting for Fuel Pizza.
- **Design and management of up-fittings:** Designed and managed 1,500 sq. ft. office up-fitting for Bob Bills Nationwide. Designed and managed 2,200 sq. ft. office up-fitting for Re/Max Real Estate.
- **Design of multifamily housing:** As a part of the Charlotte Community Design Studio, played a key role in creating the master plan for a 13-acre site for high density housing.

Other experience:
Painting and restoration of classic cars: In an award-winning classic restoration shop, was in charge of painting and preparation.
Framing and finishing of custom homes: For a custom home builder in Montana, helped frame and finish custom homes ranging from 3,000 to 5,000 sq. ft.

COMPUTERS   Proficient with software including Architectural Desktop 3.3, Adobe Photoshop, Maya 6.0, Pinnacle, InDesign, Form Z, Cadcam, and other software.
Knowledgeable of both PC and Macintosh platforms.

PERSONAL   Outstanding personal and professional references. Have been told by my boss that my greatest asset is my outgoing personality and my ability to establish strong working relationships.

Exact Name of Person
Title or Position
Name of Company
Address
City, State, Zip

ASSISTANT MANAGER

Dear Exact Name of Person: (or Dear Sir or Madam if answering a blind ad.)

I would appreciate an opportunity to talk with you soon about how I could contribute to your organization through my management experience as well as my dedication to customer service.

With more than six years of experience in property management, I have acquired strong skills related to accounting, office administration, and marketing. You will see from my resume that I have received numerous honors and awards. In one job I was named Leasing Agent of the Year, and in my next job I was named Leasing Consultant of the Quarter while also earning bonuses for exceptional performance.

In previous positions in the retail industry, I rapidly advanced to supervisory positions and became proficient in organizing employee work schedules, preparing employee performance reviews, resolving conflicts, and managing multiple simultaneous projects.

I feel certain that you would find me to be a hard-working and reliable professional who prides myself on doing any job to the best of my ability. A highly motivated individual with excellent verbal communication and interpersonal skills, I am capable of managing my time to achieve effective results.

I would like to discuss the possibility of my putting my energy and enthusiasm to work for your company. I hope you will contact me to suggest a time when we might talk about your needs. Thank you in advance for your time.

Sincerely,

Heidi Thibodeault

HEIDI THIBODEAULT

1110½ Hay Street, Fayetteville, NC 28305   •   preppub@aol.com   •   (910) 483-6611

OBJECTIVE

To benefit an organization through my management experience and real estate background as well as through my bottom-line orientation and strong customer service skills.

EXPERIENCE

ASSISTANT MANAGER. Sunny Day Apartments, Oakland, CA (2005-present). Was recruited by this organization to play a key role in managing a 356-apartment community. Am being groomed for promotion to General Manager. Utilize my strong analytical skills and bookkeeping knowledge while using Prentice Hall computer system to handle rent roll in the amount of $200,000 monthly. Troubleshoot accounting discrepancies. Handle all maintenance ordering and direct the training of leasing personnel; perform move out/in inspections, approve all applicants, and serve as Leasing Consultant.
- Named **Leasing Consultant of the Quarter,** December 2005, and July 2004.
- Earned bonuses for exceptional leasing presentations.

ASSISTANT MANAGER. Alameda Apartment Village, Oakland, CA (2000-05). Assisted manager with general administration of 276-apartment community; performed office administration and bookkeeping functions.
- Controlled rent roll in excess of $150,000 monthly; inspected apartments upon move-ins/move-outs; approved and researched applicants; handled banking transactions; maintained employment records; served as leasing agent.
- Named **Leasing Agent of the Year,** 2000.

MEMBERSHIP SUPERVISOR & CASHIER. Costco Wholesale, Berkeley and Lafayette, CA (1998-00). Was promoted to Supervisor after excelling as cashier. Supervised 14 personnel; performed bookkeeping duties; handled customer relations; assisted in outside marketing; recruited and trained new associates; set monthly goals for department.
- Named **Associate of the Month,** 1999.

TELLER. First Citizens Bank, Oakland, CA (1997-98). Performed teller duties; handled large sums of money, balanced cash drawer.

CASHIER. Costco Wholesale, Oakland, CA (1996-97). Worked part-time while attending Merritt College. Assisted customers; operated cash registers; balanced cash drawer. **Top Cashier** on two occasions; received a Letter of Commendation.

ASSISTANT CUSTOMER SERVICE MANAGER. Marshall's, Oakland, CA (1994-96). Managed cashiers; responsible for supervisory duties of employees; assisted with inventory, closed cash registers, and secured monies. Received Letter of Commendation.

SKILLS & QUALIFICATIONS
- More than six years experience as assistant manager, supervisor, and leasing agent in the management, training, and evaluation of personnel.
- Provided liaison between line staff and upper management.
- Skilled in office administration and bookkeeping functions; proficient with filing systems, statistical records; prepare narrative and detailed reports.

EDUCATION

Currently completing Business degree and previously attended Merritt College, Oakland, CA. With 100 college credit hours, am completing degree in my spare time via online courses.

PERSONAL

Known for strong personal initiative and personal resourcefulness. Outstanding references. My main hobby is reading, and I especially enjoy books on real estate and investing.

Date

Exact Name of Person
Title or Position
Name of Company
Address
City, State, Zip

BANK TELLER
with experience as
a real estate
secretary

Dear Exact Name of Person: (or Dear Sir or Madam if answering a blind ad.)

I am submitting my resume to request a transfer from Wachovia Bank in Connecticut to Wachovia Bank in Virginia. It is my desire to put my background in real estate to work for Wachovia's Construction Loan Department, and I hope one day to be in a management position in that department. My husband has been recruited for the position of City Manager with the City of Richmond, and it is my hope to transfer to a Wachovia in Richmond.

As you will see from my resume I offer extensive office-related experience, including recent experience with Wachovia Bank. I believe that my real estate background would be of great value to Wachovia's construction loan activities since I am experienced in qualifying clients for housing, performing bookkeeping related to construction loans and loan applications, and supporting an executive staff in matters related to construction sales. Based on my outstanding performance at Wachovia, the bank already realizes that I am a hard-working and reliable professional who prides myself on doing any job to the best of my ability.

I have thoroughly enjoyed my time with Wachovia Bank in Connecticut and look forward to continued dedication and success with Wachovia Bank in Virginia.

I hope you will contact me soon to suggest a time convenient for us to meet and discuss your current and future needs and how I might serve them. Thank you in advance for your time.

Sincerely yours,

Virginia Wright

VIRGINIA WRIGHT

1110½ Hay Street, Fayetteville, NC 28305   •   preppub@aol.com   •   (910) 483-6611

OBJECTIVE

I want to offer my experience in the real estate industry to Wachovia so that I can play a role in the continued profitability of its construction loan activities.

EXPERIENCE

BANK TELLER I. Wachovia Bank, Hartford, CT (2005-present). Received an award as Teller of the Month, and have become respected for my outgoing personality and strong customer service skills.
- Provided customer service and cemented relationships for the financial institution.
- Collected large deposits from commercial and personal accounts.
- Sold and cashed savings bonds, money orders, personal checks, as well as Travelers Cheques.
- Became experienced in all duties pertaining to automated teller machine.

REAL ESTATE SECRETARY. Northeastern Realty, Hartford, CT (2004-05). Typed legal documents related to small and regular estates, car transfers, guardianships, and court minutes.
- Received a **Certificate in Real Estate from Hartford Board of Realtors.**
- Provided secretarial services for real estate firm.
- Became experienced in qualifying clients for housing according to income and debt.
- Collected rent money for the houses which the firm rented.
- Completed bookkeeping transactions and banking procedures.
- Interviewed clients to determine the possibility of a probate procedure.
- Researched the feasibility of estate title transfers.
- Performed research for creditors if an estate had been opened so that a claim could be placed on the estate.
- Typed letters, envelopes, labels, invoices, and documents.
- Completed large microfilming projects.
- Ran copies on photocopying machine.
- Enrolled agents in continuing training courses.
- Entered customer data into computer terminal

ASSISTANT TO THE DEPUTY CLERK. Register of Wills/Orphans Court, Hartford, CT (2001-03). Greatly refined my research skills as I worked to provide clients with powers of attorney in the best interest of a child. Scheduled court dates when necessary
- Worked with numerous agencies including Child Protective Services and the Sheriff's Department.

DATA ENTRY & CUSTOMER SERVICE REPRESENTATIVE. Farmington Properties, Inc., Hartford, CT (2000-01). Began in an entry-level position as a Receptionist and rapidly advanced to handle challenging responsibilities. Entered large amounts of data into a database of thousands of properties. Assisted sales agents in locating information quickly. Answered a 12-line switchboard.

CARE GIVER. Blue Hills Nursing Home, Hartford, CT (1999-00).

EDUCATION

Completed secretarial and data entry courses, Trinity College, Hartford, CT, 2002-03. Graduated from Cedar Mountain High School - college preparatory courses, 2000.

PERSONAL

Outstanding references upon request. Believe that excellent customer service is the key to successful business relationships. Truly enjoy being in a support function.

Date

Exact Name of Person
Title or Position
Name of Company
Address
City, State, Zip

Dear Exact Name of Person (or Dear Sir or Madam if answering a blind ad):

With the enclosed resume, I would like to make you aware of my interest in exploring employment opportunities with your organization and introduce you to my construction industry background. I am single, hold a current passport, and am available for relocation worldwide as your needs require.

As you will see from my resume, I am currently excelling as a Carpenter with a leading construction firm in South Carolina. I am experienced in working at every stage of the construction process, and I am known for my intense commitment to safety and quality control. Although I am held in the highest regard by my current employer, I am selectively exploring employment opportunities with firms which operate worldwide. I can provide outstanding references at the appropriate time.

In prior experience, I served my country with distinction in the U.S. Army, where I began my career as a Carpenter after earning a Certificate of Completion of Apprenticeship as a Carpenter from the state of South Carolina. The U.S. Army identified my management potential and I was quickly placed in supervisory positions. I subsequently excelled as an Instructor and Training Chief, and I was then selected to receive specialized training related to the nuclear, biological, and chemical (NBC) field. After NBC training, I was handpicked for positions in which I handled the responsibility of managing NBC resources, training employees in NBC matters, and managing chemical defense programs. In one position as a Senior NBC Operations Advisor, I served as the "subject matter expert" on NBC training for Special Operations soldiers at Fort Bragg. On my own initiative, I revised and implemented the most detailed inspection checklist for NBC programs ever used in that organization, and I revised inventory control programs in order to better track equipment. I won numerous medals and other awards, including the Bronze Star, which recognized my technical expertise as well as my management skills.

While serving in the U.S. Army, I gained a reputation as an outstanding manager and mentor. I truly enjoyed helping other soldiers develop their skills to their fullest potential, and I mentored one individual who became Soldier of the Year.

If my background and skills interest you, I hope you will contact me to suggest a time when we could meet in person to discuss your needs. Thank you.

Yours sincerely,

Bryce Cunningham

BRYCE CUNNINGHAM

1110½ Hay Street, Fayetteville, NC 28305 • preppub@aol.com • (910) 483-6611

OBJECTIVE

I am single and available for worldwide relocation on an extended basis in order to apply my extensive construction background and engineering knowledge for the benefit of a company involved in global construction activities.

EXPERIENCE

CARPENTER. Williams Construction, Charleston, SC (2005-present). Expertly apply my skills as a carpenter in every phase of construction, including the framing and finishing stages of construction. Build decks and fireplace mantles and other fixtures.

STEEL ERECTOR. Cahill & Sons, Charleston, SC (2000-04). Worked as a steel erector for a Virginia company which had a contract to help build a new multimillion-dollar facility.

U.S. Army experience: Served my country with distinction and was promoted to managerial positions while gaining expert knowledge related to nuclear, biological, and chemical (NBC) matters:
OPERATIONS MANAGER. Fort Campbell, KY (1995-2000). As a proud member of the Special Forces, conducted land navigation training, managed counter-drug missions, and provided guidance in NBC matters.
- On a formal performance evaluation, was described as "proactive and dedicated to safety in a high-risk training environment."

SENIOR NBC OPERATIONS ADVISOR. Fort Bragg, NC (1991-95). Was the trusted advisor to a senior Special Forces executive on NBC matters and was the "subject matter expert" for all NBC training for Special Operations soldiers.
- Prepared detailed written documents pertaining to NBC training. Revised and implemented the most detailed inspection checklist for NBC/Language programs ever seen. Recommended and implemented significant modifications to the NBC and Language programs.
- Revised the chemical defense equipment status report to better track all group chemical equipment. Flawlessly accounted for hundreds of thousands of dollars in assets.
- On a formal performance evaluation, was commended for "flawlessly coordinating Special Forces operations for several major projects."

OPERATIONS MANAGER ("First Sergeant"). Fort Bragg, NC (1988-91). In the Army's only Special Operations support organization, was in charge of directing aviation re-fueling and warehouse support. Was praised on a formal evaluation for "unparalleled knowledge and ability in supply related procedures and knowledge."

Highlights of other military experience:
Began my military career as a **CARPENTER.** Exhibited skill while laying out job sites per blueprints and diagrams, and performed detailed carpentry work. Was promoted rapidly to **SENIOR CARPENTER & ASSISTANT SECTION CHIEF,** which placed in the position of training and managing trades personnel. Cross-trained in electrical and plumbing work.

EDUCATION

Completed more than two years of college-level training through the U.S. Army.
Received **Certificate of Completion of Apprenticeship as a Carpenter,** South Carolina Apprenticeship Council.
Graduated from the U.S. Army **Chemical School** and **Chemical Staff Specialist School.**

PERSONAL

Can provide excellent personal and professional references.

CAREER CHANGE

Date

Exact Name of Person
Title or Position
Name of Company
Address
City, State, Zip

**CERTIFIED RESIDENTIAL
APPRAISER**

Dear Exact Name of Person: (or Dear Sir or Madam if answering a blind ad.)

With the enclosed resume, I would like to make you aware of my interest in exploring employment opportunities with your organization.

As you will see from my resume, I have spent more than 15 years in the residential appraisal and real estate brokerage business, and I have become a respected member and president of numerous professional organizations. I am proud to say that my reputation is that of an honest person with unquestioned integrity. I have also become respected for my technical appraisal skills, and because of that I have been contacted by FEMA and other hurricanes in the aftermath of natural disasters.

A recent project in New Orleans after Hurricane Katrina stimulated me to think "outside the box," and I realize that I would like to utilize my strong analytical skills and appraisal knowledge within the insurance industry. I am single, and all my children are grown, so I would cheerfully travel and relocate as your needs require.

I hope you will call or write soon to suggest a time convenient for us to meet and discuss your current and future needs and how I might serve them. Thank you in advance for your time.

Sincerely,

Alexander Smith

Alternate last paragraph:
I hope you will welcome my call soon to arrange a brief meeting at your convenience to discuss your current and future needs and how I might serve them. Thank you in advance for your time.

ALEXANDER SMITH

1110½ Hay Street, Fayetteville, NC 28305   •   preppub@aol.com   •   (910) 483-6611

OBJECTIVE   I want to contribute to an organization that can use an appraiser of residential properties who offers a proven ability to interact with customers as well as the numerous agencies involved in the residential appraisal business.

LICENSES   Idaho **Certified Residential Appraiser,** #A-6611
Idaho **Licensed Real Estate Broker,** #B-283051
FHA Direct Endorser Approved
Have worked full time in the Real Estate business since 1990

EDUCATION &   Completed extensive yearlong **Residential Appraisal Program,** Northwestern Appraisal
TRAINING   Institute, Boise, Idaho. 1990. Courses included the following:
R1- Introduction to Real Estate Appraisal
R2- Valuation Principle and Procedures
R3- Applied Residential Property Valuation
G1- Introduction to Income Property Appraisal
Seminars and continuing education:
Uniform Standards of Professional Appraisal Practice
Valuing Small Properties by the Income Approach
Fair Lending and the Appraiser
Uniform Standards: Limited Reports and Departure
Appraising 2-4 Family Residences
U.S. Department of Housing and Urban Development

Completed **B.S. in Management**, Boise State University, Boise, Idaho, 1995. Earned degree in my spare time while working full-time in a job that required frequent travel.

MEMBERSHIPS   Am a current member of the following professional organizations:
American Association of Realtors
Idaho Association of Realtors
Boise Association of Realtors, past president
American Association of Realtors Appraisal Section, past president
Ada County Regional Appraiser Group, current president

EXPERIENCE   **CERTIFIED RESIDENTIAL APPRAISER.** Daniels Appraisal Service & Real Estate Brokerage, Boise, ID (1990-present). For a respected appraisal service, travel four days a week to surrounding counties to appraise residences. Have appraised thousands of properties, new and existing, and am an expert on the policies of the VA, Fannie Mae, FHA, and other regulators. Coordinate with real estate brokers as well as with the owners of residential property.
- On my own initiative, developed a new approach to residential appraisal that was very successful with multimillion-dollar homes. For $750, produced and published a detailed book after each appraisal that helped discerning buyers of premium properties.
- Became acknowledged as an authority on residential appraising, and have contributed articles to numerous newspapers and books designed for home buyers and sellers.
- During numerous national disasters including Hurricane Katrina, was sought out by the Federal Emergency Management Agency (FEMA) and the VA to undertake a special project to visit the distressed area to perform residential appraising.

PERSONAL   Believe strongly in personal integrity and honesty. My word is as strong as my signature.

Date

Exact Name of Person
Title or Position
Name of Company
Address
City, State, Zip

CONTROLLER

An impressive background and a track record of exceptional results as shown on her resume ought to fetch numerous interviews.

Dear Exact Name of Person: (or Sir or Madam if answering a blind ad)

With the enclosed resume, I would like to formally make you aware of my interest in exploring employment opportunities within your organization.

As you will see from my resume, I have excelled in a variety of assignments which required outstanding accounting, customer service, and management skills. In my current position as Controller, I prepare monthly financial statements and year-end financials while also supervising ten people in the accounting department including an assistant controller as well as the MIS and accounts payable/receivable personnel. I wrote this 30-year-old company's first policies and procedures manual. While in control of $5 million in inventory, I developed procedures which led the company to process inventory by barcode at its nine locations.

In my prior job, I rose to Chief Financial Officer for a diversified corporation with holdings in the construction industry and restaurant business. For one of the company's divisions, I was personally responsible for leading the limited partnership's reorganization out of Chapter 11 bankruptcy and, after leading the company out of bankruptcy, the company posted a 7% net profit within the first year.

I am knowledgeable of software including Depreciation Solution, Computer Systems Dynamics (CSD) programs, and Microsoft Office. I have demonstrated my capabilities in operational areas including contract development and negotiation, debt structure reorganization, and information systems/data processing administration.

If you can use a hardworking professional with knowledge in numerous operational areas, I hope you will contact me to suggest a time when we might meet to discuss your needs and how I might serve them. I can provide outstanding personal and professional references. Thank you in advance for your time, and I would appreciate your holding my interest in your company in the strictest confidence at this point.

Yours sincerely,

Michelle Bazaldua

MICHELLE BAZALDUA

1110½ Hay Street, Fayetteville, NC 28305　•　preppub@aol.com　•　(910) 483-6611

OBJECTIVE　　To contribute to an organization that can use a skilled accounting professional with experience related to financial analysis and financial statement preparation, auditing, cash management, AR/AP, general ledger, payroll, collections, and automated systems.

EXPERIENCE　　**CONTROLLER.** Quality Building Supply, Springfield, VA (2004-present). Prepare monthly financial statements and year-end financials while supervising ten people in the accounting department including an assistant controller, AP and AR personnel, and the MIS Director.
- For this 30-year-old company, wrote its first policies and procedures manual.
- Implemented new computer systems for automated payroll with swipe cards.
- Am in control of over $5 million in inventory; developed procedures in processing inventory by barcode for the company's nine locations.
- Implemented new software called CSD, a program for the building supply industry.

For The Jason G. Roth Company, was promoted from Controller to Chief Financial Officer, and worked in two main divisions of the company (1995-2003):

2001-03: CHIEF FINANCIAL OFFICER & GENERAL MANAGER. Stone Mountain, GA.
- For a chain of three premier restaurants, was personally responsible for leading the limited partnership's reorganization out of Chapter 11 bankruptcy; personally renegotiated the company debt structure and reduced food, labor, and liquor costs by as much as 12% within six months.
- After leading the company out of bankruptcy, achieved a 7% net profit within the first year.
- Supervised all business operations at three establishments which employed more than 150 employees while producing annual sales of $4.6 million.
- Was the hands-on manager in charge of daily operations, marketing and promotions, purchasing, inventory control, and alcohol management.
- Was in charge of transition planning as the businesses were readied for sale to a new management team; directed the liquidation of assets not included in the sale.

1995-2001: CONTROLLER and PROPERTY & PROJECT MANAGER. Lester Springs, GA. For the Real Estate Development Division, oversaw on-site and off-site construction of new buildings and tenant improvements in addition to performing all financial and property management functions for 32 industrial properties valued at $128 million.
- Collaborated with the owner and architects during the preliminary planning stages of each project; took bids, awarded contracts, and provided oversight of the construction phase through completion.
- Marketed properties, negotiated leases, and handled all property management duties.
- Was in charge of all accounting for this entire real estate portfolio; in addition to managing investment instruments, negotiated secured/unsecured loans up to $41 million.
- Oversaw cash management, mortgage management, and auditing.
- Served as liaison to company attorneys and accountants.
- Supervised projects valued at $61 million, saving $1.2 million as general contractor.
- Generated more than $7 million in net profits through the careful management of company-owned stocks, bonds, and mutual funds.

ACCOUNT CLERK II. County of Siddell, In-Home Supportive Services, Siddell, GA (1990-95). Prepared regular financial reports for the State of Georgia while also reviewing, auditing, and approving grants valued at $10.8 million on a bimonthly basis.
- Initiated and implemented the county's first computerized Medicare issuance system.

EDUCATION　　**Associate of Arts Degree in Accounting,** Hazelton Junior College, GA.

PERSONAL　　Knowledgeable of software including Depreciation Solution, CSD, and Microsoft Office.

Date

Exact Name of Person
Title or Position
Name of Company
Address
City, State, Zip

CORPORATE RELOCATION MANAGER

Dear Exact Name of Person: (or Dear Sir or Madam if answering a blind ad.)

This letter is in response to the ad placed in the Sunday, <u>Bloomington Daily News</u>. Please find enclosed my resume describing my qualifications.

As you will see from my resume, I offer extensive experience in the corporate relocation process. I travel more than 50% of the time as I make PowerPoint presentations to Fortune 500 companies and other organizations seeking to relocate employees in the most affordable way. In nearly every situation, I have helped companies save money in the relocation process.

In previous jobs in the real estate and banking industry, I gained knowledge of real estate while working in a real estate banking group and in the commercial lending department of a bank. I financed 100% of my college education and pursued my degree at night while excelling in full-time, demanding jobs which required excellent problem-solving and decision-making skills.

I hope you will contact me to suggest a time when we might discuss your needs. I can provide outstanding references at the appropriate time.

Sincerely,

Louise Obermeier

LOUISE OBERMEIER

1110½ Hay Street, Fayetteville, NC 28305   •   preppub@aol.com   •   (910) 483-6611

OBJECTIVE   I want to contribute to an organization that can use a dynamic professional with extensive knowledge of corporate relocation and property management issues.

EDUCATION   **Bachelor of Science in Business Administration,** Indiana University at Bloomington, IN, 2003.

EXPERIENCE   **CORPORATE RELOCATION MANAGER.** Bloomington Property Management Company Welcome Center, Bloomington, IN (2004-present). Train and staff and seven-person office while overseeing all aspects of goal setting for this small and highly motivated team.
- Prepared the annual budget for this division of the company.
- Made presentations to Fortune 500 companies (Microsoft, AT&T, Black & Decker) that were relocating employees to the area. Developed and used PowerPoint presentations.
- Marketed 30 apartment communities which we managed (market availability less than 1% during this time).
- Coordinated exhibits for the Bloomington Chamber of Commerce Small Business Expo and the State of Indiana Human Resource Managers Conference.
- Directed a project installing a new local area network (LAN) in our seven-person office.
- Handled accounts payable.
- Designed ads for various publications.
- Motivated staff members to set and achieve ambitious productivity goals.

ADMINISTRATIVE ASSISTANT. Bank One Real Estate Banking Group, Bloomington, IN (2002-03). Was specially recruited for this position which involved providing support for four busy executives.
- Supported the department Vice President and three Assistant Vice Presidents maintaining current loans.
- Set up and maintained the credit file system for the department.
- Coordinated the relocation of the Detroit division to Bloomington.

ADMINISTRATIVE ASSISTANT. CitiFinancial Commercial Lending Department, Bloomington, IN (1998-02). Supported a Senior Vice President and Vice President in the Commercial Lending Department.
- Prepared documents for all types of commercial loans.
- Researched any customer account problems, handled customer complaints.

SALES ASSISTANT. Bullards Furniture, Indianapolis and Bloomington, IN (Part-time 1999-05). Assisted customers with selecting and purchasing 18th and 19th century furniture reproductions and accessories.
- Managed inventory.
- Designed, implemented and maintained displays.

COMMUNITY   Active in the Bloomington Chamber of Commerce
INVOLVEMENT   Boys & Girls Club Volunteer – Bloomington, IN

COMPUTERS   Highly proficient with computer software including Word, Excel, Access, and PowerPoint.

PERSONAL   Outstanding references upon request. Offer a personal reputation of integrity.

Date

Exact Name of Person
Title or Position
Name of Company
Address
City, State, Zip

**FOREMAN &
SUPERINTENDENT**

Dear Exact Name of Person (or Dear Sir or Madam if answering a blind ad):

I would appreciate an opportunity to talk with you soon about how I could contribute to your organization through my experience in managing people and projects.

As you will see from my resume, I offer considerable construction industry experience. As a teenager in New Jersey, I began working for builders and then became a self-employed contractor of roofing, framing, and siding jobs. After that I served my country with distinction and excelled in numerous challenging assignments. In one job at West Point, I coached the U.S. Military Academy Parachute Team to its first national championship competition in 34 straight years and then to its first national title. That was a thrill for me because, although my predecessor had three national titles and many world competitions to his credit, I led the West Point team to its first national title through strengthening its training program, reorganizing physical facilities for better utilization, and by applying my strong leadership style.

Since leaving the military I have excelled as a foreman and superintendent on residential and commercial jobs, and I offer skills in all aspects of residential and commercial building. I can provide outstanding personal and professional references. I will cheerfully relocate according to your needs.

I hope you will write or call me soon to suggest a time when we might meet to discuss your current and future needs and how I might serve them. Thank you in advance for your time.

Sincerely yours,

Clem K. Hammer

Alternate last paragraph:
I hope you will welcome my call soon to arrange a brief meeting at your convenience to discuss your current and future needs and how I might serve them. Thank you in advance for your time.

CLEM K. HAMMER

1110½ Hay Street, Fayetteville, NC 28305   •   preppub@aol.com   •   (910) 483-6611

OBJECTIVE

To benefit an organization that can use a skilled organizer, resourceful problem solver, and versatile manager with strong communication, negotiating, and motivational abilities.

EXPERIENCE

FOREMAN/ACTING SUPERINTENDENT. Briar Builders, Lincoln, NE (2005-present). Because of my excellent reputation for both personal character and construction expertise, was recruited by this construction industry firm to oversee its residential development activities; handled all duties of a superintendent.

- Purchased lots and coordinated clearing and footings; built multiple single-family homes in the $85,000-$140,000 price range in new residential developments.
- Was actively involved in selling many of the homes we built; coordinated with real estate brokers for the sale of some of the properties.
- Prepared all written materials related to construction including description of materials needed, documents for appraisals and building permits, and other paperwork.
- Hired and supervised workers from every construction trade.

SUPERINTENDENT. PNC Builders, Lincoln, NE (1998-05). Played a key role in this company's enjoying the most profitable period in its history; acted as a superintendent for residential developments and for commercial projects.

- Supervised construction of five commercial office buildings in MT, NE, and WY; my attention to detail and expert management brought these projects in at a cost of 30% less than had been bid by the next highest bidder.
- Negotiated the purchasing of residential lots; prepared documentation for appraisal with VA and mortgage companies, filed building permits, selected and negotiated terms with subcontractors, and supervised all work from land clearing through finished project stage while handling all job costing, accounting, disbursements, and finances.

SELF-EMPLOYED REMODELER. Lincoln, NE (1997-98). After my honorable discharge from military service, performed renovations and remodeling of residential properties; built/remodeled kitchens and bathrooms and designed/built home additions.

Highlights of military experience: U.S. Army, locations worldwide. During the following highlights of my military experience, was promoted ahead of my peers and was selected for difficult assignments which required excellent organizational and management skills.

- **Operations Sergeant.** Was selected for a job at West Point supervising riggers in the repair of parachute equipment; supervised airdrops of people/assets.
- Was handpicked for a position as **Coach, U.S. Military Academy Parachute Team.** Coached the team to its first-ever national title.

Other construction industry experience: Began working for builders in New Jersey and then became a self-employed contractor of roofing, framing, and siding jobs; became a skilled carpenter and learned to operate heavy construction equipment while prospecting for customers, negotiating contracts, ordering materials, and preparing payroll.

EDUCATION

Excelled in more than three years of U.S. Army training related to management, industrial safety, and other areas.
Completed the General Contractor's Course, Lincoln Technical Community College.

PERSONAL

Am known for common sense and honesty. Can provide strong references. Offer exceptionally strong crisis management skills. Held Top Secret security clearance.

CAREER CHANGE

Date

Exact Name of Person
Title or Position
Name of Company
Address
City, State, Zip

FRONT DESK CLERK

with experience as an
assistant property
manager

Dear Exact Name of Person: (or Dear Sir or Madam if answering a blind ad.)

I would appreciate an opportunity to talk with you soon about how I could contribute to your organization through my versatile skills and experience along with my personal qualities of honesty, dependability, and high personal standards.

As you will see from my resume, I offer an extensive background in real estate and property management. In one of my earliest jobs, I learned a great deal while working for one of the nation's largest real estate brokerages. Subsequently recruited for a position as a property manager, I was credited with helping the condominium project I managed achieve new levels of profitability. In that job I discovered my ability to handle multiple simultaneous tasks, and I also recognized that I have a knack for remaining calm in a crisis. In an subsequent job in the property management field, I supervised a staff of seven professionals.

Although I am held in high regard by my current employer and have been assured of rapid advancement, I am interested in returning to the property management field. I can provide excellent personal and professional references.

I would welcome your call soon to suggest a time convenient for us to meet and discuss your current and future needs and how I might serve them. Thank you in advance for your time.

Sincerely,

Myrna Senter

Alternate last paragraph:
I hope you will welcome my call soon to arrange a brief meeting when we might meet to discuss your needs and goals and how my background might serve them. I can provide outstanding references at the appropriate time.

MYRNA SENTER

1110½ Hay Street, Fayetteville, NC 28305   •   preppub@aol.com   •   (910) 483-6611

OBJECTIVE   I want to contribute to an organization that can use an outgoing professional who offers a background involved in serving customers and managing property assets for maximum profitability.

EXPERIENCE   **FRONT DESK CLERK.** Radisson Hotel, Nashville, TN (2005-present). Checked guests in and out, operated a switchboard, took reservations, and performed data entry.
- Handled sales and catering as well as payroll, typing, and filing; assisted with scheduling.
- Was strongly encouraged to enter the company's management training program, and was commended on my executive abilities which are well suited to the hospitality industry.
- Accepted this position after my husband and I relocated to Nashville in 2005.

ASSISTANT PROPERTY MANAGER. Turfland Apartments, Lexington, KY (2002-04). Supervised a staff of seven in maintenance and administrative duties.
- Performed bookkeeping transactions and maintained accounts receivable/payable.
- Prepared lease agreements; handled credit applications and refunds; received tenant payments; inspected rentals.
- Prepared company payroll and calculated deductions; prepared bank deposits.
- Marketed apartment complex to corporate accounts.
- Generated a monthly tenant newsletter; planned complex activities.
- Inventoried maintenance supplies and prepared purchase orders.
- Filed court eviction notices.

PROPERTY MANAGER. Meadowbrook Condominiums, Lexington, KY (1998-02). Trained, supervised, and evaluated five personnel.
- Maintained accounts payable/receivable transactions; prepared payroll utilizing computer.
- Processed bank deposits and prepared rent deposit refunds.
- Prepared leases, collected rents, inspected units, and performed tenant credit checks.
- Prepared a monthly newsletter and planned tenant activities.
- Filed court eviction notices.

OFFICE MANAGER. Coldwell Banker, Lexington, KY (1996-98).
- Maintained accounts payable/receivable transactions.
- Performed data entry of daily check activity.
- Prepared payroll and bank deposits. Collected on returned checks.

HIGHLIGHTS OF QUALIFICATIONS
- A professional with over 12 years of experience in the administrative field including over seven years in property management
- Gained valuable experience working with Section 8 government subsidized housing.
- Experience in payroll, bookkeeping, and preparing bank deposits
- Skill in recruiting, training, and supervising personnel
- Developed computer proficiency while using the Windows XP operating systems along with Microsoft software; type 55/60 wpm; 10-key by touch
- Meet established goals and deadlines. People- and results-oriented

EDUCATION   Completed 70+ hours in the Business program, University of Kentucky, Lexington, KY.

CAREER CHANGE

Date

Exact Name of Person
Title or Position
Name of Company
Address
City, State, Zip

Dear Exact Name of Person: (or Dear Sir or Madam if answering a blind ad.)

    With the enclosed resume, I would like to make you aware of my strong interest in the job of Housing Coordinator for the Kansas Indian Housing Authority which you recently advertised.

    As you will see from my resume, I offer expertise in all areas related to housing production, housing rentals, and homeownership. Throughout my career in the housing industry, I have counseled individuals seeking to make decisions about their housing needs, and I have negotiated with lenders, attorneys, and others related to the sale and resale of property.

    With strong oral and written communication skills, I also offer a reputation as a fair and honest businessman. I have established a network of contacts in the real estate and construction industries in counties throughout Kansas, and I am very knowledgeable of Kansas building codes. I also offer expert knowledge of VA, FHA, and HUD regulations and procedures, and I have a network of contacts within those organizations. My experience includes helping select housing for acquisition and rehabilitation and building sites for new construction.

    I hope you will give me the courtesy of an interview so that I may show you in person that I am someone who could significantly enhance your organization's goals. I can provide outstanding references at the appropriate time, and I would consider it an honor to be associated with the aims of the Kansas Indian Housing Authority.

Sincerely,

Russell Hooper

RUSSELL HOOPER

1110½ Hay Street, Fayetteville, NC 28305　　·　　preppub@aol.com　　·　　(910) 483-6611

OBJECTIVE　　To offer my experience in sales, marketing, and management to an organization that would benefit from my strong bottom-line orientation and results-oriented style.

EDUCATION　　**B.S., Business Administration with a minor in Recreation**, Newman University, Wichita, KS, 1998.
A.S. degree, Wichita State University, Wichita KS, 1996.

EXPERIENCE　　**MANAGER.** Kansas Homes, Inc., Wichita, KS (2005-present). Was specially recruited by this family business to assist in establishing four sales locations and set up accounting systems for a newly started manufactured home business.
- Worked with the corporate accountant to set up accounting systems using QuickBooks Pro.
- Negotiated and signed contracts with lending institutions.
- Prospected for site locations and negotiated property leases for business locations in Topeka, Salina, and Wichita.
- Applied my knowledge of HUD, VA, and FHA lending procedures while working with attorneys and financial institutions.

REAL ESTATE SALES REPRESENTATIVE. Sunflower State Realty, Inc., Wichita, KS (2002-05). Sold residential properties while also participating in developing subdivisions and remodeling existing homes.
- Established a network of contacts in both Sedgwick and Butler counties.
- Became skilled in all aspects of prospecting for leads while listing and selling homes.

MANAGER. Shadduck Homes, Hutchinson, KS (1999-02). Managed a one-location dealership of a manufactured home business located northwest of Wichita.
- Managed all daily operations of the business including hiring and training employees.
- Trained employees in effective sales techniques.
- Handled a considerable amount of financial responsibilities related to land procurement, loan closings, negotiating with lenders, and obtaining permits.
- After the sale, provided oversight for all matters related to service.

SALES REPRESENTATIVE. Mobile Housing Center, Wichita, KS (1997-99). Refined my sales skills while learning the manufactured home business.

Other experience: After college, excelled in a job selling time share condominiums.
Built own home through HUD sweat-equity program.

AFFILIATIONS　　Vice President, Sedgwick County Club
Have extensively volunteered my time with Habitat for Humanity
As a native Lumbee Indian, have donated my time to charitable causes which benefit minority Indian students who seek financial assistance in obtaining college educations.

COMPUTERS　　Proficient with software including Word, PowerPoint, Excel, and Access.

PERSONAL　　Innovative, self-motivated, persistent, and goal-oriented professional who quickly develops rapport with people. Excellent problem-solver and enjoy finding creative solutions to stubborn problems. Outstanding references available on request.

CAREER CHANGE

Date

Exact Name of Person
Title or Position
Name of Company
Address
City, State, Zip

INDEPENDENT CONTRACTOR

Dear Exact Name of Person (or Dear Sir or Madam if answering a blind ad):

I would appreciate an opportunity to talk with you soon about how I could contribute to your organization through my reputation as a talented manager with strong abilities in motivating employees and guiding them to meet high performance standards by setting an example of true professionalism and dedication to excellence.

While serving my country in the U.S. Air Force, I consistently earned the respect and praise of my superiors for my ability to take on challenges and excel in the tough jobs. I thrive on solving problems and on using my ability to maximize the potential of each employee, thereby achieving higher levels of productivity while eliminating methods which waste valuable time, money, and human resources.

Presently I operate two independent businesses. I am a licensed real estate agent while also involved in running a paint contracting company with four employees. Throughout my military career I displayed my adaptability and versatility in two main fields of concentration: the development and management of training programs and the supervision of supply operations.

I would like to emphasize that my strongest abilities are in building teams, providing quality training, and motivating others to excel and maximize their own individual talents. I possess sound judgment and decision-making skills along with the ability to react quickly and handle the pressure of deadlines and stressful situations.

I hope you will welcome my call soon to arrange a brief meeting at your convenience to discuss your current and future needs and how I might serve them. Thank you in advance for your time.

Sincerely yours,

Rhoda C. Walnut

Alternate last paragraph:
I hope you will call or write me soon to suggest a time convenient for us to meet and discuss your current and future needs and how I might serve them. Thank you in advance for your time.

RHODA C. WALNUT

1110½ Hay Street, Fayetteville, NC 28305   •   preppub@aol.com   •   (910) 483-6611

OBJECTIVE   To offer superior managerial and motivational abilities to an organization in need of a creative problem solver who excels in increasing productivity and morale while guiding employees to outstanding results through my talent for bringing out the best in others.

EXPERIENCE   **INDEPENDENT CONTRACTOR.** Lexington, KY (2005-present). Am simultaneously involved in two independent business activities: market and sell residential real estate and operate a paint contracting company, where my responsibilities include making estimates and scheduling four workers in cooperation with other contractors.

With a reputation as a talented manager of human, material, and fiscal resources, advanced in supply/logistics as well as property management, U.S. Air Force:
PROPERTY MANAGER & MANAGER OF SUPPORT SERVICES. Clark AFB, TN (1997-04). Described as a solid leader who could be counted on to solve difficult problems, controlled multimillion-dollar assets while supervising 38 flight services/supply specialists supporting 95 aircraft.
- Located sources for parts for a 15,067-line-item inventory valued in excess of $98 million.
- Took on a problem area, and in five months had succeeded in increasing parts availability from 36 to 65%; reduced unavailable parts rates 14%.
- Implemented strong measures for following up on difficult-to-locate parts and maintained 90% availability in one area where the Air Force's standard was 75%.
- Revitalized the awaiting-parts program and freed $400,000 in daily operating expenses.
- Established a training and job rotation system which produced thoroughly cross trained personnel and eliminated production losses due to absences for training.
- Reduced critical spares unavailability 20% by locating and correcting database errors.

PROGRAM MANAGER. Clark AFB, TN (1995-96). Transformed a substandard operation into one recognized for outstanding achievements while building a new atmosphere of cooperation and team work; managed a special equipment inventory in a program which prepared for rapid response to worldwide emergencies.
- Implemented a data base capable of monitoring assets valued in excess of $25 million.
- Was credited with making a broad range of improvements, including a comprehensive training plan, which greatly increased capabilities.
- Handpicked for a quality assessment team, developed a unit self-assessment plan.

INSTRUCTOR. Pope AFB, NC (1992-94). Consistently produced first-rate results as the senior instructor and role model for 400 basic trainees annually.

MANAGER, SUPPLY RECEIVING DEPARTMENT. Germany (1990-1991). Known for my initiative, technical supply knowledge, and expertise as a motivator, supervised ten people.
- Prepared discrepancy reports; worked with stock control personnel to solve problems.
- Eliminated sea and land shipment detention charges which had been $30,000 in 1990.
- Guided my section to recognition with a monthly incentive award six times in one year.

EDUCATION   Studied Business Management, Central Texas College.
& TRAINING   Completed extensive training in logistics and property management; currently studying for a real estate broker's license at the Lexington Real Estate Academy.

PERSONAL   Anticipate the potential for problems and have a keen ability to develop remedies. Highly intuitive and resourceful problem solver. Outstanding references upon request.

Date

Exact Name of Person
Title or Position
Name of Company
Address
City, State, Zip

INTERIOR DESIGNER   Dear Exact Name of Person: (or Dear Sir or Madam if answering a blind ad.)

I would appreciate an opportunity to talk with you soon about how I could contribute to your organization through my sales and communication skills, interior design expertise, as well as my initiative and ability to work independently.

As you will see from my resume, I have been working since I was 16 years old, and I financed 80% of my college education through summer and part-time jobs. A highly motivated self-starter, I was nominated for numerous honors at Maryville University because of the leadership I provided on campus, to my sorority, and in the community. I am especially proud of the fact that, as my sorority's elected president, I transformed a poorly performing organization with serious financial problems into a respected entity which won the "most improved chapter" award.

I have found that my leadership is a valuable asset in business, too. I have a knack for motivating people, and I am respected for my ability to troubleshoot difficult problems and satisfy even the fussiest customers. You would certainly find me to be a hard worker who would enjoy contributing to your goals, and I would be delighted to provide outstanding personal and professional references at the appropriate time.

I hope you will welcome my call soon to arrange a brief meeting at your convenience to discuss your current and future needs and how I might serve them. Thank you in advance for your time.

Sincerely yours,

Joy Ann Honour

Alternate last paragraph:
I hope you will call or write me soon to suggest a time convenient for us to meet and discuss your current and future needs and how I might serve them. Thank you in advance for your time.

JOY ANN HONOUR

1110½ Hay Street, Fayetteville, NC 28305　•　preppub@aol.com　•　(910) 483-6611

OBJECTIVE　　To contribute to an organization that can use a creative and dynamic young professional with expertise related to interior, commercial, and residential design who offers very strong leadership, motivational, communication, and sales skills.

EDUCATION　　**Bachelor of Science (B.S.)** degree in **Human Environmental Sciences**, Maryville University, Maryville, SC, 2000.
- As elected president of my sorority, Delta Zeta, transformed a disorganized operation into the "most improved chapter in NC and SC"; was personally named "Outstanding President for NC and SC" and inducted into the Greek Hall of Fame.
- Was elected Student Legislator, Student Government Association; was elected Secretary of the legislature's Rules and Judiciary Committee.
- Was nominated for several prestigious awards for campus, community, and sorority leadership; received the respected Artemis Award.
- Personally financed 80% of my college education through part-time and summer jobs.

MEMBERSHIP　　Member, American Society of Interior Designers since 2000; presently an Allied Practitioner.

EXPERIENCE　　**INTERIOR DESIGNER.** The Decorator Store, Charleston, SC (2004-present). Have worked with this family-owned business since I was 16 years old, and have become an expert in all aspects of residential interior design in a shop that is well known for its creation of quality window treatments.
- Hired and supervised other employees.
- Am known for my skill in working with "fussy" clients in this custom business.
- Applied my leadership skills by helping this store to expand from its solid niche in window treatments into interior design consultation services.
- Have become skilled in figuring the actual fabrication of window treatments.
- Used my sales and organizational skills to improve customer relations/service.
- Because of my strong communication and motivational skills, am the interior designer who troubleshoots stubborn problems when they arise.

INTERIOR DESIGN INTERN. U.S. Government, Directorate of Engineering and Housing — Design Branch, Ft. Bragg, NC (2001-03). Received a letter of praise and appreciation and was complimented for my initiative and independence while excelling in an internship which required me to design an entire building; specified carpets, tile, and paints; performed some architectural sketching; redesigned a map.
- Worked on interior design recommendations for the new medical center at Ft. Bragg.
- Studied the design of local churches.
- Received an "A" for my internship; invited to participate in meetings on the new hospital.

COMPUTER OPERATOR. Maryville Technical Community College, Maryville, SC (2000-01). Processed information for a tire recycling project using the Apple computer; data processed the results of others research, and inputted mailing lists.

TYPIST. World Travel, Maryville, SC (2000). Typed letters, delivered tickets, and set up displays of travel brochures; took pride in doing very small jobs to the best of my ability.

PERSONAL　　Believe my leadership qualities are very valuable as they help me sell and motivate people. Am interested in gaining expertise in every aspect of interior design.

Date

Exact Name of Person
Title or Position
Name of Company
Address
City State, Zip

INTERIOR DESIGNER   Dear Exact Name of Person: (or Dear Sir or Madam if answering a blind ad.)

With the enclosed resume, I would like to make you aware of my background as an Interior Designer as well as my interest in exploring suitable employment opportunities with your organization. I am in the process of relocating to the Seattle area in order to be near my family, and I am approaching organizations in the Seattle market which might be in need of a strong and resourceful young design professional.

Design of Commercial and Educational Facilities

As you will see from my resume, I am currently excelling as an Interior Designer in Minneapolis, MN. While impressing both clients and my employer with my knowledge of finishes and furnishings as well as my expertise related to design/color, I have become known for my exceptionally strong communication skills and team leadership ability. Design projects I have worked on have included a middle school and elementary school, agricultural center, research building, and signage for a prominent university. Highly computer literate, I utilize AutoCAD on a daily basis and am proficient with Word.

Extensive Healthcare Design Experience

In my previous position as an Interior Designer in Duluth, MN, I oversaw the details of coordinating repair and construction projects as well as facility enhancements throughout the university hospital facilities. While becoming skilled in healthcare design, I handled specifications, budget analysis, and project design for projects which included the university's burn center, gynecology unit, ICU waiting area, pulmonary unit, ambulatory center, imaging department, pediatric waiting room, radiology waiting room, and the food and nutrition lounge.

Residential Design Knowledge

I also offer experience related to residential design. Immediately after graduating from University of Minnesota with a B.A. degree in Interior Design, I worked as an Interior Design Assistant and Sales Associate for a company in Coon Rapids, MN. In that job I assisted two interior designers in all aspects of residential design.

I hope you will contact me to suggest a time when we might meet to discuss your needs. Although I can provide outstanding references at the appropriate time, my current employer is unaware of my plans to relocate, so I would appreciate your keeping my approach confidential at this point. I am frequently in the Seattle area looking at housing, and I can make myself available to meet with you at your convenience. Thank you in advance for your professional courtesies.

Sincerely,

Simon Lawrence

SIMON LAWRENCE

1110½ Hay Street, Fayetteville, NC 28305   •   preppub@aol.com   •   (910) 483-6611

OBJECTIVE

To contribute to an organization that can use an innovative and resourceful interior designer who offers exceptionally strong communication, planning, and problem-solving skills.

EXPERIENCE

INTERIOR DESIGNER. Twin Cities Architectural Collaborative, Minneapolis, MN (2004-present). Have refined my team leadership skills while working on a variety of design projects ranging from Healthcare design to educational design.

- Utilize AutoCAD routinely to perform millwork/casework drawings, interior architectural details, flooring patterns, as well as space planning and interior layouts; room finish schedules; writing specifications; composing finish boards.
- Have been praised by clients and management for my outstanding communication skills; on a recent outstanding performance evaluation, was told that my strongest abilities are knowledge of finishes and furnishings, working with clients, and design/color.
- Projects include:

Hospital Family/Birthing Center	Twin Cities Hospital, St. Paul, MN
Designed a nurse station as a standard	Twin Cities Hospital, St. Paul, MN
Administrative Office area	Twin Cities Hospital, St. Paul, MN
Cancer Treatment Center	Twin Cities Hospital, St. Paul, MN
Psych/Rehab renovations	Coon Rapids Community Hospital, MN
Wellness Center	UniCare, Minneapolis, MN
UM Learning Center	University of Minnesota, Minneapolis, MN
Medical office building	St. Paul Medical Center
Twin Cities High School	Twin Cities Public Schools, St. Paul, MN
Lake Harriet Elementary School	Twin Cities Public Schools, St. Paul, MN

INTERIOR DESIGNER. University of Minnesota Hospitals, Duluth, MN (2002-04). Oversaw the details of coordinating repair and construction projects as well as facility enhancements throughout the university hospital facilities.

- Hired for a 200-hour internship, stepped into the designer's job when it was unexpectedly left vacant and became involved in working with the department supervisor to restructure the position and eliminate problems which had existed for some time.
- Assisted in restructuring the facility enhancement portion of the budget ($450,000) including combining budgeted figures into a concise report for the hospital administrators.
- Handled operational areas including ordering products and overseeing installation and repair.
- Consulted with physicians, nurses, and other involved administrative staff members to get their input into design projects for areas which directly affected them and the end users.
- Handled specifications, budget analysis, and design of projects such as:

Burn center renovations	Sleep disorders clinic	Pediatric clinics
Rehab in-patient unit	Dialysis in-patient unit	Hospital satellite clinics

EDUCATION

B.A. degree in Interior Design, University of Minnesota, Minneapolis, MN, 2002.

- Was instrumental as a member of the class which completed all the preliminary work resulting in gaining the program FIDER (Foundation for Interior Design Education Research) accreditation; this degree program is the model for the university's future.
- Coordinated formal and social events as well as serving on the standards board which helped promote a positive image for Beta Alpha Chi sorority.

PERSONAL

Highly creative and resourceful self-starter who excels in working with others.

CAREER CHANGE

Date

Exact Name of Person
Title or Position
Name of Company
Address
City, State, Zip

Dear Exact Name of Person (or Dear Sir or Madam if answering a blind ad):

With the enclosed resume, I would like to make you aware of my interest in exploring property management employment opportunities with your organization.

Extensive experience in interior design

As you will see from my enclosed resume, I am an experienced interior designer with nearly 20 years of experience in the field. Until 2005, I was associated with a construction firm which I helped to establish "from scratch" in 1988. The company built approximately 30 speculative houses a year, and I took care of the interior designing and financial management of the firm while my partner tended to the construction side of the business. The company created new subdivisions and built homes in all price ranges, from $100,000 to $500,000. When the firm relocated to Jackson in 2005, I decided not to move, and I have been self-employed as an Interior Designer. Most recently I have made major contributions to new homes in Pascagoula which expressed contemporary, southern living, and traditional styles.

In-depth understanding of the construction and loan processing business

My background includes experience as a Senior Loan Processor with a major mortgage corporation, where I was involved in construction analysis, construction management, and loan processing. I hold a General Contractor's license in the state of Mississippi, and I am skilled at working with architectural plans, drawings, and blueprints.

If you can use a talented manager who possesses a gift for being able to visualize the final result and bring the customer's dreams to reality, I hope you will contact me to suggest a time when we might meet to discuss your needs. I offer versatile administrative and creative abilities which I am confident could be of value to a company such as yours. Thank you in advance for your time, and I hope to have the pleasure of meeting with you.

Yours sincerely,

Kate Marquand

KATE MARQUAND

1110½ Hay Street, Fayetteville, NC 28305 • preppub@aol.com • (910) 483-6611

OBJECTIVE

To become associated with an organization and with individuals who seek to employ a professional with experience in home decorating and interior design along with an in-depth understanding of construction, home building, land development, and loan processing.

EXPERIENCE

INTERIOR DESIGNER. Self-employed, Pascagoula and Gulfport-Biloxi, MS (2005-present). Designed and implemented the home decorating plans for three new homes in Pascagoula: a 6,000-sq. ft. home and two 3,000-sq. ft. homes expressing contemporary, southern living, and traditional tastes.
- Redlined plans and made changes to architectural drawings based on how the families would live in the house; fixed serious design flaws. Selected light fixtures, tile colors, paint colors, brick colors, carpets and draperies, and other items.

INTERIOR DESIGNER & FINANCIAL MANAGER. Southern Mississippi, Inc., Gulfport-Biloxi, MS (1988-05). Was part of a two-person team that started up "from scratch" a successful new homebuilding business that ultimately built 30 new speculative houses a year in a community which experienced continuous turnover of military personnel.
- Managed the bookkeeping and interior design aspects of the business while my partner tended to the technical aspects of homebuilding and construction. Controlled finances and reviewed subcontractor bids and bills. Managed payables and receivables. Prepared financial reports.
- Supervised colors and accessories for the interior and exterior of homes. Worked with homes at the planning stage in order to assure the most beautiful staging of the house and its amenities. Chose fabrics, colors, and fixtures which appealed to home buyers. Anticipated changing trends in styles, materials, and colors and integrated my knowledge into the interior decorating stage.
- Played a major role in developing new subdivisions; determined brick, siding, and paint exteriors and designed the interiors of those homes in suitable ways.
- The business moved to Jackson. I chose not to relocate and have worked freelance.

SENIOR LOAN PROCESSOR & CONSTRUCTION ANALYST. Harrison County Mortgage Corporation, Gulfport, MS (1982-88). Began in an entry-level receptionist position, and was rapidly promoted to supervise personnel, handle loan processing, and review construction plans.
- **Construction analysis:** Reviewed construction plans and set up lines of credit for contractors. Approved payment of funds. Coordinated reports detailing the sold/unsold status of properties.
- **Construction management:** Established new office. Managed employees refinancing mortgages.
- **Loan processing:** Became an expert in underwriting and processing FHA, VA, FNMA, and NC housing loans. Interviewed prospective customers. Reviewed and submitted guarantee documents and closing instructions.

EDUCATION

A.A.S. in Business Management; William Carey College, MS, 1982. Was named to the Dean's List every semester. Received the Business Achievement Award and was selected by teachers as "Best All-Around Student."

LICENSE

General Contractor's license, state of Mississippi

PERSONAL

Outstanding references on request. Skilled in organizing complex activities.

Date

Exact Name of Person
Title or Position
Name of Company
Address (number and street)
Address (city, state, and zip)

LEASING CONSULTANT

Dear Exact Name of Person (or Sir or Madam if answering a blind ad):

I would appreciate an opportunity to talk with you soon about how I could contribute to your organization through my experience in apartment lease/rental operations as well as through my reputation as a people-oriented, enthusiastic, and energetic young professional.

Known as quick learner, I can be depended on for personal integrity, resourcefulness, and dedication to excellence in everything I attempt. As you will see from my enclosed resume my most recent jobs have been as a Leasing Consultant in Colorado Springs, CO. For ABC Investments, Inc., I was entrusted with managing a large 280-unit property and a smaller 78-unit property. Earlier with Alpha Financial Services, Inc., I earned advancement after only a month with the company and gained a strong interest in continuing to grow and provide excellent services in this field.

I hope you will welcome my call soon to arrange a brief meeting to discuss your current and future needs and how I might serve them. Thank you in advance for your time.

Sincerely,

Pearl N. Golden

Alternate last paragraph:
I hope you will call or write me soon to suggest a time convenient for us to meet and discuss your current and future needs and how I might serve them. Thank you in advance for your time.

PEARL N. GOLDEN

1110½ Hay Street, Fayetteville, NC 28305   •   preppub@aol.com   •   (910) 483-6611

OBJECTIVE

To offer my knowledge and experience in the area of property management and apartment rental and leasing operations to an organization that can use an enthusiastic young professional known for well-developed customer service and human relations skills.

EXPERIENCE

LEASING CONSULTANT. ABC Investments, Inc., Colorado Springs, CO (2004-present). Was credited with increasing the occupancy rate for the company's rental units while managing a 280-unit property and a smaller 78-unit property.
- Organized the operations of the property management office and provided excellent customer service through my professionalism in providing the highest quality services.
- Maintained records on leased apartments and prepared weekly and monthly reports.
- Balanced records of rent received as well as other cash income.
- Displayed a mature and professional manner while managing the office to include answering phones, walking prospective renters through unoccupied units, and completing lease arrangements.
- Was entrusted with full charge of the office when the Property Manager was away and counted on for sound judgment and decision-making skills.
- Created flyers promoting the complex and took them to various local companies for display; resulting in increasing awareness of the complex, thereby producing more leased units.
- Earned units toward my CAM — Certified Apartment Manager — designation.

LEASING CONSULTANT. Alpha Financial Services, Inc., Colorado Springs, CO (2000-04). Demonstrated interest, enthusiasm, and strong communication and "people" skills which led to my advancement to this position after only a month with the company.
- Learned the proper and ethical ways to succeed in this business and was given increasingly more responsibility in showing, leasing, and managing rental/leased properties.

TEACHER and **EARLY CHILDHOOD EDUCATION SPECIALIST.** Manana/La Casa Unified School District, Manana, CA (1999). Planned and oversaw age-appropriate classroom activities; supervised three aides while ensuring each child was learning in a safe and interesting environment.
- Refined my planning and time management skills while earning 24 units in Early Childhood Education.

SITE DIRECTOR. Poco Hills Family YMCA, Manana, CA (1995-98). Originally hired as a Counselor, took on full responsibility for an after-school program for 35 school-age children at its start up.
- Was selected from a group of four counselors to provide leadership and supervision for all phases of the new program.
- Planned activities and ensured that social, emotional, and physical developmental needs of the children were being met and that they were in a safe and healthy environment.

EDUCATION

Completed two years of college course work with concentrations in Child Development and Nursing, Mt. San Antonio College, Walnut, CA.

TRAINING

Attended a training program sponsored by the Apartment Association of Colorado Springs, CO, with an emphasis on legal and motivational training as well as resident relations.

PERSONAL

Am a quick learner and work well with people as a member of a team or independently.

Date

Exact Name of Person
Title or Position
Name of Company
Address
City, State, Zip

LOAN CLOSING SPECIALIST & LEGAL ASSISTANT
for a private real estate practice

Dear Exact Name of Person: (or Dear Sir or Madam if answering a blind ad.)

I would appreciate an opportunity to talk with you soon about how I could contribute to your organization through my training as a Loan Closing Specialist/Legal Assistant.

Currently employed as a Loan Closing Specialist/Legal Assistant for Kevin H. Fuller, a well-known Attorney in Springfield with a private real estate practice, I assist in preparing loan packages and closings while preparing legal documents, conducting title searches, and providing customer service. In a previous position as a Loan Processing Clerk for the Springfield Federal Reserve Bank, I became skilled in all aspects of loan processing while handling mortgage banking and loan processing within a budget of over one million dollars. I submitted loans, coordinated appraisals, prepared legal documents, and compiled loan packages as well as interviewed loan applicants and prepared applications. I also coordinated with a wide range of real estate attorneys, appraisers, residential and commercial sales professionals, and VA/FHA officials.

While earning a Bachelor of Arts degree in English from the Chaminade University of Honolulu, Hawaii, I completed courses in Public Speaking, Business Writing, and English Literature. I am also skilled in utilizing various accounting and banking programs being proficient with Windows XP, Microsoft Word, Excel, and PowerPoint.

I hope you will welcome my call soon to arrange a brief meeting at your convenience to discuss your needs and goals and how I might serve them. Thank you in advance for your time.

Yours sincerely,

Tina M. Shaver

Alternate last paragraph:
I hope you will call or write soon to suggest a time convenient for us to meet and discuss your current and future needs and how I might serve them. Thank you in advance for your time.

TINA M. SHAVER

1110½ Hay Street, Fayetteville, NC 28305   •   preppub@aol.com   •   (910) 483-6611

OBJECTIVE   To benefit an organization that can use a hard-working professional experienced in office operations with specialized knowledge of loan closing procedures, accounting/bookkeeping, and marketing/publicity.

EDUCATION   Earned **B.A. in English**, Chaminade University of Honolulu, Honolulu, HI, 1999.
In my spare time, am completing courses toward a B.S. degree in Management, University of Illinois, Springfield, Illinois.

COMPUTERS   Skilled in utilizing various accounting and banking programs; proficient with Windows XP, Microsoft Office, and MLS.

EXPERIENCE   **LOAN CLOSING SPECIALIST & LEGAL ASSISTANT.** Kevin H. Fuller, Attorney-at-Law, Springfield, IL (2003-present). For a private real estate practice, assist in preparing loan packages and closings while also preparing legal documents, conducting title searches, and providing customer service.
- Use Windows operating system with specialized software.

LOAN PROCESSING CLERK. Springfield Federal Reserve Bank, Springfield, IL (2002-03). Became skilled in all aspects of loan processing while handling mortgage banking and loan processing within a budget of over one million dollars.
- Submitted loans, coordinated appraisals, prepared legal documents, and compiled loan packages.
- Interviewed loan applicants and prepared applications; provided customer service.
- Coordinated with a wide range of real estate attorneys, appraisers, residential and commercial sales professionals, and VA/FHA officials.

ACCOUNTING SPECIALIST. Morrison Business Services, Honolulu, HI (1997-02). Played a key role in the substantial growth of this small business which provided accounting services for small businesses.
- On my own initiative, developed and implemented aggressive marketing programs which coordinated telemarketing and direct mail activities with persistent follow-up.
- Provided all accounting support for small businesses: prepared P&Ls, payroll, general ledgers, and journals.
- Trained small businesses in recordkeeping procedures and performance reporting activities.

MARKETING COORDINATOR. Felder-Marcum, Inc., Honolulu, HI (1995-97). Developed and implemented national and local marketing programs for restaurants in Honolulu, Kahului & Laie.

MARKETING REPRESENTATIVE. Hampton Golf Club, Springfield, IL (1993-95). Excelled in a key position in marketing and public relations and worked closely with Hampton's founder and Springfield native Michael Bradford.
- Was instrumental in the development of the company's first marketing manual.
- Designed and published a golf course magazine; coordinated national tournaments and reporting results.

PERSONAL   Excellent references. Possess excellent written and verbal communication skills and work well with people at all ages. Congenial personality.

Date

Exact Name of Person
Title or Position
Name of Company
Address
City, State, Zip

MARKETING ASSOCIATE   Dear Exact Name of Person: (or Dear Sir or Madam if answering a blind ad.)

With the enclosed resume, I would like to make you aware of my interest in exploring employment opportunities with your organization.

As you will see from my resume, I entered the property management field immediately after graduating from high school, and I demonstrated my ability to excel in handling multiple simultaneous tasks as Assistant Manager of two apartment complexes. Because of my outstanding personal reputation, I was recruited by an apartment complex to serve as Leasing Manager for two complexes with more than 500 units. I was subsequently promoted by my employer to serve as Marketing Associate of a troubled complex with numerous delinquency and tenant problems. Through my strong problem-solving and public relations skills, I have reduced delinquencies by 80% while aggressively collecting more than $150,000 in monies owed the corporation.

Although I am held in high regard in my current position and am being groomed for further promotion, I am selectively exploring other opportunities. Although I can provide outstanding references at the appropriate time, I ask that you not contact my current employer until we have a chance to talk about your needs.

I hope you will call or write soon to suggest a time convenient for us to meet and discuss your current and future needs and how I might serve them. Thank you in advance for your time.

Sincerely,

Amber Nevak

Alternate last paragraph:
I hope you will welcome my call soon to arrange a brief meeting at your convenience to discuss your current and future needs and how I might serve them. Thank you in advance for your time.

AMBER NEVAK

1110½ Hay Street, Fayetteville, NC 28305   •   preppub@aol.com   •   (910) 483-6611

OBJECTIVE

To offer my knowledge and experience in the area of property management as well as apartment rental and leasing operations to an organization that can use an enthusiastic young professional with outstanding communication and negotiation skills.

EXPERIENCE

Have excelled in the following track record of advancement to increasing responsibilities with PRP of NH, LLC (2004-present).

MARKETING ASSOCIATE. Merrimack Apartments, Concord, NH (2005-present). Was promoted by PRP to a job equivalent to Assistant Manager with this 356-unit complex, and have been credited with decreasing the number of delinquent accounts through my diligence and willingness to collect door-to-door, when necessary; have become proficient in handling cases through Small Claims Court.

- Lease apartments and process applications; familiarize new residents with our lease and policies; conduct move-in and move-out inspections.
- Am knowledgeable of eviction procedures.
- Process weekly reports promptly.
- Oversee two corporate accounts.
- Supervise and train one employee.

LEASING MANAGER & ASSISTANT MANAGER. Penacook Lake Apartments, Merrimack Apartments, and Little Pond Woods Apartments, Concord, NH (2004-05). Began employment with the company as a floating leasing agent and was assigned for two months to the 253-unit Little Pond Woods Apartments complex and then to Penacook Lake Apartments before being promoted to Assistant Manager of the 280-unit Merrimack Apartments.

- Handled leasing of apartments and processed applications, lease signings, as well as move-in and move-out inspections.
- Collected rent and bank deposits; was responsible for lease renewals.
- Processed weekly reports and wrote a monthly newsletter.
- At Merrimack Apartments, brought in one corporate account with 24 apartments.

Other experience:

ASSISTANT MANAGER. Rollins Park Apartments (managed by Green Meadow Associates), Concord, NH (2001-04). After excelling as part-time Leasing Agent working at both Pinebrook and Rollins Park Apartments, was hired as a full-time Assistant Manager at Rollins Park Apartments where I signed leases, processed applications, and leased apartments.

- Was interim Manager for two months while the manager was on maternity leave.

AFFILIATION

Received NALP designation, Merrimack County Apartment Association.

EDUCATION

Completed extensive hands-on and formal training related to property management sponsored by my employers.

Graduated from Concord High School, Concord, NH, 2001. Was on the varsity basketball team and the varsity soccer team for four years. Named MVP of my soccer team in my senior year.

COMPUTERS

Experienced with Rent Roll and Prentice Hall property management programs. Proficient with software including Word, Excel, and Access.

PERSONAL

Excellent references upon request. Known for my strong work ethic. Am single (never married). Have family in the Concord area, which I consider home.

Date

Exact Name of Person
Title or Position
Name of Company
Address
City, State, Zip

**MARKETING
COORDINATOR**

Dear Exact Name of Person: (or Dear Sir or Madam if answering a blind ad.)

With the enclosed resume, I would like to make you aware of my interest in exploring employment opportunities with your organization.

As you will see from my resume, I have excelled in a variety of jobs in the real estate and property management field. In one job as a Telemarketer for time share condominiums, I gained insight into the real estate industry as I learned how the most successful sales agents represented properties so that buyers could appreciate the advantages. In subsequent positions as a Leasing Agent, I showed property to prospective tenants, handled maintenance requests, and performed moving in and moving out inspections.

My interpersonal skills are very strong, and I have been commended by all my employers for my ability to remain calm under pressure and take the most prudent action in an emergency. In my experience, working in the property management field is all about satisfying customers and solving problems, and I offer a proven ability to excel in both areas.

I hope you will call or write soon to suggest a time convenient for us to meet and discuss your current and future needs and how I might serve them. Thank you in advance for your time, and I will cheerfully provide outstanding references at the appropriate time.

Sincerely,

Catherine Jackson

Alternate last paragraph:
I hope you will welcome my call soon to arrange a brief meeting at your convenience to discuss your current and future needs and how I might serve them. Thank you in advance for your time.

CATHERINE JACKSON

1110½ Hay Street, Fayetteville, NC 28305   •   preppub@aol.com   •   (910) 483-6611

OBJECTIVE   To benefit an organization that can use a talented marketing professional with excellent communication and "people" skills along with the dedication to excel in sales and marketing.

EDUCATION   **Associates Degree, Marketing and Retailing**, Alaska Pacific University, Anchorage, AK, 2005.
Certificate, Travel Agent Training, Alaska Travel Academy, Anchorage, AK, 2000.

EXPERIENCE   **MARKETING COORDINATOR.** Denali Advertising, Inc., Anchorage, AK (2004-present). Invite members of the community to come and share in a dinner and presentation to promote Inlet Corporation's new housing development. Display model homes.

LEASING AGENT. Tudor Apartments, Anchorage, AK (2003-04). Showed property to prospective tenants. Typed rental leases and other forms and prepared petty cash reports. Performed market surveys and mailed literature on available apartments. Answered phones and scheduled move in/out appointments. Filed paperwork, helped check invoices and bills, accepted rent payments and provided receipts. Logged all contract work for maintenance, maintained key control policy, monitored maintenance inventory, and kept a visitor log.

FRONT DESK CLERK. Marriott Hotel, Anchorage, AK (2002). Checked guests in/out of hotel; provided assistance in locating rental cars and placing restaurant reservations. Informed guests on tour availabilities and flight schedules. Maintained key inventory, compiled shift reports, and made reservations as needed. Prepared end-of-shift reports and balanced drawer after each shift. Accepted phone calls coming into the front desk and covered operator phone as needed.

LEASING AGENT. Parks Management Inc., Eagle River, AK (2001-02). Was given a great deal of responsibility due to my maturity and ability to perform calmly and productively under pressure. Showed model units to prospective tenants. Performed move in/out inspections. Prepared lease agreements and other forms in addition to filing and faxing paperwork. Maintained maintenance inventory, helped write rent receipts, balanced ledgers at the end of each month, and performed market surveys. Maintained cleanliness of club house and kept a log of visitors and their needs.

SALES ASSOCIATE. Gottschalks, Eagle River, AK (1999). Set up displays, maintained and stocked inventory, operated cash register, and assisted customers with purchases. Was one of the highest ranking sales persons and was offered an Assistant Manager position which, unfortunately, conflicted with my college schedule.

TELEMARKETER. Midnight Sun Village, Anchorage, AK (1998). Contacted people by phone to provide information on time share condos, and set appointments for interested persons to view the resort and speak to sales representatives.

Highlights of other experience:
SALES SPECIALIST. Various locations, Fairbanks, AK (1995-97). Provided fashion tips to customers requiring assistance, rang purchases on cash register, prepared layaways, and took inventory. Performed slight stocking, house cleaning, and modeled new clothes at employee meetings. Maintained very high sales volume.

PERSONAL   Have acquired a talent for selling an idea or product. Outstanding references on request.

CAREER CHANGE

Date

Exact Name of Person
Title or Position
Name of Company
Address
City, State, Zip

**MORTGAGE BROKER &
ESTATE PLANNER/
EXECUTOR**

Dear Exact Name of Person: (or Dear Sir or Madam if answering a blind ad.)

I would appreciate an opportunity to talk with you soon about how I could contribute to your organization through my finance, sales, and management experience.

As you will see from my resume, I have excelled as a mortgage banker and can provide outstanding personal and professional references. For eight years after graduating from college, I advanced in a track record of promotion with Chaves Financial Services. As a Mortgage Broker I became skilled in debt restructuring and financial analysis. I then became the company's inhouse expert on credit matters, and I played a key role in developing and implementing a new program for underwriters. I demonstrated my ability to adapt to change when I personally trained associates after my employer changed the nature of its mortgage business to the straight referral of applications. Because of my leadership ability and conceptual skills, I was promoted to Division Manager.

In 2006, I voluntarily resigned from my position in order to assume full-time responsibilities as executor of my father's estate after he passed away. I felt it was my responsibility to make prudent decisions for my siblings on matters related to his business and personal assets. Now that I have completed this personal project, I am ready to return to the mortgage brokerage field.

Although the door is open for me to return to my previous employer, I am selectively exploring opportunities with other companies that can use a hard charger with a proven ability to positively impact the bottom line. I feel certain that you would find me to be a hard-working and reliable professional who prides myself on doing any job to the best of my ability.

I hope you will welcome my call soon to arrange a brief meeting at your convenience to discuss your current and future needs and how I might serve them. Thank you in advance for your time.

Sincerely yours,

Kurt Gainey

KURT GAINEY

1110½ Hay Street, Fayetteville, NC 28305   •   preppub@aol.com   •   (910) 483-6611

OBJECTIVE

To benefit an organization that can use a versatile young professional who has excelled in sales and management through applying my excellent analytical and problem-solving skills as well as my ability to train and motivate employees.

EDUCATION

B.S. degree in Economics with a minor in Industrial Engineering, New Mexico State University, Las Cruces, NM, 1998.
Completed extensive training related to financial services sponsored by my employer.

EXPERIENCE

MORTGAGE BROKER & ESTATE PLANNER/EXECUTOR. Bottomless Lakes Mortgage, Inc., Roswell, NM (2006-present). Use my sales and public relations skills to prospect for and generate new accounts while brokering loans to underwriters.
- After the resignation of my father, took over the responsibility of administering his estate; made decisions related to the disposition of business assets, personal assets, and real property while settling accounts with customers, collecting accounts receivable, and determining investment strategies.

DIVISION MANAGER/MORTGAGE BROKER. Chaves Financial Services, Inc., Roswell, NM (1998-06). Was promoted in the following track record of advancement:
2004-06: After being promoted to Division Manager, maintained the highest closing ratio in the company while supervising five account executives and playing a key role in developing the company's strategic marketing plans.
- Maintained accounts, developed new underwriters, and hired/trained new employees.
- Succeeded in an industry which has an extremely high turnover rate.
2001-04: As an Assistant Manager/Broker, trained new employees and supervised other brokers during a time when the company changed its mortgage business to the straight referral of applications; generated and closed my own accounts.
2000-01: As a Loan Originator, played a key role in implementing the company's new program to "Table Fund" mortgage loans; worked applications generated by Chaves and then closed loans and sold them to underwriters.
- Gained expertise in completing all the paper work and documentation related to mortgage processing, including verifications and appraisals.
1999-00: As an Assistant Manager, oversaw a new corporate program which provided applications in specific regions to our underwriters; reviewed all applications taken daily and designated them to appropriate underwriters.
- Became the company's "in-house expert" on matters pertaining to credit requirements, income requirements, and specific programs for determining proper destination.
1998-99: Began with this company as a Mortgage Broker after graduating from college; contacted customers with loans financed at a high rate and motivated them to refinance.
- Became skilled in areas including debt restructuring and financial analysis; learned to examine individual financial situations and identify needs.

SALES REPRESENTATIVE/COLLECTIONS AGENT. New Mexico Cable Services, Albuquerque, NM (1996-98). Excelled in sales during a full-time summer job and was then invited to take a part-time job in collections when I resumed a full load as a college student.

PERSONAL

Can provide excellent personal and professional references. Enjoy golf, tennis, running, scuba diving, and guitar. Thrive on the challenge of making a contribution to the "bottom line." Was known by customers for my high ethical standards in selling products/services of real value. Am single and open to relocation and travel.

Date

Exact Name of Person
Title or Position
Name of Company
Address
City, State, Zip

**MORTGAGE
CONSULTANT**

One interesting feature
of this resume is that it
is in a semi-functional
format, which may
interest those of you
who are curious about
functional resumes.
Even his cover letter is
set up in a functional
format, so that he can
identify key areas of
competency to
prospective employers.

Dear Exact Name of Person: (or Dear Sir or Madam if answering a blind ad.)

With the enclosed resume, I would like to inquire about employment opportunities in your organization and make you aware of my extensive background related to sales and marketing, customer service, and management.

Sales, customer service, and marketing background

As you will see from my resume, I have most recently excelled in handling sales and customer service responsibilities in both the financial services and automobile sales field. In my earliest positions as an Auto Sales Representative, I refined my communication and negotiating skills and then advanced in a track record of accomplishment as a Sales Manager and then General Sales Manager. In my current job in the financial services field, I am excelling as a Mortgage Consultant in a highly competitive marketplace, and I am known for my excellent communication and negotiating skills.

Experience in contracting and purchasing

In a previous job, I refined my decision-making and problem-solving skills as an Assistant Contract Officer. I was authorized to approve contracts under $500,000 for the procurement of goods and services, and I was commended for my ability to maintain excellent working relationships while overseeing strict quality assurance related to the expenditure of public money.

Military and security background

As a young airman in the Air Force, I proudly served my country and was entrusted with one of the nation's highest security clearances: Top Secret. After military service, I worked in the law enforcement and corrections field and continued to serve my country in the National Guard in administrative capacities.

I can provide outstanding references at the appropriate time, and I would enjoy an opportunity to talk with you in person about your needs. If you can use a versatile young professional who is accustomed to excelling in multifaceted complex assignments, I hope you will contact me. Thank you in advance for your time.

Yours sincerely,

Mark R. Graham

MARK R. GRAHAM

1110½ Hay Street, Fayetteville, NC 28305 • preppub@aol.com • (910) 483-6611

OBJECTIVE

I want to contribute to an organization that can use an accomplished sales professional who offers a proven ability to establish strong working relationships, generate profitable bottom-line results, and provide outstanding customer service.

EDUCATION

College: Completed three years of college at these institutions: studied **General Studies** and **Sociology**, Boston College, MA; studied **Business Administration**, Northeastern University, MA; and studied **Business Administration**, Boston Business College, MA.
Military Training: Completed technical training and professional development courses sponsored by the U.S. Air Force; areas studied included administration and operations management.
Sales: Completed numerous courses related to sales and customer service sponsored by my employers.

EXPERIENCE

Sales and Financial Field:
MORTGAGE CONSULTANT. New England Mortgage, Brookline, MA (2004-present). As a mortgage consultant for a regional mortgage brokerage company, provide services related to debt consolidation while refinancing VA, FHA, conforming, and nonconforming loans.

GENERAL SALES MANAGER. Peter David Used Cars, Lexington, MA (2000-04). Was recruited by the founder of the company to serve as his General Sales Manager; supervised up to ten sales professionals including assistant sales managers.
- Trained sales professionals in winning techniques related to sales and customer service.
- Helped my sales staff become skilled at "closing the sale" and negotiating final details.

SALES MANAGER. Revere Chrysler-Suzuki, Lexington, MA (1995-99). Was credited with being a major force in helping the company achieve gross sales of $32 million a year along with an extremely healthy after-tax income.
- Resigned from this job when I was recruited by my former employer, Peter David, to become his General Sales Manager.

Corrections and Law Enforcement Field:
CORRECTIONAL OFFICER. (1990-94). Worked in a 1,000-man corrections facility in Maryland State Penitentiary, Potomac, MD and in the Bethesda City Jail, Bethesda, MD.

Contracting and Finance Field:
ASSISTANT CONTRACT OFFICER. Defense Control Administrative Services, Bethesda, MD (1985-90). Was authorized to approve contracts under $500,000 for the procurement of goods and services for the U.S. government; refined my communication and negotiating skills while fine-tuning the details of complex contracts.

Military Service:
ADMINISTRATIVE SPECIALIST. Strategic Air Command, Andrews AFB, MD (1980-84). Held a Top Secret security clearance and was entrusted with receiving Top Secret documents and other classified documents. Was promoted rapidly from Airman to Sergeant.

PERSONAL

Enjoy helping others and being in business situations in which my product knowledge can help consumers make a wise decision about products and services. Have proven my ability to provide the finest customer service in a highly competitive marketplace.

Date

Exact Name of Person
Title or Position
Name of Company
Address
City, State, Zip

MORTGAGE LENDING SUPERVISOR

Dear Exact Name of Person: (or Dear Sir or Madam if answering a blind ad.)

With the enclosed resume, I would like to make you aware of my interest in exploring employment opportunities with your organization.

As you will see from my resume, in my current position as a Mortgage Lending Supervisor, I have increased loan growth 24% in an economy hindered by high interest rates. While training and supervising 10 professionals, I have led the department to record levels of productivity while minimizing risk and losses.

In previous experience as a Mortgage Loan Processor with Bank of America, I became skilled in originating, preparing, processing, and closing mortgages, and I led a satellite office to produce over $46 million a year in mortgage loans.

With a reputation as a resourceful and creative executive, I can provide outstanding references at the appropriate time. My husband has accepted a position in Atlanta, and I am hoping to transfer my real estate and mortgage loan expertise to a financial institution in your area. I hope you will call or write soon to suggest a time convenient for us to meet and discuss your current and future needs and how I might serve them. Thank you in advance for your time.

Sincerely,

Theresa O'Sullivan

Alternate last paragraph:
I hope you will welcome my call soon to arrange a brief meeting at your convenience to discuss your current and future needs and how I might serve them. Thank you in advance for your time.

THERESA O'SULLIVAN

1110½ Hay Street, Fayetteville, NC 28305 • preppub@aol.com • (910) 483-6611

OBJECTIVE

To benefit an organization seeking a hardworking professional with an extensive background in consumer and mortgage lending who also possesses outstanding analytical, decision-making, and customer relations skills.

EDUCATION

Bachelor of Science degree in Industrial Personnel Psychology, Stetson University, Deland, FL; minored in **Business Administration,** 1998.
Executive training: Have attended a wide range of professional development continuing education courses, including the Consumer Banking School in Daytona Beach, FL, and classes in management skills, leadership, and mortgage and consumer lending.

LICENSURES

Licensed Florida Real Estate Broker.
Hold series 6 & 63 licenses with the National Association of Security Dealers.

EXPERIENCE

MORTGAGE LENDING SUPERVISOR. Bank of America, Deland, FL (2005-present). Oversee the daily operations of a mortgage lending department which holds $30 million in deposits and loans; supervise and evaluate ten employees.
- Hold lending authority to approve the full spectrum of loans and credit, including mortgages, consumer loans, and revolving credit. Increased loan growth 24%, consistently surpassing both personal and company goals.
- Design and apply loan growth policies; minimize risks and losses.

MORTGAGE LOAN PROCESSOR. Bank of America Mortgage Corporation/Bank of America, Deland, FL (2002-05). Applied my extensive background in loan environments while refining my problem-solving skills handling a variety of functions related to originating, preparing, processing, and closing mortgages; processed approximately 1,000 mortgages.
- Was instrumental in helping this satellite office produce over $45 million a year in mortgage loans. Prepared documents, obtained needed loan information, and maintained all records according to state and federal guidelines.

MORTGAGE LOAN PROCESSOR. Beville United Mortgage Company, Deland, FL (2001-02). Refined financial knowledge and skills while researching and processing mortgage loans for this well known financial institution.
- Screened customers for loan approval, prepared documents for underwriting and closing loans, and prepared closed mortgages for guaranty to government agencies.

RENTAL MANAGER. State Farm, Daytona Beach, FL (1996-01). Utilized my administrative and financial skills overseeing the maintenance of 270 rental properties and handling $1.5 million in escrow and trust accounts annually.
- Researched customer credit histories and designed advertising materials.

LOAN PROCESSOR. Re/Max Executive Realty, Daytona Beach, FL (1995-96). Discovered my ability for lending while preparing and coordinating mortgages and personal loan arrangements among buyers, sellers, mortgage companies, and attorneys.
- Deposited and disbursed funds, reconciled bank statements, and prepared and presented reports to top-level management.

PERSONAL

Am a versatile, dedicated professional known for attention to detail, integrity, and organizational skills. Enjoy challenges and maximizing my resources. Have consistently received excellent work evaluations. In process of relocating to Atlanta.

Date

Exact Name of Person
Title or Position
Name of Company
Address
City, State, Zip

MORTGAGE LOAN
ORIGINATOR

Dear Exact Name of Person: (or Sir or Madam if answering a blind ad.)

With the enclosed resume, I would like to make you aware of an experienced finance professional with exceptional supervisory, communication, and organizational skills who offers a track record of success in financial planning and loan origination as well as sales and customer service.

As you will see from my resume, I have been in the financial services field since 2001, when I became associated with Upstate Financial as a Manager Trainee. I also worked in the financial services field as a Finance and Supply Management Officer with the U.S. Army Reserves.

In my current job as a Mortgage Loan Originator, I have excelled in all aspects of my job. In December, I closed loans totaling $239,700 in volume–the most loans closed in the branch; this allowed our branch to earn $1,765,700 in volume which put us in the top spot in our region. I have earned a reputation as a highly effective communicator with the ability to discuss sophisticated concepts with attorneys and industry experts as well as the ability to talk in "layman's language" and explain technical and abstract concepts to average consumers.

Although I am highly regarded by my present employer and can provide outstanding references at the appropriate time, I would ask that you not contact my current employer until after we talk.

If you can use a sharp young professional with outstanding supervisory, communication, and organizational skills, I hope you will contact me to suggest a time when we might meet to discuss your needs and how I might serve them. I can assure you in advance that I have an outstanding reputation and would quickly become a valuable asset to your organization.

Yours sincerely,

Matthew Parsons

MATTHEW PARSONS

1110½ Hay Street, Fayetteville, NC 28305 • preppub@aol.com • (910) 483-6611

OBJECTIVE   To benefit an organization that can use an experienced finance professional with exceptional supervisory, communication, and organizational skills who offers a background in financial planning and loan origination as well as sales and customer service.

EDUCATION   **Bachelor of Arts degree in Communications and Public Relations**, Jefferson Community College, Watertown, NY, 2001.

COMPUTERS   Familiar with the operation of Windows XP; Microsoft Word, Excel, PowerPoint, and Access;

EXPERIENCE   **MORTGAGE LOAN ORIGINATOR.** Watertown Financial Services, Inc., Watertown, NY (2003-present). Provide customers with financial planning and consumer loan information for this busy mortgage loan broker. Process VA, FHA, conforming and non-conforming first and second mortgages while handling debt consolidations, refinancing, and other financial arrangements.
- Perform research to assess property value, determine lien status, and assess credit worthiness of the prospective client.
- Consult with attorneys, VA and FHA officials, appraisers, and other construction and lending officials in matters related to loan conveyance and loan closings.
- Develop consumer mortgage loan programs and devise financial plans to assist the customer in regaining control over their financial situation.
- Demonstrate my exceptional communication skills while marketing and explaining to the customer products and services that are not well-understood by the average consumer.
- Have the highest closing percentage (nearly 30%) on marketing leads provided by CMC.
- In Dec, I closed seven loans totaling $239,700 in volume–the most loans closed in the Branch; this allowed our branch to earn $1,765,700 in volume, to lead the region.

FINANCE and SUPPLY MANAGEMENT OFFICER. U.S. Army Reserves, Fort Drum, NY (2001-present). As a 1st Lieutenant in the Army Reserves, provide finance, logistics and support, and transportation services; served in Afghanistan during Operation Enduring Freedom. Continue as a "weekend warrior" once a month in order to serve my country.
- Supervise up to 30 employees, managing and tracking all cargo movements throughout the European theater. As Finance Officer, ensure the timely processing of per diem and finance issues. Provide technical assistance to all Department of Defense customers receiving outbound shipments of cargo. Serve as Training Officer for the Directorate of Logistics and manage training requirements for the organization.
- Processed more than 126 Transportation Movement Control Documents, 73 Hazardous Cargo Declaration forms, and 11 aircraft worth of equipment for deployment in three days, in support of a noncombatant evacuation mission to Kuwait.
- Coordinate movement requirements for the U.S. Army throughout Europe, providing sustainment operations and support in Afghanistan for Operation Enduring Freedom.

MANAGER TRAINEE. Upstate Financial, Watertown, NY (2001-02). Performed a variety of customer service, computer support, loan origination, and collections tasks for this busy national lender. Held fiscal responsibility for over $300,000 in accounts; reduced the branch's exposure to losses while increasing our customer base.
- Performed financial analysis and developed proposals for handling accounts; maintained account records and control forms. Maintained over 300 customer accounts by collecting on overdue accounts, developing sales plans, and selling debt consolidation proposals.

PERSONAL   Excellent personal and professional references are available upon request.

CAREER CHANGE

Date

Exact Name of Person
Title or Position
Name of Company
Address
City, State, Zip

MORTGAGE LOAN PROCESSOR

Dear Exact Name of Person: (or Dear Sir or Madam if answering a blind ad.)

With the enclosed resume, I would like to make you aware of my interest in exploring employment opportunities with your organization.

As you will see from my resume, I am currently excelling as a Mortgage Processor for the National Bank of Hawaii. I came to the National Bank of Hawaii with vast experience in the field, since I had previously worked for 20 years as a Loan Officer and Branch Manager with Bank of America. I have been able to put my experience to work for the National Bank of Hawaii in resourceful ways that improved profitability. For example, I spearheaded a new initiative that led to the creation of a database of potential customers. That new database has resulted in a $10 million increase in annual profits for the mortgage loan division.

Although I am held in the highest regard in my current position and can provide outstanding references, I am interested in exploring the possibility of applying my skills outside the banking community. I am confident that my strong analytical skills as well as my "instincts refined through experience" could be useful to a company seeking astute professionals who can analyze financial documents and make prudent strategic recommendations.

I hope you will call or write soon to suggest a time convenient for us to meet and discuss your current and future needs and how I might serve them. Thank you in advance for your time.

Sincerely,

Anthony Edwards

Alternate last paragraph:
I hope you will welcome my call soon to arrange a brief meeting at your convenience to discuss your current and future needs and how I might serve them. Thank you in advance for your time.

ANTHONY EDWARDS

1110½ Hay Street, Fayetteville, NC 28305 • preppub@aol.com • (910) 483-6611

OBJECTIVE I want to contribute to an organization that can use an experienced mortgage loan processor who offers savvy executive abilities related to discerning risk and identifying potential problems as well as a commitment to the highest levels of profitability and quality control.

EDUCATION **B.A. Economics and Social Studies**, Chaminade University of Honolulu, HI, 1988.
General Academic, Hawaii Pacific University, 1984-86.
Extensive professional training related to mortgage loan processing, financial administration, and customer service.

LICENSE Hold a Hawaii Real Estate Broker's License.

COMPUTERS Proficient with popular software programs including Microsoft Word, Excel, Access, and PowerPoint.
Experienced in utilizing customized software in the financial services industry and mortgage loans processing business.

EXPERIENCE **MORTGAGE LOAN PROCESSOR.** National Bank of Hawaii, Honolulu, HI (2005-present). Work in Honolulu, HI, in the main office and branch making construction and housing loans.
- As needed, serve in the main office of O'ahu (NBH) in Mililani Town, HI, working in administration with the bank's special assets including problem loans, foreclosures, bankruptcies, and the liquidation of foreclosed and repossessed property.
- Spearheaded a new initiative that led to the creation of a database of potential clients. This database allowed a new cadre of telemarketers to identify potential new clients and make appointments for mortgage processors, with the result that revenue grew by an additional $10 million in one year.

LOAN OFFICER & BRANCH MANAGER. Bank of America and Trust Company, Honolulu, HI (1990-05). Began my career at the Bank of America in collections and advanced to Loan Officer with responsibilities including examining and evaluating applications for lines of credit and installment loans.
- Authorized loan approvals up to $1 million.
- Analyzed applicant's financial status, credit, and property evaluation to determine feasibility for granting loan requests.
- Served as Installment Loan Manager in Waialua and Wai'anae, HI.
- Was promoted to Branch Manager, Pearl City, HI.
- Screened customers for loan approval, prepared documents for underwriting and closing loans, and prepared closed mortgages for guaranty to government agencies.

FIELD ENGINEER. Hawaii Company, Honolulu, HI (1988-90). Performed field work for housing sites for a company that provides engineering work on subdivisions for land developers.

MILITARY U.S. Army National Guard; Rank: Sergeant (Inactive), 1988-94

MEMBERSHIPS Member of Lions and Kiwanis Clubs

PERSONAL An avid reader of books related to entrepreneurship and business. Outstanding references.

CAREER CHANGE

Date

Exact Name of Person
Title or Position
Name of Company
Address
City, State, Zip

MORTGAGE LOAN SPECIALIST

This sales professional is actually seeking to transfer her skills into a new industry. She is hoping to convince employers in the pharmaceutical industry that she could excel in pharmaceutical sales through applying the same highly motivated nature which has helped her achieve outstanding results recently in banking and earlier in the human services field.

Dear Exact Name of Person: (or Dear Sir or Madam if answering a blind ad.)

With the enclosed resume, I would like to make you aware of my interest in employment as a Pharmaceutical Healthcare Representative with Pfizer. I believe you are aware that Don Smith, one of your Healthcare Representatives, has recommended that I talk with you because he feels that I could excel in the position as Pharmaceutical Healthcare Representative.

As you will see from my enclosed resume, I offer proven marketing and sales skills along with a reputation as a highly motivated individual with exceptional problem-solving skills. Shortly after joining my current firm as a Mortgage Loan Specialist, I was named Outstanding Loan Officer of the month through my achievement in generating more than $20 million in loans.

I believe much of my professional success so far has been due to my highly motivated nature and creative approach to my job. For example, when I began working for my current employer, I developed and implemented the concept of a postcard which communicated a message which the consumer found intriguing. The concept has been so successful that it has been one of the main sources of advertisements in our office and the concept has been imitated by other offices in the company.

In addition to my track record of excelling in the highly competitive financial services field, I have also applied my strong leadership and sales ability in the human services field, when I worked in adult probation services. I am very proud of the fact that many troubled individuals with whom I worked told me that my ability to inspire and motivate them was the key to their becoming productive citizens.

If you can use a creative and motivated self starter who could enhance your goals for market share and profitability, I hope you will contact me to suggest a time when we could meet in person to discuss your needs and goals and how I could meet them. I can provide strong personal and professional references at the appropriate time.

Yours sincerely,

Irene S. Lane

IRENE S. LANE

1110½ Hay Street, Fayetteville, NC 28305 • preppub@aol.com • (910) 483-6611

___

OBJECTIVE   To offer my experience in sales, marketing, and customer service to an organization that would benefit from my aggressive style of developing customer relationships and my desire to work for an organization that seeks to maximize market share and profitability.

EDUCATION   **B.S. in Business Administration,** University of San Diego, CA 1998.
- Completed this degree in my spare time while excelling in my full-time job.

EXPERIENCE   **MORTGAGE LOAN SPECIALIST.** First Mortgage Services, San Diego, CA (2004-present). Have continuously excelled in this position which requires excellent sales, customer service, decision making, and problem solving skills.
- Was named Outstanding Loan Officer for generating more than $20 million in loans.
- Process VA, FHA, conforming, and nonconforming first and second mortgages while handling debt consolidations, refinancing, and other financial arrangements.
- Consult with attorneys, VA and FHA officials, appraisers, and other construction and lending officials in matters related to loan conveyances and loan closings.
- Research property to assess value, ensure liens, and assess credit worthiness of clients.
- Am known for my gracious style of communicating with the public and for my ability to explain technical concepts in language that is understandable to lay people.
- Have gained valuable experience in marketing services which are not well understood by the average consumer.

MORTGAGE LOAN SPECIALIST. Ramsey Mortgage, San Diego, CA (2000-04). Gained expertise in all aspects of mortgage loan processing while becoming an expert in handling slow payments and credit repairs.

ADULT PROBATION SERVICES OFFICER. California Department of Corrections, San Diego, CA (1990-99). Because of my exceptional work performance, excellent attitude, and superior work performance, was promoted in the following track record:
1994-99: Adult Intensive Probation Parole Officer. Was promoted to a supervisory position which involved providing guidance and supervising a case load of 50 clients per week.
- Earned widespread respect for my ability to establish rapport and cordial relationships with individuals from troubled backgrounds and with turbulent case histories.
1990-94: Adult Probation/Parole Officer. Took pride in the fact that an extremely high percentage of my clients completed their probation and went on to become well adjusted and productive citizens; was frequently told that it was my leadership and motivation skills which made the difference in their lives.
- Provided supervision and guidance for up to 150 clients per month who were on court-ordered probation; completed paperwork and reports in a timely fashion.

DEPUTY CLERK. County Clerk of Superior Court, San Diego, CA (1988-90). Processed affidavits for court traffic tickets, misdemeanors, and felonies in the Criminal Division; was known for my professional style of interacting with others.

Other sales experience: Gained sales experience as an Account Representative for a company which sold sleep systems; also worked as a Sales Representative for a company marketing the Canon Facsimile line.

PERSONAL   Enjoy tackling, achieving, and exceeding ambitious goals through my ability to work effectively with others. Excel in prospecting for new business. Resourceful and high energy.

CAREER CHANGE

Date

Exact Name of Person
Title or Position
Name of Company
Address
City, State, Zip

OFFICE MANAGER   Dear Exact Name of Person: (or Dear Sir or Madam if answering a blind ad.)

With the enclosed resume, I would like to make you aware of the considerable administrative, clerical, sales, and management abilities I could put to work for you. I am responding to your ad for a Property Manager.

As you will see from my resume, I am skilled in all aspects of office activities and am proficient with the Windows XP program including Word, Excel, and Access. I am a very cheerful and adaptable person, as has been demonstrated by my ability to adapt rapidly and become quickly productive while working in long-term and short-term temporary assignments for major corporations, small businesses, and utility companies. I am skilled at operating a multi-line switchboard system.

A resourceful and enthusiastic individual, I have always found resourceful ways to contribute to increased efficiency in all of my jobs. For example, in one job with an electrical supply company, I developed ideas which resulted in increased efficiency in supply parts ordering. In another job with a prominent retailer, I was named Sales Representative of the Month and was credited with playing a key role in increasing repeat business through my customer service and sales skills.

In one of my first professional positions, I was promoted rapidly by a children's entertainment company to responsibilities which involved traveling to conventions to book shows and negotiate contracts.

If you can use a versatile young professional known for an excellent attitude as well as superior work habits including reliability, dependability, and honest, I hope you will contact me to suggest a time when we might meet to discuss your needs. I can assure you in advance that I could rapidly become an asset to your organization.

Sincerely,

Elaina Curtis

ELAINA CURTIS

1110½ Hay Street, Fayetteville, NC 28305   •   preppub@aol.com   •   (910) 483-6611

OBJECTIVE

To contribute to an organization that can use a hard worker and fast learner with extensive computer operations experience, proven skills in business management and business development, along with expertise related to marketing, advertising, and public relations.

EDUCATION

With a 3.87 GPA, have completed three years of college studies in Economical Finance, Charleston College, Charleston, SC; pursuing completion of the degree in my spare time.

SPECIAL SKILLS

Skilled in utilizing a variety of software for maximizing business performance:

Quicken Pro   One Write Plus
Windows XP, including Word, Excel, and Access

- Experienced in accounts receivable and payable as well as inventory control. Operate multi-line telephone systems. Excel in newsletter development and graphic layout.

EXPERIENCE

OFFICE MANAGER. Re/Max Homeowners, Ltd., Charleston, SC (2005-present). For a real estate company, function as the "right arm" to the owner as she concentrated her energies in sales while I manage all business and office functions; completed Real Estate School.

- Perform strategic business planning and development while also coordinating all marketing and advertising activities; design effective advertising.
- Handle all areas of accounting including payables and receivables.
- Process all the company's real estate contracts and perform liaison with customers.
- Schedule appointments for clients with the builder, interior decorator, insurance company, and closing attorney.
- As Office Manager, perform work previously done by two people; saved the company money by reorganizing office procedures and the filing system for greater efficiency.

MANAGER. JCI Dance, Charleston, SC (2004-05). Made significant contributions to the bottom line of this company which specialized in teaching the art of Ballroom dancing; handled all accounting matters, including the preparation of weekly and monthly reports, while also planning and implementing innovative campaigns to boost the numbers of students.

- Developed and implemented business plans that increased the customer base.
- Coordinated marketing and advertising activities.
- Prepared/analyzed reports pertaining to business development and strategic planning.
- Hired, trained, and supervised new employees including dance instructors.
- Played a key role in diversifying the types of dance instruction offered to include Country Western and Latin as well as Ballroom. Planned dance competitions and special events including parties; became known for my meticulous attention to detail in all matters.

MANAGER. Military Surplus, Charleston, SC (2002-04). For a small wholesale distribution company, excelled in numerous roles simultaneously; in this one-person office, handled sales, customer service, accounting, inventory control, and liaison with the parent company.

OFFICE MANAGER. Little People Entertainment, Charleston, SC (2001-02). For a children's entertainment company, was promoted to Junior Vice President (the youngest person ever to hold this title in the company); traveled extensively throughout the country to entertainment conventions to book shows.

- Oversaw accounts payable/receivable, tax preparation, employee hiring/training, as well as coordination with customers. Learned to negotiate contracts and close business deals.

PERSONAL

Have a cheerful, outgoing personality suited to customer service and property management.

Date

Exact Name of Person
Title or Position
Name of Company
Address
City, State, Zip

OFFICE MANAGER   Dear Exact Name of Person: (or Dear Sir or Madam if answering a blind ad.)

With the enclosed resume, I would like to make you aware of my interest in exploring employment opportunities within your organization.

As you will see from my resume, I offer considerable skills related to bookkeeping and accounting, office management, and computer operations. I loyally served my most recent employer, and the owners of the business will provide glowing references. I began my employment as a Receptionist and quickly became known for my enthusiastic style and intelligence. I was promoted to Office Manager and made many major contributions to the firm's profitability. I provided the leadership which convinced the owners to purchase new software for this real estate firm, and the firm is now operating in a state-of-the-art fashion with listings available on the Internet.

In addition to handling numerous administrative and management responsibilities, I was responsible for balancing checking accounts for five different companies. This included handling sales escrow accounts, accounts payable and receivable, property management accounts, and tenant security accounts. Through my initiative in computerizing bookkeeping, and through my leadership in computerizing rental income, we were able to free up precious time for management to engage in activities which improved the bottom line by 25%. I created numerous sales, production, and other reports which allowed the owners to analyze multiple factors related to profitability and cash flow.

Highly proficient in operating computers and in training employees and managers to use them, I am skilled at using Windows XP, Excel, Word, RealFast Forms, and spreadsheets. Experienced in troubleshooting computer problems, I can nearly always resolve computer problems without calling a hardware or software expert. I offer a proven ability to rapidly master new software and applications.

If you can use a vibrant communicator and enthusiastic hard worker, I hope you will contact me to suggest a time when we might meet to discuss your needs. I can assure you in advance that I could become a valuable asset to your organization.

Yours sincerely,

Agatha Shields

AGATHA SHIELDS

1110½ Hay Street, Fayetteville, NC 28305   •   preppub@aol.com   •   (910) 483-6611

OBJECTIVE   I want to contribute to an organization that can use my extensive background related to office management, computer operations, customer service, and public relations.

COMPUTERS   Highly proficient in operating and maintaining computers; utilize Windows XP; RealFast Forms, Excel Communications, Top Producer, Word, spreadsheets.
Office equipment: Utilize typewriters, calculators, scanners, copiers, fax machines.

EXPERIENCE   **OFFICE MANAGER.** Haikey, Hunter & Associates Real Estate, Tulsa, OK (2001-present). Began as a Receptionist and was promoted to Office Manager; made many contributions to this business through my strong personal initiative, outstanding organizational skills, expertise in bookkeeping and accounting, and computer knowledge.
Computer operations and administration:
- When I started with the firm, this real estate organization had two computers in the office; convinced the owners that multiple computers would result in more efficiency and boost profitability. By computerizing the rental department's bookkeeping, we were able to free up the rental manager's time to put more rental properties under contract, with the result that rental income increased 25%.
- Play a major role in assuring that the office is very up-to-date and efficient; that all real estate agents are on the Internet, that all the firm's listing are on line, and that out-of-town sellers could pull up their houses listed on the Internet.
- Became extremely skilled at troubleshooting computer problems, and learned how to rapidly pinpoint a problem and fix it myself without calling in a computer expert.
Reports:
- On my own initiative, compiled and created many different types of reports for my employers which they did not have before; these reports allowed them to identify where excess money was being spent and where the most income was being generated, and they praised me for enhancing their management decision-making process.
- Prepare payroll reports, production reports, sales reports, and other reports.
Accounting and bookkeeping:
- Balance checking accounts for five different companies including property management and tenant security deposit accounts and sales escrow account.
- Handle all accounts payable and receivable.
Customer service and public relations:
- Expertly handled the public while answering a 15-line switchboard as a receptionist.
- Learned the Tulsa Area Board of Realtors Multiple Listing Service, and provide highly professional support to the agents at Haikey, Hunter & Associates.

PROGRAM ASSISTANT. Oklahoma City Offices, Muskogee, OK (1999-01). At a time when this office was receiving new computers, I played a role in fielding and implementing new equipment and software. Trained employees. Made commodity loans; handled data entry.

EDUCATION   Studied Real Estate Licensing Law, Tulsa Real Estate Academy, Tulsa, OK, 2005.
Studied Accounting, Muskogee Community College, Muskogee, OK, 1997.
Completed numerous real estate programs and training updates, 1995-05.

LICENSE   Obtained my real estate license 2005.

PERSONAL   Have a strong sense of loyalty to my employer, and always give more than 100% to my job. In my spare time, enjoy walking and jogging, cross stitching, and refinishing furniture.

CAREER CHANGE

Date

Exact Name of Person
Title or Position
Name of Company
Address
City, State, Zip

**OFFICE MANAGER &
LICENSED OFFICE
REPRESENTATIVE**

Dear Exact Name of Person (or Dear Sir or Madam if answering a blind ad):

With the enclosed resume, I would like to make you aware of my desire to become a Real Estate Agent with your organization.

As you will see from my resume, I have excelled as Office Manager of B.J. Moore's Nationwide Insurance Office in New Castle, PA. In my spare time, I have earned my Bachelor of Science degree and am licensed to sell auto, life and health, and the full range of fire insurance products. I played a key role in helping this agent become a Legion of Honor Agent on multiple occasions, and I have become knowledgeable of all aspects of managing an insurance agency for maximum profitability. We continually re-underwrite our book of business to remain profitable, and we maintain vigilant quality control of our multiline single-line business in order to maintain a quality book of business.

Although I am held in high regard by my employer and have been strongly encouraged to make a career in the insurance business, I have decided that I wish to pursue a career in real estate sales and property management. I want to live and work in New Castle, where I grew up and where my strongest personal and professional relationships exist. I am confident that my outgoing personality, strong administrative skills, and ability to manage my time for maximum effectiveness will enable me to become very successful in real estate sales.

I hope you will contact me soon to suggest the next step I should take in exploring the opportunities for a real estate career with your company. Thank you in advance for your courtesies.

Sincerely,

Summer Reign

SUMMER REIGN

1110½ Hay Street, Fayetteville, NC 28305 • preppub@aol.com • (910) 483-6611

OBJECTIVE   To contribute to an organization that can use a dedicated hard worker who excels in establishing and maintaining effective working relationships while providing excellent personal service and applying my outstanding sales and marketing skills.

EDUCATION   Completed **Bachelor of Science degree in Education**, New Castle Community College, New Castle, PA, 2005.
- Completed this degree in my spare time while excelling in my full-time job.
- Excelled academically; graduated **magna cum laude.**

LICENSE   Licensed Insurance Agent, Property and Casualty as well as Life, Accident, and Health, with the State of Pennsylvania.

TRAINING   Extensive training in all aspects of quoting and writing insurance applications for Auto; Fire (Homeowners, Renters, Boat Owners, Personal Liability Umbrella, Inland Marine, and Commercial); Life and Health.

EXPERIENCE   **OFFICE MANAGER & LICENSED OFFICE REPRESENTATIVE.** Nationwide Insurance, B.J. Moore's Office, New Castle, PA (1999-present). Became employed by my mother's insurance agency shortly after graduating from high school; have become a Licensed Insurance Agent while also acting as Office Manager.
- Quote and write insurance applications for Auto; Life and Health; and Fire coverage including homeowners, renters, boat owners, personal liability umbrella, inland marine, and commercial.

- Have become skilled in all aspects of managing an insurance agency, including the necessity of re-underwriting our book of business in order to remain a profitable agency; have also learned how to operate a multi-line single-line business in order to maintain a quality book of business.

- Have gained expert understanding of Nationwide policies, procedures, and practices.

- Prospect for new customers and work with existing clients to determine their need for certain products and to tailor those products to their particular needs and situations.

- Although I am working in my mother's office, have gained the respect and loyalty of the customers we service because of my sincere concern for their well-being and my professional approach to serving their needs.

- Have learned that the insurance business is a relationship business, and have established warm relationships with all of our policyholders.

- Have a great respect for B.J. Moore and the way she does business; have played a key role in her being named a Legion of Honor Agent multiple times.

PERSONAL   Have grown up in the insurance business and have learned valuable sales and public relations skills. I am confident that I could be successful in the highly competitive business of real estate sales. Derive much personal satisfaction from selling products for specific situations. Can provide outstanding personal and professional references.

Date

Exact Name of Person
Title or Position
Name of Company
Address
City, State, Zip

Dear Exact Name of Person: (or Dear Sir or Madam if answering a blind ad.)

I would appreciate an opportunity to talk with you soon about how I could contribute to your organization through my skills in office management and knowledge of office administrative procedures.

As you will see from my resume, I am currently the Office Manager for a real estate agency where I also handle responsibilities as Rental Property Manager. In August of last year, I took on the extra responsibilities of overseeing a secretary and a receptionist and expanded job requirements. A highly motivated self-starter, in my spare time I completed the Real Estate Program at the Columbia Real Estate Institute and became licensed by the state to sell real estate.

Prior to joining Carolina Properties, I greatly refined my administrative and computer operations skills while working for the Fort Jackson, SC school system. In addition to spending the bulk of my time in records management in the administrative offices of that system, I filled in at various schools as a receptionist and library clerk.

Through my practical office management and technical computer operations skills, I offer a background of maturity and adaptability sure to make me a valuable asset to your organization.

I hope you will welcome my call soon to arrange a brief meeting at your convenience to discuss your current and future needs and how I might serve them. Thank you in advance for your time.

Sincerely yours,

Charlotte Greene

Alternate last paragraph:
I hope you will call or write soon to suggest a time convenient for us to meet and discuss your current and future needs and how I might serve them. Thank you in advance for your time.

CHARLOTTE GREENE

1110½ Hay Street, Fayetteville, NC 28305   •   preppub@aol.com   •   (910) 483-6611

OBJECTIVE   To apply my outstanding skills in office management and administration to an organization that can use a mature professional with a versatile background of accomplishments.

LICENSES   Certified as a Notary Public, 2005.
Licensed Real Estate Salesman, 2006. Completed 150-hour training program at Columbia Real Estate Institute, 2006.

EXPERIENCE   *Advanced in this progression with Carolina Properties, Columbia, SC*:
OFFICE MANAGER & RENTAL PROPERTY MANAGER. (2006-present). Was promoted to oversee two employees while handling all day-to-day functions related to managing approximately 25 rental properties.
- Apply my communication skills while working closely with appraisers to ensure they receive complete and accurate information.
- Enter new listings into the computer system and distribute appropriate information to each agent. Collect details on each home sale, enter data into computer system, and inform each agent of the sale.
- Make disbursements to agents and maintained ledgers on each property.
- Coordinate with home owners as I represent the rental company. Polish troubleshooting skills while "ironing out" problems and defusing irate buyers to sellers.
- As the point of contact for questions, attend and take notes of each sales meeting.
- Prepare records of each month's new construction closings and listings received.
- Create monthly and yearly reports for brokers which include information of each agent's production.

RENTAL PROPERTY MANAGER. (2004-06). Listed and sold residential real estate in addition to handling the rental department.
- Reached the $1.1 million mark in sales in just six months with the company!

RECEPTIONIST and **ADMINISTRATIVE ASSISTANT.** Fort Jackson Schools, SC (2001-04). Displayed my adaptability while working in the personnel department of the administrative offices of the Fort Jackson school system as well as in the libraries and offices of various schools in the system at a large military base.
- Maintained confidential files for approximately 520 employees. Helped new employees complete their life and health insurance forms and various forms required for working for the military school system. Received and routed calls using a 15-line phone system.
- Provided help for parents, job applicants, salesmen, and others with business in the school's offices—both in person and on the phone. Compiled weekly enrollment summaries for each school as well as personnel breakdowns for the entire system and monthly principal's reports. Ordered supplies and typed special order requests.

Highlights of other experience:
- Maintained accurate and complete financial records for the PTA (Parent-Teacher Association) as Treasurer for both a junior high and an elementary school.
- Polished office management abilities as the Assistant Manager of an Equestrian Center.
- Gained experience in working with the public as a Bank Teller.

EDUCATION   Studied English with a minor in speech, University of South Carolina, Columbia, SC.

COMPUTERS   Highly proficient with spreadsheets as well as software including Word and Excel.

Date

Exact Name of Person
Title or Position
Name of Company
Address
City, State, Zip

OFFICER MANAGER
and SALES ASSISTANT

Dear Exact Name of Person: (or Dear Sir or Madam if answering a blind ad.)

With the enclosed resume, I would like to make you aware of my interest in exploring employment opportunities with your organization.

As you will see from my resume, I am experienced in working in the fast-paced atmosphere of a successful real estate company. When I joined the company, I applied my strong administrative and computer operations skills, but I rapidly learned that I tremendously enjoy working with the public and "making a sale." I was frustrated that I could not communicate many matters to the homeowner, so I decided to spend my spare time obtaining my real estate license. Now that I am licensed, I am interested in establishing a career in real estate sales at one of the leading real estate firms.

You would find that I am a highly motivated individual who has a "knack" for dealing with the public. I believe that real estate programs can teach the technical knowledge needed by agents, but I also believe that the key to success in real estate is the ability to cultivate warm relationships through persistence and hard work. I am willing to put in the long hours and use my outgoing personality to help make my employer (and me) very successful.

I hope you will call or write soon to suggest a time convenient for us to meet and discuss your current and future needs and how I might serve them. Thank you in advance for your time.

Sincerely,

Ashley Davis

Alternate last paragraph:
I hope you will welcome my call soon to arrange a brief meeting at your convenience to discuss your current and future needs and how I might serve them. Thank you in advance for your time.

ASHLEY DAVIS

1110½ Hay Street, Fayetteville, NC 28305 • preppub@aol.com • (910) 483-6611

OBJECTIVE

To benefit an organization that can use a hard-working, dependable, and loyal professional who offers a strong customer service background and excellent communication skills as well as real estate office experience.

EDUCATION & TRAINING

Hold a TN Real Estate License issued in 2004; successfully completed indoctrination into the Board of Real Estate.
- Member of MLS (Multiple Listing Service).

Graduated from Nashville High School, Nashville, TN, 2001.
- Graduated as the Salutatorian with a 97% average.
- Nominated by peers as Class President.
- Played varsity soccer and tennis. Was named MPV of my soccer team in my senior year.

EXPERIENCE

OFFICER MANAGER and **SALES ASSISTANT.** Opry Mills Real Estate, Nashville, TN (2004-present). Provide administrative support and performed sales duties while contributing to the success of this busy office during this training internship through Nashville Job Training Corp.
- Make cold calls to gain additional clients.
- Handle most of the "leg work" for the agents.
- Show rental properties and handled payroll and accounts payable/receivable; file client lists and tax records.
- Work closely with bank representatives and VA to help process client proposals; handled VA contracts.
- Create PowerPoint presentations and then make oral presentations to the owners to advise them on the status of areas such as maintenance and occupancy.

ADMINISTRATIVE CLERK (temporary). Employment Security Commission, Nashville, TN (2003). Answered multi-line phone system.
- Refined computer skills.
- Offered assistance to clients to help them better understand the program.
- Was commended for my efficiency in being able to cut through work.

ADMINISTRATIVE ASSISTANT and **SALES REPRESENTATIVE.** Nashville Realty, Nashville, TN (1999-02).
- Wrote contracts and collected payments in addition to selling.
- Provided excellent customer service while also performing administrative functions such as filing and answering telephones.

CASHIER (Part-time). Linens & Things, Nashville, TN (1999-01). Worked in this job in my junior and senior year of high school.
- Assisted customers while also making cash transactions and packaging purchased merchandise.
- Provided warm and friendly service to ensure repeat business.

PERSONAL

Offer honesty and a genuine love for working and communicating with the public. Give 100% to any task and take pride in a job well done. Have worked extensively on computers using software including Word, Excel, Access, and PowerPoint.

Date

Exact Name of Person
Title or Position
Name of Company
Address
City, State, Zip

OPERATIONS ASSISTANT
with property
management experience

Dear Exact Name of Person (or Dear Sir or Madam if answering a blind ad):

With the enclosed resume, I would like to make you aware of my exceptional customer service, communication, and customer service skills as well as my background in purchasing, accounts receivable, sales, and property management.

Administrative and account management skills

In my most recent position, I performed administrative and customer service tasks while assisting in the management of multimillion-dollar accounts. I dealt with clients and continuously resolved transportation and logistics problems. I became known for my ability to remain calm in a crisis, and I discovered that patient listening is one of the best tools for handling customer issues. I am known for my ability to soothe and satisfy customers who are upset.

Sales, communication, and customer service experience

In a previous position, I utilized my sales and customer service ability, maintaining a 78% show rate from appointments that I scheduled–the highest percentage in the company. I also demonstrated my ability to quickly learn new computer systems, mastering the proprietary software used by the company. My exceptional computer skills were tested when I was tasked with translating and editing documents into English, and I have mastered numerous proprietary software programs as well as popular programs such as Word, Excel, and Access.

With a Bachelor of General Studies degree with majors in Psychology, Behavioral Studies, and Criminal Law/Juvenile Delinquency, I was pursuing an Advanced Masters program in Public Administration when my spouse was transferred. Now that I have permanently relocated to Washington state, I would like to develop a long-term, career relationship with an organization that could benefit from my skills.

If you can use an articulate communicator with strong organizational skills and a commitment to providing the highest possible levels of customer service, I hope you will contact me. I assure you in advance that I have an excellent reputation and would quickly become an asset to your organization.

Sincerely,

Angela Canete

ANGELA CANETE

1110½ Hay Street, Fayetteville, NC 28305 • preppub@aol.com • (910) 483-6611

OBJECTIVE

To benefit an organization that can use an articulate, highly motivated, and career-oriented sales or customer service professional with a versatile background in sales, customer service, purchasing, accounts receivable, and property management.

EDUCATION

Maintained a 3.5 GPA while pursuing an **Advanced Masters program in Public Administration** from the Champlain College, Burlington, VT, 2004-06.

Earned a **Bachelor of General Studies degree with majors in Psychology, Behavioral Studies, and Criminal Law/Juvenile Delinquency**, University of Maryland, Munich, Germany campus (2002).

EXPERIENCE

OPERATIONS MANAGER. United National Sales and Service, Burlington, VT (2005-present). Performed a variety of administrative and customer service tasks in this busy medical supply environment.

- While my supervisor was researching problem accounts, I handled accounts averaging nearly $5 million in sales.
- Took customer's orders via multi-line telephone and fax, maintained files documenting orders shipped and received, and handled accounts receivable.
- Employed my excellent customer service skills to successfully interact with customers whose accounts did not balance; researched these discrepancies and made adjustments when necessary.

CLIENT CONTACT SPECIALIST. Vermont Industries, Burlington, VT (2002-04). Demonstrated excellent customer service skills while contacting clients and referrals to encourage them to set up appointments with agents.

- Consistently maintained a 78% rate of scheduled appointments who actually showed – the highest appointment show rate in the entire company.
- Received formal training in data entry, telemarketing, time management and scheduling.
- Earned a certificate for successfully completing a three-day training course in sales techniques. Quickly mastered proprietary computer software designed for Vermont Industries. Attended weekly training sessions in sales.

CONSULTANT. Mercedes Motors, Munich, Germany (2000-02). Translated and edited documents into English for two different companies while living abroad in a foreign city of 13 million inhabitants.

- Trained employees of two companies in written and spoken English and grammar.

PROPERTY MANAGER. Northwest Wood Apartments, Burlington, VT (1998-00). Responsible for managing all aspects of the operation of this 16-unit apartment complex, interviewing prospective renters, collecting all rent payments, handling and coordinating all maintenance requests.

COMMUNICATIONS OFFICER. Seattle Police Department, Seattle, WA (1995-97). Assessed situations and prioritized calls in order to dispatch appropriate response teams to emergency and crime scenes.

- Maintained constant contact with eight police officers, in order to determine which units could respond most quickly to incoming calls. Familiarized myself with the dispatch area, minimizing response time and directing response team personnel to the scene.

PERSONAL

Outstanding personal and professional references are available upon request.

CAREER CHANGE

Date

Exact Name of Person
Title or Position
Name of Company
Address
City, State, Zip

PRINCIPAL BROKER
seeking a salaried
position with a
professional association

Dear Exact Name of Person: (or Dear Sir or Madam if answering a blind ad.)

    With the enclosed resume and this cover letter, I would like to make you aware of my interest in being considered for the position of Executive Director of the Washington Association of Real Estate. I would like you to know that I would be willing to cease operations of my real estate firm should I be offered the opportunity to serve the association in this capacity.

    As you will see from my resume, I offer a track record of sincere commitment to making the Tacoma and Fort Lewis community a better place to live. That same motivation is why I am seeking the position as Executive Director of an association of which I am proud to be a member. In every job I have taken on throughout my life, I have fully dedicated myself to that role. I would be equally dedicated to serving the association as its paid full-time director.

    As an elected member of the Thurston County Board of Commissioners, I have taken pride in serving my community in the political arena. I am confident that my experience in lobbying for legislation in Olympia and Washington, DC could be beneficial to the association. I also have served as President of the largest association of retailers in WA, and I presided over the organization at a time when it was rapidly re-positioning from an organization of small retailers into an organization which counted the largest retailers among its members. The annual convention I presided over as President was attended by in excess of 10,000 people, up from the previous year's head count of 7,000. I also served as President of the Tacoma Club and played a major role in starting up this new organization.

    Through my business background in addition to my political activities and significant volunteer leadership roles, I have highly refined management and organizational skills which I am certain could benefit the association. Through my experience as a commissioner, I have refined my ability to negotiate sensitive issues and I pride myself on my ability to establish and maintain outstanding relationships.

    I hope you will strongly consider my desire to serve our association and to work with the board of directors in determining and implementing the association's strategy for the next millennium. Please give me an opportunity to demonstrate to you in person that my interest is sincere and my contributions to our association could be significant and enduring. I wish you to know, too, that I would consider it a pleasure to work with Frances Sweeney and Tangie Gibbs in accomplishing the goals set by the board.

Yours sincerely,

Hector Lewis

HECTOR LEWIS

1110½ Hay Street, Fayetteville, NC 28305　　·　　preppub@aol.com　　·　　(910) 483-6611

OBJECTIVE　　To contribute to the Washington Association of Real Estate through my sincere desire to work toward the economic growth and prosperity of the organization while applying my marketing and sales abilities, my negotiating and consensus-building skills, as well as my strong leadership ability and reputation as a respected community leader.

REAL ESTATE　　Washington Association of Real Estate, Tacoma Association of Real Estate, and the United
AFFILIATIONS　　Association of Real Estate

HONOR　　In 2001, was awarded the **Department of the Army Commanders Award for Public Service** by General Thompson, commanding general of Fort Lewis and now Chairman of the Joint Chiefs of Staff; recognized for extensive contributions to Tacoma and Fort Lewis.

EDUCATION　　**B.A.,** Pacific Lutheran University, 1981; named Outstanding Alumnus, 1999.
- As an alumnus, have been active on the **Pacific Lutheran University Board of Visitors** and was a charter member of the **Pacific Lutheran University Endowment Society,** which assists in funding scholarships.
- Am also on the **Pacific Lutheran University Foundation Board**, a 30-member board which attempts to raise funding and increase community awareness.

EXPERIENCE　　**PRINCIPAL BROKER.** Hector Lewis Real Estate, Tacoma, WA (1998-present). Obtained my Real Estate Sales License in 1997 and founded the real estate firm which bears my name in 1998; the company has specialized in commercial and land transactions.

PRESIDENT. Seafood World, Tacoma, WA (1983-present). As President of a company started by my father in 1960, provide oversight of a business which has a full-time General Manager.

EXPERIENCE　　**ELECTED MEMBER, PIERCE COUNTY BOARD OF COMMISSIONERS.** With a
IN POLITICS　　strong desire to contribute to my community, have been successful in utilizing politics as my primary vehicle; have gained extensive experience in lobbying for legislation in Olympia and Washington, DC. Elected to the board in 1998 and re-elected in 2002.
- Elected Vice Chairman in 1999, Chairman in 2000 and 2003 by fellow board members.
- As a member of the **Commencement Bay Health Systems Board of Trustees,** 1998-05, am involved in making major economic decisions which affect our county.
- Member, **Tacoma Chamber of Commerce Board of Directors,** 2000 and 2003.
- Have significantly refined my negotiating, organizational, and management skills as one of seven commissioners responsible for allocating $278 million annually.

TRADE　　**PRESIDENT.** Washington Seafood Dealers Association (2001). Was elected President of
ASSOCIATION　　the largest association of retailers in WA; was groomed for the position through holding
EXPERIENCE　　numerous leadership positions over a five-year period. As President, continued the association's aggressive re-positioning from an organization of small independents into an organization joined by the largest food retailers.
- Presided over a 10,000-person annual convention, up from 7,000 the previous year.

Other community/state leadership and volunteer experience:
PRESIDENT. Tacoma Club, 2003. Played key role in obtaining the club's charter.
Appointed by Lieutenant Governor to the Washington Board of Directors, 2000-02.
Pierce County Sealife Club, National Rifle Association.
Museum of the Sound Board, 1999-00.

CAREER CHANGE

Date

Exact Name of Person
Title or Position
Name of Company
Address
City, State, Zip

Dear Exact Name of Person: (or Dear Sir or Madam if answering a blind ad.

Please accept the enclosed resume and application as the documents you have requested related to determining the best candidate for the job of Deputy County Manager.

As my resume shows, I offer a unique mix of entrepreneurial know-how, research skills, management experience, and personal relations ability. As the founder and manager of a local business which has become known for honest business practices, I am respected for my ability to use sound judgment, tact, and diplomacy in helping parties with opposing points of view work out fair and amicable solutions to problems. While handling multiple projects simultaneously on a daily basis, I also oversee budgeting, financial statement preparation, and strategic planning.

Because of my commitment to Kanawha County, I have been involved as a leader in respected local service organizations. On one occasion, I collected research and formulated a proposal for a respite shelter for neglected and abused women and children. I am committed to making Kanawha County a better place to grow up, work, and live, and I use my leisure time to work on projects which enhance the vitality of our community.

As I hope my resume shows, I offer strong analytical and research skills, and I earned a degree in paralegal technology prior to obtaining my bachelor's degree *magna cum laude*. On numerous occasions I have been told that I have a gift for rapidly assimilating large volumes of technical and financial data in order to pinpoint strategic opportunities, operational weaknesses, and "hidden" problems.

I hope you will give me an opportunity to interview for this position so that I can show you in person that I am uniquely qualified with unusually strong interpersonal, financial, communication, and decision-making abilities.

Sincerely yours,

Kelly Bradford

KELLY BRADFORD

1110½ Hay Street, Fayetteville, NC 28305　•　preppub@aol.com　•　(910) 483-6611

OBJECTIVE

To contribute to Kanawha County as its Deputy County Manager by applying my experience in working with the county's unique network of business, professional, and civic organizations along with my strong analytical, financial, supervisory, and problem-solving skills.

EDUCATION

Magna cum laude graduate of University of Charleston with a **B.A degree in Political Science**, 2002.

Earned **A.A. degree in Paralegal Technology**, University of Charleston, 2000; gained valuable skills related to conducting legal research, writing legal briefs, negotiating legal issues, and searching real estate titles.

AFFILIATIONS

Member, Charleston Area Board of Realtors

Member, Board of Directors, Better Health of Kanawha County

Member, Salvation Army

EXPERIENCE

PRINCIPAL & BUSINESS MANAGER. Kanawha Properties, Charleston, WV (2005-present). Have used my interpersonal skills and strategic planning ability to develop "from scratch" a real estate business which is known for honest business practices and aggressive marketing practices.

- Have become known for my strong problem-solving skills in a job which requires constant mediation and negotiation in order to help parties with different interests and goals find common ground. Plan, organize, and direct all aspects of daily operations.
- Oversee budgeting, financial statement preparation, liaison with accountants, and long-range financial planning; control expenditures.
- Utilize information from the public and private sector in preparing research reports and making administrative decisions. Supervise 15 office employees and sales professionals.

CUSTOMER SERVICE REPRESENTATIVE. America West, Huntington, WV (2002-05). Excelled in dealing with the public in a gracious manner while selling and writing standard airline tickets, modifying existing tickets, and making reservations at the ticket counter while also processing ticketed passengers, opening and closing aircraft, marshaling in aircraft, and providing needed loading and unloading of aircraft on the ramp.

ADMINISTRATIVE AIDE. WV Office Products Corporation, Charleston, WV (2001-02). For this large corporation handled a wide variety of tasks including reconciling a cash drawer, maintaining equipment, selling office machines, and resolving customer problems.

PARALEGAL. Sweeney, Gibbs, Forbes, and McKinney, Charleston, WV (2000). Performed real estate title searches, prepared documentation related to bankruptcies, handled investigative work, interviewed witnesses, and assisted in court and legal research and writing.

Other experience:

RESEARCHER. Researched, collected data, and then formulated a proposal for the Salvation Army for a respite shelter for neglected and abused women and children.

CHAIRMAN, CHILD ADVOCACY COMMITTEE. In a volunteer job with a local service organization, chaired its largest committee which oversees activities in six areas.

PERSONAL

Am known for my ability to provide leadership in getting individuals and organizations to work together on common goals. Offer highly refined problem-solving skills. Have a strong desire to work toward making Kanawha County an even better place to live!

CAREER CHANGE

Date

Exact Name of Person
Title or Position
Name of Company
Address
City, State, Zip

PROPERTY CHIEF

Dear Exact Name of Person: (or Dear Sir or Madam if answering a blind ad.)

I would appreciate an opportunity to talk with you soon about how I could contribute to your organization through my extensive background in property management and computer operations.

As you will see from my resume, most recently I was handpicked to take over a troubled organization as its Property Chief. Although the organization was widely regarded as being "out of control" when I took it over, I retrained staff, installed new computer programs, and corrected numerous deficiencies so that we passed a rigorous inspection with "no faults" noted. In a previous job as Supply Chief, I managed the provision of inspection, training, and consulting services related to contracting, purchasing, warehousing, financial management, and all other areas of supply administration. In that job, I also performed extensive public relations duties with activities and organizations.

You will also see from my resume that I have administered supply operations for nearly all kinds of items, from communications-electronics to clothing, as well as professional services. In one job as Operations Chief, I trained and supervised 29 people while managing purchasing and requisitioning related to a 150-page file containing 2500 pending requisitions.

Proficient with both Windows operating systems, I am experienced in using Word and Excel; and I am skilled in using spreadsheets and databases to maximize efficiency and solve problems. In addition to my extensive formal training in all aspects of supply, I have benefited from recent training in Total Quality Leadership (TQL).

I hope you will welcome my call soon to arrange a brief meeting at your convenience to discuss your current and future needs and how I might serve them. Thank you in advance for your time.

Sincerely yours,

Alice Jones

Alternate last paragraph:
I hope you will call or write me soon to suggest a time convenient for us to meet and discuss your current and future needs and how I might serve them. Thank you in advance for your time.

ALICE JONES

1110½ Hay Street, Fayetteville, NC 28305   •   preppub@aol.com   •   (910) 483-6611

OBJECTIVE   To benefit an organization that can use a versatile administrator with excellent financial and accounting knowledge, computer expertise, and property management experience.

COMPUTERS   Proficient with Word, Excel, and PowerPoint; skilled in working in Windows.
- Experienced in using spreadsheets and databases for analysis, efficiency, problem solving.
- Offer a proven ability to rapidly master new software and operating systems.

EXPERIENCE   *Rose to top positions in the property management field while serving my country in the U.S. Marine Corps in the following positions:*

PROPERTY CHIEF. Electronics School, Jacksonville, NC (2005-present). Was specially recruited for this position which involved turning around a disorganized operation riddled with accountability, human resources, and other problems; received an Achievement Medal for exceptional management results.
- Supervise four employees in a section which controlled accountability for more than $8 million in communications-electronics assets. Identify and resolve discrepancies valued at more than $300,000. Transferred records from Access to ATLASS System.
- Implemented the transfer of more than $3 million in computer assets to customer accounts.
- Was commended for my skill in reorganizing internal operations, streamlining procedures, and installing new computer programs.

SUPPLY CHIEF/CONSULTANT. Instruction and Inspection Staff, Oceanside, CA (2001-04). Managed a $60,000 budget while supporting the training for a 185-person organization; provided inspection, instruction, and consulting services related to these and other areas:

    contracting   purchasing   financial management
    warehousing   training   supply administration
- Performed public relations duties; directed food drives for the Salvation Army.

RETAIL STORE MANAGER. Defense Support Stock Control, Thailand (2000-01). Received a respected Certificate of Recognition for my bottom-line results in managing a clothing sales store which retailed up to $3,000 in uniforms monthly. Supervised two clerks.

SUPPLY COORDINATOR. Recruiting Station, Richmond, VA (1995-00). Supported the recruiting efforts of 65 recruiters located at ten recruiting sites throughout Virginia while managing the payment and accountability of $125,000 in telephone bills, $65,000 in recruiter travel claims, and other budget items valued at more than $100,000.
- Earned a medal for outstanding purchasing, contracting, and financial management.

OPERATIONS CHIEF. Material Issue Point, Camp Lejeune, NC (1993-95). Trained, motivated, and supervised 29 people while overseeing a 150-page current accounts file with more than 2500 pending requisitions. Handled purchasing and requisitions management.

EDUCATION   Excelled in more than two years of college-level courses in supply administration, financial management, and human resources sponsored by the U.S. Marine Corps; courses included:
- Total Quality Leadership (TQL), 2005
- Supply Service and Property Management Schools, 1990-05

PERSONAL   Highly motivated self starter. Excellent personal and professional references. Offer the ability to solve difficult problems through analytical skills as well as through motivating people.

CAREER CHANGE

Date

Exact Name of Person
Title or Position
Name of Company
Address
City, State, Zip

**PROPERTY
INSURANCE
ADJUSTER**

Dear Exact Name of Person: (or Dear Sir or Madam if answering a blind ad.)

With the enclosed resume, I would like to make you aware of my interest in exploring employment opportunities with your organization. I am available for work on a contract and independent contractor basis, if that is your preference.

As you will see from my resume, I am involved in the property management and insurance adjusting field. I began my work as an insurance adjuster after successfully owning and operating auto body shops. I earned a reputation as a savvy and insightful property adjuster while working for Massachusetts Reconstruction, and I have diversified into the property adjusting field.

In recent experience, I completed a six-week project for a major insurer as I assessed property damage in multiple states in the aftermath of Hurricane Katrina. I take pride in my ability to perform thorough analysis of damaged properties and provide 100% accurate investigations of property damage.

With no children at home, I am available for long-term assignment including overseas work. I possess a current passport and can pass the most rigorous background checks.

I hope you will call or write soon to suggest a time convenient for us to meet and discuss your current and future needs and how I might serve them. Thank you in advance for your time.

Sincerely,

Paul Warren

Alternate last paragraph:
I hope you will welcome my call soon to arrange a brief meeting at your convenience to discuss your current and future needs and how I might serve them. Thank you in advance for your time.

PAUL WARREN

1110½ Hay Street, Fayetteville, NC 28305 • preppub@aol.com • (910) 483-6611

OBJECTIVE

To contribute to an organization that can use an experienced insurance adjuster who offers extensive experience related to property and automobile damage as well as liability claims.

LICENSE

Licensed by the State of Massachusetts as an Insurance Adjuster

EXPERIENCE

PROPERTY INSURANCE ADJUSTER. Warren Adjusting Services, Inc, Boston, MA (2005-present). Write estimates for home owners property damage as well as auto damage and liability claims for 18 companies.
- Am known for my excellent negotiating skills and ability to settle claims quickly and fairly.
- Am skilled at evaluating losses, coordinating removal of salvage, and handling titles.

PROPERTY ADJUSTER. Massachusetts Reconstruction, Worcester, MA (2003-05). Wrote insurance estimates for reconstruction related to fire, water, and smoke damage.
- Supervised reconstruction activities; closed contracts.
- Worked extensively with personal injury attorney Jason L. Lynch; handled auto wreck investigations and crime scene analysis.
- Testified in court proceedings about auto accidents and personal injury claims.

OWNER/OPERATOR. Suffolk Body Shop, Boston, MA (1998-03). Managed 27 people working in a body shop, used car lot, three service stations, and a garage.
- Operated a wrecker service and muffler shop.
- Operated the body shop; wrote estimates; ordered parts; dispersed work.
- Was a licensed MA Vehicle Inspector.

OWNER/OPERATOR. Warren Station, Revere, MA (1994-98). Owned and operated a full service station and auto repair shop.

Military experience: Honorable Discharge, U.S. Air Force; worked as a Munitions Specialist.

EDUCATION

One year of college in Business Administration, Boston University, MA.
A.S.E. Certified in Frame and Suspension and Alignment.
A.S.E. Certified in Heat and Air Conditioning Repair.
A.S.E. Certified in Emission Controls and Tune-up.
A.S.E. Certified in Brake Repairs.
MA Licensed State Inspector for 14 years.
Cadillac Quality Control Training.
Toyota Quality Control and Service Advisor.
- Extensive technical training in service and repair as well as numerous courses conducted by companies such as Cadillac and Toyota pertaining to refinishing, principles of four-wheel steering, transmission repair, computer operation, other areas.
- Skilled at utilizing Mitchell Estimate Sys and CCC Total Loss Evaluation as well as guide books including NADA and the Red Book; routinely use personal computer.

COMPUTERS

Proficient with numerous software programs including Word and Excel.

PERSONAL

Offer an unusual combination of exceptional organizational and communication skills along with technical knowledge of property adjusting, auto adjusting, and the insurance industry.

Date

Exact Name of Person
Title or Position
Name of Company
Address
City, State, Zip

PROPERTY MANAGER   Dear Exact Name of Person: (or Dear Sir or Madam if answering a blind ad.)

With the enclosed resume, I would like to make you aware of my interest in exploring employment opportunities with your organization. My husband and I are in the process of relocating to Peoria, IL, and I am seeking to assume property management responsibilities with a company that can use a dedicated hard worker.

As you will see from my resume, I have distinguished myself in the property management field in Salt Lake City, where I have served in leadership roles with local professional associations such as the Home Builders Association and the Salt Lake County Apartment Association. I am respected as an honest individual who knows how to profitably impact my employer's bottom line through resourcefulness and attention to detail. I have maintained 100% occupancy during the past three year-period, despite a net loss of jobs in the community. While other complexes are struggling, Lone Park has a waiting list.

I can provide outstanding references at the appropriate time, and I feel certain that you would find me in person to be an outgoing and versatile individual who offers strong management and problem-solving skills.

I hope you will call or write soon to suggest a time convenient for us to meet and discuss your current and future needs and how I might serve them. Thank you in advance for your time.

Sincerely,

Lena Mathlaw

Alternate last paragraph:
I hope you will welcome my call soon to arrange a brief meeting at your convenience to discuss your current and future needs and how I might serve them. Thank you in advance for your time.

LENA MATHLAW

1110½ Hay Street, Fayetteville, NC 28305   •   preppub@aol.com   •   (910) 483-6611

OBJECTIVE

To benefit an organization in need of an experienced property manager and sales professional who offers excellent problem-solving and customer relations skills as well as a flair for money management.

COMPUTERS

Proficient with software including Word, Excel, PowerPoint, and Access. Have become experienced in Website development while working with my husband, who is a computer programmer.

EXPERIENCE

PROPERTY MANAGER. Lone Park Apartments, Salt Lake City, UT (2002-present). For a business which is owned and managed by Sweeney, McKinney, and Anderson, Real Estate Division, I supervise three administrative and maintenance personnel while overseeing the leasing of 502 apartments, collection of rent, servicing of current residents, and performing administrative duties.

- Maintained 100% occupancy during the past three year-period, despite a net loss of jobs in the community. While other complexes are struggling, Lone Park has a waiting list.
- Greatly improved the interior and exterior appearance of the property, justifying a 20% rental increase.
- In my first year on the job, reduced turnover by 30% and thereby improved occupancy rates through my ability to interview and perform background checks on potential tenants.
- In my spare time, am active in leadership roles in local associations including the Salt Lake Home Builders Association and the Salt Lake County Apartment Association.

ONSITE PROPERTY CO-MANAGER. Wasatch Apartments, Salt Lake City, UT (1990-02). In a complex owned and managed by Wheeler, Towering, and Prople Properties, I managed ten employees while directing the leasing of this new property consisting of 332 apartments, collection of rent, servicing of current residents, and performing administrative duties.

- Was promoted from assistant manager to manager after three years.
- Maintained a consistently high occupancy rate during market slumps and periods in which apartment competition was high.

ONSITE PROPERTY ASSISTANT MANAGER. Mill Creek Apartments, Provo, UT (1989-90). In a complex managed by Parsons & Whitfield Realtors, I directed the leasing of 188 apartments, collection of rent, and overseeing the servicing of current residents while providing administrative support.

LICENSES

Received Certified Apartment Management designation, United Apartment Association. Obtained UT Real Estate Broker's License, Provo Technical Community College, Provo, UT. Received Accredited Residential Manager Certificate, Institute of Real Estate Management.

EDUCATION

Completed two years of coursework in **Business Administration**, Salt Lake Community College, Salt Lake City, UT. Pursuing completion of the degree in my spare time. Graduate of Salt Lake High School, Salt Lake City, UT. Was elected Homecoming Queen in my senior year.

AFFILIATIONS

President – Salt Lake County Apartment Association, 2005. President – Salt Lake Home Builders Association, 2005. Education Chairman – Salt Lake County Apartment Association, 2003.

Date

Exact Name of Person
Title or Position
Name of Company
Address
City, State, Zip

PROPERTY MANAGER
for manufactured housing

Dear Exact Name of Person (or Dear Sir or Madam if answering a blind ad):

Can you use an experienced project manager who offers a background in both manufactured housing as well as "spec" and custom residential construction?

As you will see from my resume, I worked full-time while earning my B.S. degree in Civil Engineering, Construction Option, at North Carolina State University.

In my current position, I am supervising the major remodeling of residential housing while also managing projects related to site-built and manufactured housing. In my previous position, I developed a profitable construction business which became known for on-time delivery and integrity. I began in the construction industry as a Carpenter's Helper, and then I accepted a position as a Rental Unit Maintenance Manager.

Although I am held in high regard in my current position, my wife and I are relocating to your area, and I am seeking an employer that can use my construction knowledge and project management experience.

I hope you will welcome my call soon to determine if there is a time when we could meet in person so that I could show you that I am a highly motivated, ambitious person who could become a valuable part of your team. Thank you in advance for your time.

Sincerely yours,

Larry E. Remington

GIL BARRY WESTERN

1110½ Hay Street, Fayetteville, NC 28305 • preppub@aol.com • (910) 483-6611

OBJECTIVE
To benefit an organization that can use a smart, cost-conscious businessman who has demonstrated the ability to grow and manage a profitable construction company through my project management skills and knowledge of both commercial and residential construction.

EDUCATION
Bachelor of Science in Civil Engineering, Construction Option, North Carolina State University, Raleigh, NC, 1990; worked full-time while earning my degree.

EXPERIENCE
PROJECT MANAGER. Brahms Construction Company , Inc., Charlotte, NC (2004-present). For both site-built and manufactured housing at three family residential subdivisions, am responsible for all budgeting, quantity surveys, material purchasing, subcontractor scheduling, permit procurement, inspection scheduling, construction supervision, as well as coordination among interior decorators, realtors, and home buyers.
- Scheduled, supervised, and assured completion of all warranty work.
- Supervised major remodeling of residential rental units.

PRESIDENT/MANAGER. Second Avenue Renovation, Charlotte, NC (1989-2004). Developed a profitable construction business and established a base of very satisfied customers while managing projects of varying sizes and complexity and completing jobs on time and within budget.
- Succeeded in this business by developing a personal reputation for quality, honesty, and reliability; now generate a significant portion of new business through word-of-mouth referrals and repeat customers.
- Became skilled in all aspects of project supervision, including management of subcontractors, liaison with suppliers, coordination with inspectors, supervision of employees, and communication with customers.
- Developed expertise related to all phases of site development as well as all aspects of planning and laying out new homes and additions.

RENTAL UNIT MAINTENANCE SUPERVISOR. Worsted Properties, Raleigh, NC (1985-89). Became knowledgeable about most areas related to the installation and upkeep of electrical and plumbing systems/fixtures while supervising construction, repairs, and maintenance performed on a diversified inventory of rental apartments and houses.
- Boosted profits and cut costs by reducing the time vacant units were "down" for repairs.
- Gained experience in property maintenance, public relations, and coordination.
- In a simultaneous job as **Night Manager** for Sophie's Subs in Raleigh, increased kitchen productivity by 25%, thereby reducing the need for additional workers.

CARPENTER'S HELPER. Allen Framing Contractors, Raleigh, NC (1984-85). Achieved an exceptionally high volume of production, reducing the need for additional crew.
- Was involved in the production and transportation of wall components for a 200-unit apartment complex.
- Learned to use power and air tools as well as surveying practices and instruments.
- Learned the basic principles of concrete construction and was a highly productive worker while building and setting forms for concrete construction.

PERSONAL
Offer a proven ability to relate effectively to all participants in a construction project. Am known as a talented planner, organizer, and scheduler with excellent skills.

Date

Exact Name of Person
Title or Position
Name of Company
Address
City, State, Zip

PROPERTY MANAGER   Dear Exact Name of Person (or Dear Sir or Madam if answering a blind ad):

With the enclosed resume, I would like to make you aware of my interest in exploring employment opportunities with your organization.

While completing my B.S. degree in Urban and Regional Planning from West Virginia University, I was aggressively recruited by the largest industrial materials supplier in the world, Smith Enterprises, Inc., upon college graduation, and I rapidly advanced from inside sales to outside sales. As an inside sales representative, I managed 85 accounts worth $3 million and increased the profit margin by 15%. I restored confidence in some of the company's largest regional accounts, and I established outstanding relationships with all customers. After being promoted to outside sales with the Builder Sales Division, I took over an underperforming territory and, within four months, tripled sales.

I was recruited for my current job as Project Manager with a construction company by a customer whom I served while at Smith. Quality Construction created a new position especially for me, and I have been instrumental in developing sales of a new division to the $1 million per annum level. I excel in working with customers, subcontractors, city and state officials, as well as insurance personnel. I am in charge of 300 independent subcontractors who all work for me on various projects, and I have earned the confidence of veteran construction industry professionals because of my technical construction knowledge.

I gained considerable construction industry experience while in college as I worked up to 30 hours a week as a Carpenter and Residential Framer. I also managed crews for various jobs, and am skilled at utilizing a wide variety of construction industry tools and can safely operate various vehicles and equipment. One of the accomplishments of which I am proud is the fact that I financed all of my college education through loans and part-time jobs in the construction industry.

If you can use an aggressive young professional with a wealth of knowledge related to the construction industry, I hope you will contact me to suggest a time when we might meet to discuss your needs. I can provide outstanding personal and professional references at the appropriate time, but I ask that you please not contact my current employer until after we have a chance to meet and discuss your needs.

Yours sincerely,

Nathan Dawson

NATHAN DAWSON

1110½ Hay Street, Fayetteville, NC 28305 • preppub@aol.com • (910) 483-6611

OBJECTIVE

I want to contribute to an organization that can use an experienced young professional with extensive sales, customer service, and management experience.

EDUCATION

Bachelor of Science (B.S.) degree in Urban and Regional Planning, West Virginia University, Blacksburg, WV, 1998.
- Acquired technical knowledge of the design of cities, neighborhoods, and traffic flow.
- In a summer internship, designed landscaping including sprinkler systems.

COMPUTERS

Experienced with Autocad, ArcInfo, ArcView, 3D Walkthrough, and many other programs.

EXPERIENCE

PROJECT MANAGER. Quality Construction Co., Blacksburg, WV (2002-present). Was recruited by a company which was a customer account of mine when I worked for Smith Enterprises; have excelled in a new position created specially for me and have been instrumental in developing a new division, increasing sales to the level of $1 million per annum in less than a year; the owner recently hired a second Project Manager to help with the work.
- Am in charge of 300 independent subcontractors working for me on various projects; have earned the respect of all subcontractors, most of whom are senior construction industry craftsmen.
- As Project Manager, 85% of my work is concerned with the repair of damaged property; perform liaison with many insurers; also work with customers adding to their homes.
- Extensively research covenants and other matters.
- Excel in working with customers, insurance personnel, government officials, and others.

INSIDE AND OUTSIDE SALES PROFESSIONAL. Smith Enterprises, Inc., Blacksburg, WV (1998-02). As a graduating college senior, was recruited by the largest industrial materials supplier in the world which is owned by a British firm and headquartered in Newport News, VA.
- Of the 30 people Smith interviewed at West Virginia, I was the only one invited to the second interview and was hired after an extensive battery of tests.
- Although the company has a standard policy of starting new sales employees in the warehouse and then promoting them to inside sales in one year, I was promoted to inside sales after only two months.

Inside sales achievements: managed 85 accounts worth $3 million and increased profit margin by 15%.
- As **Inside Sales Representative,** took over a corporate account worth $1.7 annually to Smith and restored confidence which had been lost through my predecessor's lack of follow through; established outstanding relationships.
- Inherited the $200,000 Smithfield Packing account which was "on the ropes" and quickly restored the customer's confidence in Smith's products and customer service.
- Handled debits/credits; was the primary contact for industrial firms within a 60-mile radius including Monsanto, Smithfield Packing, Lundy's, Carolina Foods, and others.

Outside sales achievements: took over an underperforming territory producing $17,000 and, within four months, increased sales to $53,000.
- As **Outside Sales Representative,** established strong rapport with all customers.
- Managed a two-person installation crew, a one-person showroom staff in Blacksburg, a two-person showroom staff in Pinehurst, and two employees in Sanford.

PERSONAL

Highly motivated hard worker with unlimited personal initiative. Excellent references.

Date

Exact Name of Person
Title or Position
Name of Company
Address
City, State, Zip

PROPERTY MANAGER   Dear Exact Name of Person (or Dear Sir or Madam if answering a blind ad):

With the enclosed resume, I would like to make you aware of my interest in exploring employment opportunities with your organization and introduce you to my background.

As you will see from my resume, I graduated from Troy State University at Montgomery, AL, where I pursued a major emphasizing sales, marketing, communications, and customer service. After graduation, I accepted two positions in two different companies, and I have become a master at "juggling" my time for maximum efficiency while excelling in jobs in two industries. As a Property Manager for apartment units in AL and GA, I oversee all aspects of bookkeeping while also managing small crews performing repairs and maintenance. As a Marketing Consultant with an insurance company, I have increased sales 5% in six months, and the company projects a 15% annual increase. I am an extremely hardworking and ambitious individual with strong communication and problem-solving skills, and I have learned a great deal by working simultaneously in the insurance business and property management industry.

While earning my degree at TSU, I worked as a Commissioned Sales Associate, and I played a key role in boosting overall appliance department sales by 15%. Even before my sales experience with Home Depot, I was accustomed to influencing others through my strong communication skills and leadership ability. In high school, I was elected Captain of my varsity soccer team and President of the French Club. I am a highly motivated individual to whom others naturally turn for leadership and direction.

I have decided that I wish to make a permanent career in real estate sales, and I am confident I could make major contributions to the bottom line of an organization that appreciates persistent hard chargers with intellect and charisma. I offer a proven ability to focus my energies in order to maximize profitability and customer satisfaction.

If my background and skills interest you, I hope you will contact me to suggest a time when we could meet in person to discuss your needs. Thank you.

Sincerely,

Aaron Friedman

AARON FRIEDMAN

1110½ Hay Street, Fayetteville, NC 28305 • preppub@aol.com • (910) 483-6611

OBJECTIVE
To positively impact the "bottom line" of an organization that can use an ambitious self-starter with strong communication, sales, and problem-solving skills.

EDUCATION
B.A., Business Management, Troy State University, Montgomery, AL, 2004.
- Excelled in numerous courses which refined my written communication skills including Business Negotiations and Sales Theories, Macro and Micro Economics, Small Group Communications, and Economics.
- My major emphasized the development of strong sales, marketing, customer relations, and personnel management skills.

Graduated from Garrett High School, Montgomery, AL, 1998.
- Elected **President,** French Club. Selected **Captain,** Varsity basketball team.
- Named **All Conference** and **All State,** soccer, 11th and 12th grades.

LANGUAGE
Strong working knowledge of French with speaking, reading, and writing ability.

EXPERIENCE
After graduating from TSU in December 2004, I accepted offers of employment from two different organizations and currently work for two companies. Although I work up to 80 hours a week, I welcomed the opportunity to acquire experience in two different industries. Can provide outstanding references from both employers. Columbus, GA (2004-present).

PROPERTY MANAGER. Woodstream Properties, Inc., Columbus, GA, and Montgomery, AL. Coordinate the work of up to eight people while coordinating renovations and overseeing rental management for multiple apartment units. Oversee all aspects of bookkeeping while personally handling any tenant issues and complaints which arise.
- Travel extensively to supervise needed repairs and unit management of units in GA, AL, and SC. Have managed the on-time and within-budget renovation of six rental units.

MARKETING CONSULTANT. William Wallis Insurance Agency, Columbus, GA (2004-present). Have increased sales by 5% in six months and anticipate an annual sales increase of 15%. Revamped the advertising program to target new markets; suggested new sales approaches and marketing techniques which were successfully implemented.
- Introduced the concept of cross-selling, and developed a plan to train experienced insurance agents in cross-selling techniques. This concept has refined the sales skills of the firm's insurance professionals. Stimulated sales and prospected for new accounts through my strong telemarketing skills.

COMMISSIONED SALES ASSOCIATE. Home Depot, Montgomery, AL (2001-03). Worked up to 40 hours a week in order to partially finance my college education.
- Became one of the store's leading sales producers. Received a 5% commission on all appliance products which I sold, and played a key role in boosting overall appliance department sales by 15%. Coordinated with sales representatives from wholesalers, and negotiated excellent terms for Home Depot.

FOREMAN. Southern Construction, Montgomery, AL (1999-01). Began as an entry-level laborer and advanced to Foreman. Managed all projects on time and within budget.
- Supervised a crew of 4-6 people, and exercised total authority for hiring and terminating employees. Refined my ability to communicate with and supervise employees.

PERSONAL
Highly motivated individual who wishes to contribute to corporate profitability. Excellent references. Am single and available for worldwide relocation. Will travel as needed.

Date

Exact Name of Person
Title or Position
Name of Company
Address
City, State, Zip

PROPERTY MANAGER   Dear Exact Name of Person: (or Dear Sir or Madam if answering a blind ad.)

I am writing to express my strong interest in a position with your company. With the enclosed resume, I would like to make you aware of my background as an articulate professional with an extensive track record of success in customer service, sales, and management which could be of benefit to your organization.

As you will see from my resume, my involvement in sales and customer service environments extends throughout my career, from my earliest positions as Assistant Manager, through jobs in the airline and car rental industries, to my current position as a Property Manager. In addition, my maturity and responsibility have led to consistent advancement into supervisory positions, where I have excelled as a trainer and manager, leading by example while providing the highest possible levels of customer service.

Through the years, I have built a reputation as an energetic, reliable employee. I feel that my dedication to ensuring the continued success of my employers, as well as my outstanding communication and motivational skills, have been the keys to my advancement throughout my career.

If you can use an individual whose sales and customer service skills have been proven in a variety of challenging environments, I hope you will write or call me to suggest a time when we might meet in person to discuss your goals and how my background might serve your needs. I can provide outstanding references at the appropriate time.

Sincerely,

Robert Quinn

ROBERT QUINN

1110½ Hay Street, Fayetteville, NC 28305 • preppub@aol.com • (910) 483-6611

OBJECTIVE   To benefit an organization that can use an experienced manager with exceptional communication and organizational skills who offers a track record of accomplishment in customer service, training and staff development, and management.

EDUCATION   Completed three years of course work towards a Bachelor of Science in Communications; maintained a 3.45 cumulative GPA.

EXPERIENCE   **PROPERTY MANAGER.** Quinn Rentals, Phoenix, AZ (2005-present). Responsible for all aspects of the management for 40 rental properties, including maintenance and upkeep of the physical structure and grounds, inspection and cleaning of individual units, showing of rental properties to potential clients, and collections.
- Conduct exit inspections to determine if tenants have caused damage to the property; clean and inspect individual units prior to showing them to prospective tenants.
- Perform minor carpentry, electrical, and plumbing repairs; hang, prepare, patch, and repair sheet rock; prepare and paint interior walls and ceilings. Oversee major and minor renovations to the interior and exterior of the buildings, as well as landscape maintenance.

ASSISTANT BRANCH MANAGER. Avis Car Rental, Phoenix, AZ (2004-05). Supervised and trained two manager trainees; in the absence of the Branch Manager, managed the operation of this local car rental company with a $500,000, 85-car inventory.
- Completed a number of administrative reports, tracking the number of cars rented as well as the per diem cost to the customer and profit to the company on each vehicle rented. Provided exceptional customer service, delivering vehicles to customers and providing detailed information about rental rates, mileage, and insurance.

ASSISTANT BRANCH MANAGER. Hertz Rent-A-Car, Phoenix, AZ (2000-04). While training and directing six manager trainees and a training assistant, assisted in overseeing operations of a car rental company with a 200-vehicle inventory worth more than $1 million.
- Was responsible for scheduling all preventive maintenance, as well as major and minor repairs for all vehicles in the fleet. Conducted daily inventory of all vehicles and completed visual and mechanical inspections at vehicle delivery and turn-in.

STATION AGENT. Continental Airlines, Phoenix, AZ (2000-02). While simultaneously pursuing my college education and working in the above position, took on a second, part-time job assisting Continental passengers at Phoenix Sky Harbor International Airport by verifying their flight and/or checking them in on the computer.
- Refined my customer service skills while dealing with the public in a tactful and diplomatic manner in situations where the customer was frequently tired, frustrated, and hostile. Loaded and unloaded cargo and filled out baggage claim reports.

Highlights of earlier experience: Began my career in sales and customer service by quickly advancing to **ASSISTANT MANAGER** in my first position with Cactus, Inc.; managed six employees in the Building Materials department, overseeing inventory control and quality assurance, as well as ensuring that the department met all sales quotas. Coordinated directly with the manager in developing and maintaining compliance with budget forecasts.

PERSONAL   Excellent personal and professional references are available upon request. Am single and can travel or relocate to meet the needs of my employer.

Date

Exact Name of Person
Title or Position
Name of Company
Address
City, State, Zip

PROPERTY MANAGER   Dear Exact Name of Person: (or Dear Sir or Madam if answering a blind ad.)

I would appreciate an opportunity to talk with you soon about how I could contribute to your organization through my versatile skills related to managing people, finances including leasing and bookkeeping, property, and marketing/sales activities.

I consider myself a dynamic self-starter and go-getter who is comfortable being placed in situations which require excellent problem-solving and opportunity-finding skills in order to be successful.

In my current position as Property Manager, I have been promoted rapidly based on my proven negotiating skills as well as my ability to "juggle" dozens of simultaneous responsibilities. With an eye always watching the bottom line, I am currently in charge of every aspect of managing 285 rental units while supervising a full-time maintenance staff, screening potential residents and conducting showings, and preparing weekly and monthly financial reports. Through my attention to detail and management skills, I have improved profitability, customer relations, and external business relationships.

You would find me to be an enthusiastic young person who prides myself on my ability to take on a lot of responsibility and rapidly master new tasks.

I hope you will write or call me to suggest a time when we might meet to discuss your needs and how I might serve them. I can provide outstanding personal and professional references. Thank you in advance for your time.

Yours sincerely,

Olga Graves

OLGA GRAVES

1110½ Hay Street, Fayetteville, NC 28305 • preppub@aol.com • (910) 483-6611

OBJECTIVE
To contribute to an organization that can use a highly motivated self-starter who offers strong public relations and communication skills along with experience in managing people, property, finances, and daily business operations.

EXPERIENCE
PROPERTY MANAGER. PREP Realty, Denver, CO (2005-present). Have been rapidly promoted to jobs of greater responsibility in this large real estate/property management business; currently manage 168 rental units in Marston Lake Apartments and was selected for this job based on my excellent performance as assistant manager for the 285 units at Cherry Creek.

- *Maintenance management*: Supervise a full-time maintenance staff; coordinate and schedule staff and independent contractors.

- *Public relations*: Screen potential residents and conduct rental showings.

- *Negotiation*: Negotiate with the U.S. Naval Base Housing Department at The Rockies.

- *Administration*: Prepare weekly and end-of-month reports for top management while also preparing lease renewals, marketing plans, and data for computer entry.

- *Leasing consulting*: Began with this company as a Leasing Consultant and negotiated contracts for six months.

FLIGHT ATTENDANT and **AIR CHECKMAN.** Alaska Airlines, Denver, CO (2002-04). Was commended for my strong customer relations skills and problem-solving abilities while serving passengers on international flights.

PROPERTY MANAGER/OWNER. Bear Creek Property Management, Inc., Denver, CO (2000-02). Managed 300 commercial and residential units.

- *Accounting and bookkeeping*: Performed bookkeeping tasks and completed expense vouchers and time budgets.

- *Inventory control*: Ordered and controlled a diversified inventory.

- *Communication and negotiation*: Negotiated Section 8 H.U.D. contracts and dealt with social service agencies.

- *Financial reporting*: Prepared end-of-month reports for investors.

PROPERTY MANAGER. Cottonwood Properties, Inc., Denver and Colorado Springs, CO (1999). Was praised for my honesty and meticulous accounting practices while managing 250 rental units for two owner-investors.

EDUCATION
Associates degree in Business/General Studies, Community College of Denver, CO.
Completed Colorado Real Estate Sales Exam.
Was selected for advanced technical training, Flight Training Center, Denver, CO.

PERSONAL
Can provide outstanding personal and professional references upon request. Pride myself on my ability to cut costs, maximize profitability, satisfy customers, and cement good relationships.

Date

Exact Name of Person
Title or Position
Name of Company
Address
City, State, Zip

PROPERTY MANAGER   Dear Exact Name of Person: (or Dear Sir or Madam if answering a blind ad.)

With the enclosed resume, I would like to make you aware of my interest in exploring employment opportunities with your organization.

As you will see from my resume, I offer extensive experience in property management. In my current position, I manage a large apartment complex where I raised occupancy by 17% in a six-month interval. In previous experience with State Farm Realtors, I handled maintenance management, public relations, inspections and inventory, administration, court liaison, and negotiation with tenants. I also previously excelled as a Realtor, when I became a $1.2 million dollar producer in my first 12 months. Although I was successful as a Realtor, I found that I enjoyed the property management field and I was recruited by the State Farm organization to direct its property management department in Washington, DC.

My husband and I are relocating to the Tampa area, and I am seeking to join an ambitious organization in need of an experienced manager. I am accustomed to meeting aggressive goals for occupancy and customer satisfaction.

I hope you will call or write soon to suggest a time convenient for us to meet and discuss your current and future needs and how I might serve them. Thank you in advance for your time.

Sincerely,

Kaylee Knowles

Alternate last paragraph:
I hope you will welcome my call soon to arrange a brief meeting at your convenience to discuss your current and future needs and how I might serve them. Thank you in advance for your time.

KAYLEE KNOWLES

1110½ Hay Street, Fayetteville, NC 28305 • preppub@aol.com • (910) 483-6611

OBJECTIVE
I want to contribute to an organization that can use a highly motivated self-starter who offers strong public relations and communication skills along with experience in managing people, property, finances, and daily business operations.

EXPERIENCE
PROPERTY MANAGER. Georgetown Community, Midlands, TX (2005-present). While managing this large apartment complex, raised and maintained occupancy by 17% in a 6-month time interval. Collect rent, make deposits, and balance books at end of each month.
- Prepare activity, occupancy, and market reports for Broker-in-Charge and property owner.
- Coordinate with contractors. Oversee maintenance; lease apartment, process applications, and expedite lease agreements; use Prentice Hall and Property Pro-On Site System.

Began with State Farm Realtors company in 2000, and have excelled in handling both sales/marketing and property management responsibilities on a large scale:
PROPERTY MANAGER. State Farm Realtors, Property Management Department, Washington, DC (2000-05). Excelled as a property manager for one of the area's most well-known real estate/property management firms; was responsible for an inventory of between 180 to 200 residences.
- *Maintenance Management:* Supervised maintenance activities; coordinated and scheduled staff and independent contractors; obtained estimates for work to be performed and monitored major repairs as work proceeds.
- *Public relations:* Screened potential residents and conducted rental showings.
- *Inspections and inventory:* Conducted bi-annual inspections of every property and conducted house inventories; ordered goods and materials as needed.
- *Administration:* Prepared reports for top management while also preparing lease renewals, inspection reports, and other paperwork.
- *Negotiation:* Mediated between owners and tenants as needed in situations where disputes arose over damages, security deposits, or rent owed.
- *Accomplishments:* Made significant contributions to office operations through organizing office policies and procedures; brought 125 new properties into management.

REALTOR. Re/Max Realtors, Washington, DC (1998-2000). Became a $1.2 million dollar producer within 12 months! Gained valuable skills in sales, marketing, and contract negotiating while acquiring expert knowledge of most aspects of the real estate business.

OFFICE ADMINISTRATOR. Cape Fear Real Estate Corp., Roanoke, VA (1995-98). Processed sales contracts and revisions; verified sales prices, financing, option pricing, and lot premiums with approved documents; deposited and accounted for all earnest money received; prepared sales, closings, and construction reports; maintained land files including settlement statements and title insurance commitments.

PROPERTY MANAGEMENT OFFICER/MEDICAL SUPPLY SPECIALIST. U.S. Army, locations worldwide (1990-95). As Property Management Officer, ordered and received all non-medical supply items for the Logistics Division; maintained all files of local purchase items ordered and received; maintained quarterly budgets.

EDUCATION
Completed nearly two years of college coursework toward two-year degree, University of the District of Columbia; am only six credit hours short of earning my degree.

PERSONAL
Have utilized Word and Excel, and the Multiple Listing Service System (MLS).

CAREER CHANGE

Date

Exact Name of Person
Title or Position
Name of Company
Address
City, State, Zip

PROPERTY MANAGER

Dear Exact Name of Person: (or Dear Sir or Madam if answering a blind ad.)

Please accept the enclosed resume as an indication of my strong interest in receiving consideration for a supervisory or managerial position with your organization. I am highly interested in the field of airline catering and feel that I offer the organizational and communications skills needed for success in this competitive business.

With a bachelor's degree, I have completed extensive professional training in supervisory and managerial principles, personnel management, and motivational/team building skills. I offer a proven track record of success based on my proactive problem-solving and decision-making skills, business know-how, and customer service background. With no prior experience in property management, I stepped into my current position and quickly learned the inner workings of a large apartment complex. After restructuring all facets of operations, productivity increased, expenses were reduced, and apartments were available for tenancy 30% faster than before.

In a previous position I was promoted from a sales position to District Manager for a public utility company. I made significant contributions while developing and implementing new procedures and programs which resulted in lowered costs, increased customer satisfaction, and increased productivity. My accomplishments included reconfiguring service areas for a 50% reduction in response time, achieving the highest employee retention rates, and posting the best safety records of all the districts in our region.

You can be assured that I possess the initiative, creativity, team building/ motivational ability, leadership, as well as the planning and organization skills needed in the professional you seek. I can provide outstanding personal and professional references. I am single and will travel and/or relocate as your needs require.

I hope you will call or write me soon to suggest a time when we might meet to discuss your current and future needs and how I might serve them. Thank you in advance for your time.

Sincerely,

Justin Sears

JUSTIN SEARS

1110½ Hay Street, Fayetteville, NC 28305   •   preppub@aol.com   •   (910) 483-6611

OBJECTIVE To offer proven supervisory and managerial abilities along with a background of effectiveness in establishing goals, applying sound judgment to the decision-making and problem-solving process, and motivating others through proven communication and team-building skills.

EDUCATION & TRAINING Hold a **B.A. in Liberal Arts with a concentration in History**, University of Central Florida, Orlando, FL.
Attended seminars emphasizing supervisory and management principles along with effective personnel management and motivational skills, Valencia Community College, Orlando, FL.

EXPERIENCE **PROPERTY MANAGER.** Lake Apopka Estates, Winter Garden, FL (2005-present). For the city's second-largest apartment complex which has 617 units, supervise 14 employees in the building & grounds and maintenance departments while developing improvements to operating procedures which impacted favorably on productivity and the bottom line.
- Developed and implemented projects during which a warehouse and workshop were completely renovated to OSHA standards; this resulted in more efficient use of space.
- Manage personnel administration actions as well as purchase orders, contractor billing, and the process for selecting contractors.
- Reduced time needed to prepare vacant apartments for new tenants 30% by coordinating maintenance requirements with improved purchasing and inventory procedures.
- Introduced new planning measures and developed maintenance schedules and control procedures which maximized employee efficiency and overall productivity.

DISTRICT MANAGER. Florida Natural Gas, Orlando, FL (1989-04). Was promoted in a track record of advancement after joining the company as a Salesman.
1992-03 (District Manager): Received numerous awards for my accomplishments related to developing and implementing creative ways of operating with significant cost savings, increased customer satisfaction, and improved productivity for the district office of a public utility company.
- Supervised a nine-person staff which provided financial services such as billing and accounts receivable along with service, sales, and personnel administration functions.
- Implemented creative ideas to include reconfiguring the district into service areas which improved service response times an impressive 50% while reducing expenses.
- Established aggressive customer service, sales, and new customer acquisition programs.
- Provided oversight and direction for functional areas which included public relations and support services for industrial accounts.
- Received numerous quarterly management performance and safety awards; **was credited with playing a key role in the recognition of the district with the highest employee retention rate and best safety record.**
1989-92 (Sales Representative): Excelled as a Sales Representative and was selected for management training on the basis of my contributions and knowledge of corporate structure, sales theories, and distribution systems; was a valued member of a successful sales team and instrumental in engineering the introduction of new lines in areas without gas.

ASSISTANT NATIONAL SALES MANAGER. John Lake Industries, Winter Garden, FL (1983-88). Advanced to Assistant National Sales Manager for John Lake Industries.

CIVIC HONORS Elected **President** of the Orlando Club (2001-02).
Served as **President** of the Central School Parent Teacher Organization, 1998-00.
Elected **Senior Warden** and **Treasurer,** Methodist Church, 1995-00.

Date

Exact Name of Person
Title or Position
Name of Company
Address
City, State, Zip

PROPERTY MANAGER   Dear Exact Name of Person: (or Dear Sir or Madam if answering a blind ad.)

With the enclosed resume, I would like to make you aware of my background in property management as well as my interest in applying my skills for the benefit of your organization. I am eager to join a company that can use a highly motivated self-starter with extensive experience in property management. I can provide outstanding references.

As you will see from my resume, I have excelled in a track record of promotion with National Joint Realty Trust DBA Seaview Apartments. The company is a large apartment owner in the major markets, and I have been recognized on several occasions for my significant contributions to the bottom line.

I began with the company in 2004, as a Weekend Marketing Manager and was quickly promoted to Assistant Community Director (Assistant Property Manager) of an apartment complex. In 2005, I became Community Director (Property Manager), and I have excelled in every aspect of my job. While training, supervising, hiring, terminating, and maintaining payroll records for employees, I have supervised all details of move-ins, maintained outstanding relationships with residents, and ensured adherence to the highest standards of property management.

If you can use a hard-working and reliable professional who could make valuable contributions to your economic goals, I hope you will contact me to suggest a time when we might meet to discuss your needs. I would certainly enjoy the opportunity to meet with you in person.

Sincerely,

Laverna Johnston

LAVERNA JOHNSTON

1110½ Hay Street, Fayetteville, NC 28305 • preppub@aol.com • (910) 483-6611

OBJECTIVE

To benefit an organization that can use an enthusiastic young professional who has excelled in property management, customer service, sales, and marketing through applying my strong organizational and communication skills as well as my ability to juggle numerous simultaneous priorities.

EDUCATION

Completed nearly three years of college course work toward a **B.S. degree in Business Administration and Marketing**, University of North Carolina at Wilmington, NC.
* Am completing the degree in my spare time, as my work schedule permits.
Extensive training related to property management, sales, and customer service.

EXPERIENCE

PROPERTY MANAGER ("Community Director"). National Joint Realty DBA Seaview Apartments, Wilmington, NC (2004-present). For a rapidly expanding company which is a large apartment owner in the major Sunbelt markets, have excelled in every aspect of this job while emphasizing resident retention, maintaining the highest occupancy standards, and remaining within budget guidelines.
* Began with the company as a **Weekend Marketing Associate** in June, 2004; then was promoted to **Assistant Community Director** in June, 2005, and stepped up to **Community Director (Property Manager)** in January, 2006.
* Manage six employees in this 248-unit apartment complex.
* Became proficient in Word, Excel, Windows XP, and Rent Roll. Have been trained in property management by a company which is the second largest real estate investment trust (REIT) in the country in terms of apartments owned.
* Played a key role in my apartment complex's being named a qualifying winner in the National Joint Occupancy Award; met extremely high occupancy goals to qualify and received a trophy as remembrance. Train, supervise, hire, terminate, and make recommendations regarding employees; maintain accurate payroll records for employees.
* Actively market and promote apartment rentals and move-ins; collect rents; handle delinquents; supervise outside contractors on the property.
* Supervise all details of move-ins and maintained excellent resident relations.
* Working within established budgets, notify District Manager of any variations; enforce policies and procedures. Maintain high work ethic and a cooperative attitude. Supervise maintenance staff and service manager; assure adherence to federal, state, and local laws and regulations.
* Maintain maximum occupancy with minimal collection and/or vacancy loss; ensure that all interiors and exteriors of the property met company safety and appearance standards.
* In 2005, met all expectations $127,045 below budget; exceeded ROI by $112,394 YTD.
* Became known for my excellent use of company resources, and excelled in utilizing strong income generation techniques by using software for analysis.

Other experience:
SALES ASSOCIATE. Lord & Taylor Department Store, Wilmington, NC (2000-03). Began as a Sales Associate in the jewelry department and worked my way to Counter Manager in the Cosmetics Department; Learned to work in an environment in which I had to handle multiple tasks while priorities were constantly changing.
SWITCHBOARD OPERATOR. Tyson Seafood Company, Wilmington, NC (1998-2000). Became known for my strong customer service and public relations skills while operating a multi-line switchboard for a major seafood wholesaler.

PERSONAL

Excellent personal and professional references are available upon request.

Date

Exact Name of Person
Title or Position
Name of Company
Address
City, State, Zip

PURCHASING MANAGER   Dear Exact Name of Person: (or Dear Sir or Madam if answering a blind ad.)

With the enclosed resume, I would like to introduce myself and make you aware of the considerable experience in purchasing, contracting, property management, finance, and operations management which I could put to work for you. I am currently in the process of relocating to the Florida area where my extended family lives, and I would appreciate an opportunity to talk personally with you about how I could contribute to your organization.

With my current employer, I have been promoted to Senior Purchasing Manager. I am responsible for the property management of more than 5,000 houses and apartments, including a fleet of 72 service vans. I also prepare and resourcefully utilize a budget of more than $1.6 million annually for repair parts, outside services, support equipment, and materials. On my own initiative, I have totally streamlined the bidding process. In consultation with the System Manager, I implemented a new computer program to track bids, thereby transforming a previously disorganized manual process into an efficient computerized system. Additionally, I streamlined purchasing procedures while taking over a job which had previously been done by two people. Using available software, I have also established accounting and budgeting programs for a small business.

In all my previous jobs, I have been recognized—sometimes with cash bonuses— for developing new systems which improved efficiency and customer service. For example, while working for the U.S. Embassy in Miami, I created a computerized method of financial reporting which greatly enhanced the budgeting and fiscal accountability functions. In another job as a Purchasing Agent, I exceeded expected standards while handling critical functions including making decisions on the most advantageous sources, assisting in bidding solicitations, and evaluating quotations for price discounts and reference materials.

I have never been in a job where I did not find creative and resourceful ways to cut costs, improve bottom-line results, and strengthen relationships with customers.

I hope you will call or write me soon to suggest a time convenient for us to meet and discuss your needs and how I might serve them. Thank you for your time.

Sincerely,

Robert Rountree

ROBERT ROUNTREE

1110½ Hay Street, Fayetteville, NC 28305   •   preppub@aol.com   •   (910) 483-6611

OBJECTIVE   To contribute to an organization that can use a resourceful purchasing manager who is skilled in contract negotiation, operations management, and personnel administration.

EDUCATION   Completed one year of master's degree work in Urban Management, Texas State University, Mercerville, TX, 1995-96.
Earned B.S. in Health Education, University of Washington, Washington, DC, 1991.
Received A.A. in General Education, Miami Dale Community College, Miami, FL, 1986.
Completed executive development and non-degree-granting training programs in:

Cost Accounting	Managerial Accounting	Procurement
Computer Operations	Inventory Control	Budget Administration

COMPUTERS   Word, Excel, PowerPoint, Quick Books Pro, Windows, other software.

EXPERIENCE   **PURCHASING MANAGER.** Briley & Co., Ft. Hood, TX (2000-present). Have acquired a broad understanding of government contracting procedures while achieving an excellent track record of promotion in the finance and purchasing field.
- Was originally employed as a Purchasing Agent to replace two buyers; have been promoted to Senior Purchasing Manager in charge of five associates.
- Am responsible for an annual budget of approximately $2.1 million of which $1.6 million is used by me to purchase repair parts, outside services, support equipment, and materials.
- Responsible for property management: within a $150,000 monthly budget oversee maintenance and repairs performed on 5,000 housing units and a fleet of 72 vans.
- In a formal letter of appreciation, was commended for saving at least $400,000 annually by combining my extensive purchasing knowledge with my creative problem-solving skills.
- On my own initiative, streamlined the bidding process; developed a new system for obtaining price quotes from potential vendors and worked with the System Manager in developing a computer program to track quotes: this transformed the manual quotation to an efficient new process which reduced the time necessary to prepare quotes.
- Established excellent working relationships with vendors all over the country, and am known for my ability to quickly find difficult-to-obtain parts for critical needs.
- Knowledgeable of government contracting and new product testing.

CONSULTANT & VICE PRESIDENT OF FINANCE. Branson Enterprises, Miami, FL (1991-99). Played a key role in helping the owner build a new business; established budgeting and accounting systems. Negotiated the details of the company's largest contract.

PURCHASING MANAGER. Contracting Division of the U.S. Air Force, Washington, DC (1989-91). Handled critical functions including making decisions on the most advantageous sources, assisting in bidding solicitations and acceptance, and evaluating quotations for price discounts as well as delivery/transportation costs. Developed outstanding relationships and received a Laudatory Best Operation performance appraisal with cash bonus.

PROCUREMENT OFFICER. The American Embassy in Miami (1986-89). Began working for the Embassy as a Warehouse Manager and, holding a **Top Secret** security clearance, excelled in managing warehouse operations and in relocating warehouse contents to new facilities.
- Because of problem-solving ability, was promoted to Procurement Officer; took over a disorganized operation and created a computerized method of reporting Local Operational Funds (LOF) which enhanced efficiency of the budgeting and fiscal functions.

PERSONAL   Outstanding personal and professional references. Will cheerfully travel/relocate.

Date

Exact Name of Person
Title or Position
Name of Company
Address
City, State, Zip

**REAL ESTATE
AGENT**

Dear Exact Name of Person: (or Dear Sir or Madam if answering a blind ad.)

I would appreciate an opportunity to talk with you soon about how I could contribute to your organization through my experience and personal qualities.

As you will see from my resume, I excelled in the accounting and bookkeeping field prior to finding my way into real estate. Although I enjoyed the mechanics of performing bookkeeping in the construction industry, I realized that I most enjoy interaction with the public, and since childhood I have demonstrated my ability to befriend others and establish strong relationships.

After earning my real estate license, I quickly earned monthly recognition for total number of listings, and I became a Million Dollar Producer in my first year after licensing.

With skills and abilities that could make me a valuable part of your team, I am a hard-working and reliable professional who prides myself on doing any job to the best of my ability. I can provide excellent personal and professional references.

I hope you will welcome my call soon to arrange a brief meeting at your convenience to discuss your current and future needs and how I might serve them. Thank you in advance for your time.

Sincerely yours,

Bridget Carlson

BRIDGET CARLSON

1110½ Hay Street, Fayetteville, NC 28305 • preppub@aol.com • (910) 483-6611

OBJECTIVE

To contribute to a company that can use a dedicated hard worker with exceptional attention-to-detail skills.

LICENSE

Licensed real estate agent since 2005

EXPERIENCE

REAL ESTATE AGENT. Re/Max Realtors, Columbus, GA (2005-present). Write sales and listing contracts on new and existing homes including showing the homes to perspective buyers.

- Demonstrate my communication skills while showing rental properties and making sure that potential home buyers and renters understand the financial details. Advise young buyers on credit issues and personal finance.
- Received Agent of the Month twice in 2006 based on record total listings. Became a Million Dollar Producer in my first year on the job.
- Applied my talent for rapidly establishing rapport with strangers.

ACCOUNTING CLERK. Nationwide Insurance, Columbus, GA (2001-05). Handled accounts receivable and posted premiums to proper accounts; conducted premium check claims for current status.

- Worked up out-of-state premiums for break down of state.
- Filed reinsurance; filed and posted statistical records, commissions, and claims.

BOOKKEEPER. Muscogee Construction, Columbus, GA (2001). Managed bank journal, disbursement journal, and inventory summary sheets; recorded individual contractors for calendar year.

- Controlled payroll, filing, and accounts receivable/payable.
- Posted invoices, answered the phone and mobile radio.
- Set up appointments and distributed payroll.

PAYROLL CLERK/BOOKKEEPER. Patterson Planetarium, Columbus, GA (1993-00). Maintained the general ledger, accounts receivable/payable, payroll, insurance claims filing, scheduling, appointment setting, as well as expense and income recording.

Highlights of other experience:

- Developed attention-to-detail and quick eye-to-hand coordination skills while working industrial labor for Riverland Industries.
- Handled a 20-line switchboard while working at a busy real estate office.

COMPUTERS

Proficient with software including PowerPoint, Word, Excel, and Access. Am experiencing in data collection, and have created spreadsheets and databases designed to aid in rapid information retrieval.

**EDUCATION &
TRAINING**

Hold certifications in both electrology and cosmetology.
Earned certification in computers.
Successfully completed training in accounting.
Am a certified Christian Education Monitor.

PERSONAL

Always willing to go the extra mile for a job well done. Can get along exceptionally well with anyone. Have adopted as my motto "an honest day's work for an honest day's pay."

CAREER CHANGE

Date

Exact Name of Person
Title or Position
Name of Company
Address
City, State, Zip

REAL ESTATE AGENT
This talented individual has
succeeded at real estate
sales, but he yearns to
make a career transition
back into a management
position in a large
organization. Although he
has excelled in sales, he
has decided that he prefers
management.

REAL ESTATE AGENT

Dear Exact Name of Person (or Dear Sir or Madam if answering a blind ad):

I would appreciate an opportunity to talk with you soon about how I could contribute to your organization through my versatile management experience, organizational and program development skills, and reputation for excellence in counseling, motivating, and leading employees to achieve superior results.

As you will see by my resume, I offer a background which includes 20 years of service in the U.S. Army, culminating in executive roles as a Lieutenant Colonel. Throughout my military career, I was involved in planning and carrying out large-scale projects with international implications. In my last military assignment, I managed a $4.5 million annual operating budget at the headquarters of an organization with four separate but interlocking divisions. In one earlier job I developed operating procedures for a unique aviation unit operating teams which rotated from the U.S. and the Persian Gulf. This program involved joint cooperation with the U.S. Navy at high levels and managing more than 200 specialists operating and maintaining aircraft and equipment valued at more than $61 million.

I am a versatile professional able to adapt to rapid change, pressure, and deadlines while maximizing human and material resources to their fullest extent. I am proud of my reputation as an unquestionably honest individual and straightforward speaker. I have been successful in building teams of the highest quality by giving employees my trust and respect for their own abilities and decision-making skills.

My managerial and supervisory experience is enhanced by strong technical skills. I am familiar with data processing practices and several widely used software programs.

Additionally I offer what I feel is a rather unusual educational background. My B.S. degree is in Resource Management and I am a licensed Real Estate Broker. Since retiring from the Army, I have earned an associate degree in General Occupational Technology and in June 1995, will receive a second A.A.S. degree in Banking and Finance.

I hope you will welcome my call soon to arrange a brief meeting at your convenience to discuss your current and future needs and how I might serve them. Thank you in advance for your time.

Sincerely yours,

Perry A. Admiral

PERRY A. ADMIRAL

1110½ Hay Street, Fayetteville, NC 28305 • preppub@aol.com • (910) 483-6611

OBJECTIVE To offer experience in multilevel management to an organization in need of an intelligent, mature executive with a history of attaining exceptional results while directing large-scale operations in a variety of functional areas as a senior military officer.

EDUCATION **B.S., Resource Management,** Troy State University, Ft. Rucker, AL, 1978.
A.A.S., Banking and Finance, Tampa Technical Community College (TTCC), Tampa, FL, June 2005.
- Graduated with honors by maintaining a 3.9 GPA.

A.A.S., General Occupational Technology, TTCC, 2001.
- Achieved a perfect 4.0 GPA and was inducted into the National Vocational and Technical Honor Society.

EXECUTIVE & TECHNICAL TRAINING Completed the military's graduate-level Command and General Staff College and other graduate-level schools for top executives.
Attended 80 hours of course work in selling, evaluating, and managing real estate, Huff Real Estate School, Tampa, FL, 2005.

EXPERIENCE **REAL ESTATE AGENT, PROPERTY MANAGER,** and **STUDENT.** Tampa, FL (2000-present). While earning two associate degrees and an FL Real Estate Broker's License, handled the details of rental property management and real estate sales.

Retired from the U.S. Army with the rank of Colonel after a distinguished career directing daily operations, training, planning, and the execution of programs for organizations with as many as 10,000 employees and up to $61 million worth of equipment in locations throughout the world. Consistently earned respect for my ability to handle a myriad of details and numerous complex projects simultaneously in areas including personnel, security, operations, resource and budget management, public affairs, and aviation.

DEPUTY DIRECTOR. The Pentagon, Washington, DC (1990-99). Directed staff activities and developed and managed the $4.5 million annual operating budget at a corporate headquarters for four 1,000-person divisions, each with separate but coordinating missions, and which provided intelligence support for the military's central command.
- Inspired personnel to achieve exceptional performance ratings and praise for their professionalism and spirit of team work despite the drawback of severe turnover rates.

DIRECTOR OF OPERATIONS AND PLANNING. Persian Gulf (1987-90). Planned, coordinated, and managed a special task force with a sensitive mission in the Persian Gulf: had oversight for approximately 200 people operating in excess of $61 million worth of helicopters which were rotated regularly in teams between the U.S. and the Persian Gulf.

GENERAL MANAGER. Germany (1983-85). Turned an average company into a top performer by providing a leadership style which inspired employees to have a sense of pride; managed a 219-person aviation company with $52 million worth of equipment including 37 vehicles and 45 helicopters.

COMPUTER Knowledge of software including Adobe PageMaker, Microsoft Word, Excel, and PowerPoint.

PERSONAL Hold FAA Commercial, Single-Engine Helicopter license with 3,500 hours of flight time. Known for honesty and integrity, held a Top Secret security clearance.

CAREER CHANGE

Date

Exact Name of Person
Title or Position
Name of Company
Address
City, State, Zip

**REAL ESTATE
APPRAISER**

with experience in
credit union
management

Dear Exact Name of Person (or Dear Sir or Madam if answering a blind ad):

With the enclosed resume, I would like to make you aware of my interest in exploring opportunities which will take advantage of my knowledge related to mortgage lending as well as my experience related to banking, credit unions, and financial services.

As you will see from my resume, I offer a distinguished track record of accomplishment with Cedar Rapids area credit unions. As a Vice President with IowaUSA Federal Credit Union, I enjoyed a history of promotion to increased responsibilities as a credit union executive. I was promoted to Vice President to handle a variety of strategic responsibilities for four branches with total assets of $31 million. Among my accomplishments were significantly outperforming the annual yields for all credit unions, diversifying the total loan portfolio, reducing delinquencies, and increasing capital. While achieving excellent results in all areas of operations, I was instrumental in leading the credit union to a five-star rating from Cedar Creek Financial Reports, Inc., and a superior rating from I.O.A. Financial Publishing, Inc. Earlier as a Loan Manager, I played a key role in the rapid growth of assets of a credit union to $23 million from $10 million.

In 2005 I made a career change into real estate sales and then into the specialized field of real estate appraisal. This experience has allowed me to gain insight into the mortgage lending process from a different angle and has added to my strong background related to lending and financial services.

You would find me to be a congenial professional who is skilled at motivating employees to excel in their jobs and who is experienced in interacting with federal examiners, auditors, risk management professionals, and others with fiduciary responsibilities.

Because I am frequently in your area exploring employment and housing options, I would be available for personal interviews at almost any time at your convenience. I hope you will contact me if you can make use of my experience and expertise.

Sincerely,

Brian Monroe

BRIAN MONROE

1110½ Hay Street, Fayetteville, NC 28305   •   preppub@aol.com   •   (910) 483-6611

OBJECTIVE

To offer a versatile background which has included managing banking and credit union operations as well as real estate sales and appraisal to an organization that can use my ability to create new services, design software programs, and motivate employees to excel.

EDUCATION

Real Estate Appraisal and GRI Courses, Kirkwood Community College, Cedar Rapids, IA, 2005 and 2004.
Credit Union Executive Program, Credit Union American Association, with course work in areas including accounting, marketing, credit/collections, business law, money and banking, and financial counseling. Other college courses in computers and trust services.
Associate's Degree, Business Administration, Cedar Rapids Mercy College, IA, 1999.
Certified Financial Counselor, Drake University, Des Moines, IA, 2004.

EXPERIENCE

REAL ESTATE APPRAISER. Bill Hines and Associates, Cedar Rapids, IA (2005-present). After achieving success in real estate sales, transferred my skills to this specialized area of appraising commercial properties as well as residential property, land, farms, and estates for banks, attorneys, and individuals for mortgage lending purposes.
- Developed expertise in the area of research, and became knowledgeable of USPAP regulations and laws governing the appraisal process. Expanded computer knowledge and skills with Windows XP using Word, Excel, PowerPoint, and Access.

VICE PRESIDENT. IowaUSA Federal Credit Union, Cedar Rapids, IA (1988-05). Was promoted to handle a variety of strategic responsibilities while managing 10 employees and indirectly overseeing 29 people in a credit union with four branches and assets of $31 million. Reduced delinquencies to 1.06% and increased capital to 12.3%.
- Developed written policies and procedures for approval by the Board of Directors while managing areas including credit union and office operations, loans and collections, cash flow, business development, insurance and credit card operations, and security.
- Produced an annual yield on loans of 14.95% which significantly outperformed the annual yield of 11.45% for all credit unions. Diversified loan portfolio: increased secured loans to 45%, decreased unsecured loans to 55%, and increased loans from $6 to $20 million.
- Became skilled in interacting with a wide range of professionals from federal examiners, to risk management professionals, to others with fiduciary responsibilities.
- Involved in the process of troubleshooting software programs used by the four branches, provided expertise during the conversion to a Data General system. Developed an insurance program to provide collateral protection.
- Was instrumental in achieving a five-star rating from Cedar Creek Financial reports, Inc., and a superior rating from I.O.A. Financial Publishing, Inc.

Other experience:
LOAN MANAGER. Iowa Federal Credit Union, Des Moines, IA. Was praised by the board of directors for "never less than excellent" performance; supervised up to 18 people including eight loan officers in a site with an annual loan volume of $14 million.
- Played a key role in the rapid growth of assets from $10 to $23 million.

AFFILIATIONS

Linn County Dispute Resolution Center Chairman of the Board and volunteer. Chamber of Commerce: past member, board of directors, chairman of numerous committees. IowaUSA Credit Association past president. Licensed property and casualty insurance, and life and health insurance.

Date

Exact Name of Person
Title or Position
Name of Company
Address
City, State, Zip

REAL ESTATE BROKER

with commercial experience

Dear Exact Name of Person: (or Dear Sir or Madam if answering a blind ad.)

With the enclosed resume, I would like to make you aware of my interest in exploring employment opportunities with your organization. I am interested in the position of Commercial Real Estate Agency Manager which you recently advertised in *The Wall Street Journal.*

As you will see from my resume, I am a very successful commercial real estate agent who has been recognized among my peers as Top Commercial Agent based on having the highest number of listings in my state. I have maintained a record of multimillion-dollar sales throughout my career in the real estate business.

I have discovered, however, that I most enjoy the opportunities I have to mentor and develop my peers and associates, and I excel in motivating others. The supervisory and training responsibilities mentioned in your ad interest me very much, and I would enjoy helping each agent become more successful as the company prospers.

I hope you will call or write soon to suggest a time convenient for us to meet and discuss your current and future needs and how I might serve them. Thank you in advance for your time.

Sincerely,

Cheryl Stewart

Alternate last paragraph:
I hope you will welcome my call soon to arrange a brief meeting at your convenience to discuss your current and future needs and how I might serve them. Thank you in advance for your time.

CHERYL STEWART

1110½ Hay Street, Fayetteville, NC 28305   •   preppub@aol.com   •   (910) 483-6611

OBJECTIVE	To offer my broad-ranging experience in administration, public relations, sales, and management to an organization that can use my skills in solving problems, motivating my peers and subordinates to provide the highest level of service to the public.
EXPERIENCE	**REAL ESTATE BROKER.** Towson Realty and Sheffield-Arliss Realty, Towson, MD (2001-present). Consistently set sales records and earned recognition as a "Top Producer" with two different established real estate companies. • Was recognized as the **Top Commercial Agent** with the highest number of listings in the state of Maryland. • Maintain a record of $1 million-plus in sales during each year I have been in the real estate business. • Receive numerous Outstanding Sales Achievement awards. • Gained knowledge of rental department operations which included approximately 60 residential rental properties. • Was the top producer for four consecutive years. • Carry out other responsibilities including filing, contract preparation, answering phones, and preparing ad layouts as well as handling public relations. • Instruct classes on all aspects of the real estate business. • Complete all phases of the sales process through loan closings for all types of loans using all sources including FHA, VA, and conventional loans. **RECEPTIONIST.** University of Maryland, College Park, MD (1998-2001). In a full-time job while pursuing my college degree at night, received and routed calls on a 105-line main switchboard as well as greeting visitors and assisting them in finding the correct office or department. Worked directly for the college president. • Provided assistance to the Business and Student Services Departments including typing and filing support. **Highlights of earlier experience:** While in high school, worked in sales, inventory control, and merchandise buying for Filene's Department Store. **PLANT SECRETARY.** After graduating from high school, was hired to work in the shipping department of a company which built prefabricated homes, advanced to this position which included typing, filing, preparing OSHA reports, overseeing fire prevention activities, and providing administrative support for the plant manager. • Conducted inventories of all pieces of material used for building prefab homes. • As the "right arm" for the plant president, administered insurance policy processing for several hundred people.
COMPUTERS	Proficient with Word, Access, Excel, and PowerPoint. Experience in Internet research.
EDUCATION	**Bachelor of Science in Business Administration**, University of Maryland, College Park, MD, 2001. Completed degree in my spare time while excelling in my full-time position. Previously earned 18 credits toward **A.A.S. degree in Computer Science,** Towson University, Towson, MD. Graduated from Baltimore Real Estate Institute, Baltimore, MD, 2001.
LICENSES	Maryland Real Estate Broker's License, 2001 Maryland Real Estate Salesman's License, 2000.

Date

Exact Name of Person
Title or Position
Name of Company
Address
City, State, Zip

REAL ESTATE BROKER Dear Exact Name of Person: (or Sir or Madam if answering a blind ad.)

Can you use an enthusiastic, results-oriented sales professional who offers outstanding communication skills, a talent for reading people, and a reputation for determination and persistence in reaching goals?

With a proven background of success in sales, I have displayed my versatility while selling and marketing a wide variety of products and services including residential real estate and land, new and used automobiles, and financial products/investment services. In one job I trained and supervised a successful team of mutual fund and insurance sales agents. Most recently as an Independent Real Estate Broker with a Century 21 office in Portland, OR, I achieved the $3 million mark in sales for 2005. While excelling in all aspects of the business, I have used my experience and knowledge to create marketing strategies and tools which reached large audiences and generated much business.

Earlier experience gave me an opportunity to refine my sales and communication abilities as well as gain familiarity with business management including finance and collections, inventory control, personnel administration, and customer service. Prior to owning and managing a business which bought, reconditioned, and marketed automobiles, I was one of Tate Mercedes' most successful sales professionals, earning the distinction of being "Salesman of the Month" for 13 consecutive months and "Salesman of the Year."

If you can use a seasoned professional with the ability to solve tough business problems, maximize profitability, and increase market share under highly competitive conditions, I would enjoy an opportunity to meet with you to discuss your needs and how I might serve them. Known for my resourcefulness, I can provide outstanding personal and professional references.

I hope you will welcome my call soon to arrange a brief meeting at your convenience. Thank you in advance for your time.

Sincerely,

Brett Creger

Alternate last paragraph:
I hope you will call or write me soon to suggest a time convenient for us to meet and discuss your current and future needs and how I might serve them. Thank you in advance for your time.

BRETT CREGER

1110½ Hay Street, Fayetteville, NC 28305   •   preppub@aol.com   •   (910) 483-6611

OBJECTIVE

To offer a track record of success in sales and managerial roles where outstanding communication skills and the ability to close the sale were key factors in building a reputation as a highly motivated professional oriented toward achieving maximum bottom-line results.

EXPERIENCE

REAL ESTATE BROKER. Century 21, Portland, ME (2004-present). Reached the $3 million personal sales level for 2005 while providing a range of experience which has played a key role in boosting overall sales and profitability of a thriving agency in this highly competitive market.

- Have become known for strong interpersonal and communication skills while coordinating with potential buyers, lending institutions, construction professionals, sellers, and others.
- Negotiate all aspects of financial transactions; deal with mortgage company representatives to arrange financing and with attorneys to handle real estate closings.
- Utilize my expert marketing abilities while creating sales strategies and preparing direct mail materials which capture the interest of prospective clients and generate new business. Routinely make presentations to other agents and buyers.
- Have become skilled in all aspects of property evaluation and am skilled in comparing newly available homes with those having comparable features. Handle the details of researching information and completing paperwork for sales of homes and land.

SALES AND MARKETING REPRESENTATIVE. Self-employed, Portland, ME (1997-03). Trained and then supervised the efforts of as many as 12 agents while also personally marketing and selling mutual funds and insurance. Refined my abilities in a competitive field and excelled in developing sales and marketing techniques which increased sales.

Highlights of earlier experience:
FINANCE AND OPERATIONS MANAGER. Became highly effective in handling finances, marketing, and sales as the owner of a business with six sales professionals, a title clerk, a bookkeeper, and 12 employees in the body shop (New England Auto Shop, Portland, ME). Learned small business management while handling sales, finances, and collections.

- Created marketing and advertising plans and products which were highly effective.

SALES REPRESENTATIVE. For a major automobile dealer, consistently placed in the top three of 22 sales professionals (Tate Mercedes, Portland, ME). Was "Salesman of the Month" for 13 consecutive months and once honored as "Salesman of the Year."

FIELD SALES MANAGER. Became the youngest person in the company's history to hold this position after only a year with this national company (Amway, Portland, ME, and Los Angeles, CA). Became skilled in earning the confidence of potential customers and achieved a highly successful rate of positive responses from four out of each five people I approached: increased the amount of sales per customer.

TRAINING

Completed corporate training programs in areas such as real estate law, brokerage, finance, and securities as well as life, accident, and health insurance.
Am licensed as a real estate salesman, broker, and life/accident/health insurance agent.

PERSONAL

Am known for my ability to see "the big picture" while managing the details. Offer a proven ability to develop strategic plans that maximize profitability and market share in competitive environments. Am a results-oriented, persistent individual who can be counted on to finish any project on time and within budget. Can provide outstanding references.

Date

Exact Name of Person
Title of Person
Name of Company
Address
City, State, Zip

REAL ESTATE
BROKER

Dear Exact Name of Person: (or Sir or Madam if answering a blind ad.)

Can you use an enthusiastic, results-oriented sales manager who offers outstanding communication skills, a talent for reading people, and a reputation for determination and persistence in reaching goals?

With a proven background of success in sales, I have displayed my versatility while selling and marketing a wide variety of products and services including residential real estate and land, new and used automobiles, and financial products/ investment services. In one job I trained and supervised a successful team of mutual fund and insurance sales agents. Most recently as a Real Estate Broker and General Manager of a real estate firm, I achieved the $3 million mark in annual sales while training and developing junior associates who have become top producers. While excelling in all aspects of the business, I have used my experience to create marketing strategies which reached large audiences and generated much business.

Earlier experience gave me an opportunity to refine my sales and communication abilities as well as gain familiarity with business management including finance and collections, inventory control, personnel administration, and customer service. Prior to owning and managing a business which bought, reconditioned, and marketed automobiles, I was one of Houston Buick's most successful sales professionals, earning the distinction of "Salesman of the Month" for 13 consecutive months and "Salesman of the Year."

If you can use a seasoned professional with the ability to solve tough business problems, maximize profitability, and increase market share under highly competitive conditions, I would enjoy an opportunity to meet with you to discuss your needs and how I might serve them. I can provide outstanding references.

I hope you will welcome my call soon to arrange a brief meeting at your convenience. Thank you in advance for your time.

Sincerely,

Keith Toomey

KEITH TOOMEY

1110½ Hay Street, Fayetteville, NC 28305   •   preppub@aol.com   •   (910) 483-6611

OBJECTIVE   To offer a track record of success in sales and managerial roles where outstanding communication skills and the ability to close the sale were key factors in building a reputation as a highly motivated professional oriented toward maximum bottom-line results.

EXPERIENCE   **REAL ESTATE BROKER & GENERAL MANAGER.** Toomey Real Estate, Inc., Myrtle Beach, SC (2004-present). After founding a real estate firm which bears my name, quickly reached the $3 million personal sales level; hired, trained, and now manage three junior real estate brokers who are playing a key role in boosting overall sales and profitability of a thriving agency in this highly competitive market.
- Have become known for my strong interpersonal and communication skills while coordinating with potential buyers, lending institutions, construction professionals, sellers, and others.
- Negotiate all aspects of financial transactions; deal with mortgage company representatives to arrange financing and with attorneys to handle real estate closings.
- Utilize my expert marketing abilities while creating sales strategies and preparing direct mail materials which capture the interest of prospective clients and generate new business.
- Routinely make presentations to other agents and buyers.
- Have become skilled in all aspects of property evaluation and am skilled in comparing newly available homes with those having comparable features.

SALES AND MARKETING REPRESENTATIVE. Self-employed, Myrtle Beach, SC (1998-04). Trained and then supervised the efforts of as many as 12 agents while also personally marketing and selling mutual funds and insurance; refined my abilities in a competitive field and excelled in developing sales and marketing techniques which resulted in increased sales.

Highlights of earlier experience: Gained versatile experience in sales, inventory control, and customer service in jobs including the following:
FINANCE AND OPERATIONS MANAGER. Became highly effective in handling finances, marketing, and sales as the owner of a business with six sales professionals, a title clerk, a bookkeeper, and 12 employees in the body shop (Gene's Auto Shop, Houston, TX).
- Learned small business management while handling sales, finances, and collections.
- Created marketing and advertising plans and products which were highly effective.

SALES REPRESENTATIVE. For a major automobile dealer, consistently placed in the top three of 22 sales professionals (Houston Buick, Houston, TX).
- Was "Salesman of the Month" for 13 consecutive months and "Salesman of the Year."

FIELD SALES MANAGER. Became the youngest person in the company's history to hold this position after only a year with this national company (Fuller Brush Company, Plattsburgh, NY, and Phoenix, AZ).
- Became skilled in earning the confidence of potential customers and achieved a highly successful rate of positive responses from four out of each five people I approached; increased the amount of sales per customer.

STORE MANAGER & SUPPORT SERVICE SPECIALIST. Gained business management experience and learned to handle inventory control and funds (U.S. Navy).

TRAINING   Completed corporate training programs in areas such as real estate law, brokerage, finance, and securities as well as life, accident, and health insurance.
Am licensed as a real estate salesman, broker, and life/accident/health insurance agent.

PERSONAL   Am known for my ability to see "the big picture" while managing the details.

CAREER CHANGE

Date

Exact Name of Person
Title or Position
Name of Company
Address
City, State, Zip

REAL ESTATE LAW OFFICE ASSISTANT

for a real estate attorney seeks a career in the property field

Dear Exact Name of Person: (or Dear Sir or Madam if answering a blind ad.)

Can you use a highly motivated young professional who offers proven management ability and executive potential? I am responding to your recent advertisement for a Property Manager for the Hollywood Hills complex.

As you will see from my enclosed resume, I excelled academically in earning a B.A. degree in Pre-Law from University of Iowa while excelling in demanding part-time jobs in banking and sales in order to finance my college education. While working in various jobs as a college student, I gained valuable insights into internal banking operations and legal/real estate/loan procedures.

In my current position as a Law Office Assistant with a firm of real estate attorneys, I am involved in researching foreclosures, conducting title searches, and analyzing courthouse records. Although I am excelling in my position and can provide outstanding references, I am seeking a position such as the one described in your ad in which I can utilize my leadership ability and management skills.

You would find me to be a congenial and poised young person known for having "maturity beyond my years." I am a hard worker who understands the importance of working with others as a team in order to maximize profitability and market share in an industry.

I hope you will welcome my call soon to arrange a brief meeting at your convenience to discuss your needs and goals and how I might serve them. Thank you in advance for your time.

Yours sincerely,

Susan McFarlane

Alternate last paragraph:
I hope you will call or write soon to suggest a time convenient for us to meet and discuss your current and future needs and how I might serve them. Thank you in advance for your time.

SUSAN McFARLANE

1110½ Hay Street, Fayetteville, NC 28305 • preppub@aol.com • (910) 483-6611

OBJECTIVE

To contribute to an organization that can use a highly motivated young professional who offers excellent communication skills, a proven ability to serve the public graciously, as well as sales and banking experience which demonstrates my unlimited executive potential.

EDUCATION

Bachelor of Arts degree in **Pre-Law**, University of Iowa, Iowa City, IA, 2005.
- Extensively refined my written and oral communication skills in this degree program which stressed the development of top-notch writing, research, analytical, and public speaking ability.
- Excelled academically; was inducted into University of Iowa Political Science Honor Society and was named to the Dean's List several semesters.

COMPUTER KNOWLEDGE

Other software: Am experienced in utilizing Windows XP, Microsoft Works, Word and Excel software; offer the ability to rapidly master new software and hardware.

EXPERIENCE

REAL ESTATE LAW OFFICE ASSISTANT. McDowell & Douglass, Iowa City, IA (2005-present). Am gaining insight into legal procedures and learning the mechanics of the loan process while assisting real estate attorneys with business transactions.
- Research foreclosures, conduct title searches, and analyze courthouse records.
- Write numerous kinds of letters, and was commended for my excellent written communication skills.

BANK TELLER/DOCUMENTS ANALYST. Iowa Federal Credit Union, Iowa City, IA (2000-04). While excelling academically as a college student, worked part-time at two different locations of this financial institution and also worked at another job on the weekends; learned to manage my time wisely for maximum effectiveness in every activity.
- As a **Bank Teller**, greeted customers, introduced and sold new services, performed data entry and transactions on the computer, consolidated the day's paperwork, and balanced a drawer with thousands of dollars in credits and debits.
- As a **Documents Analyst**, worked in a busy operations center where I performed multiple duties including researching bank documents from all branches to solve account problems, retrieving account records, and stocking cancelled checks.
- Gained an understanding of internal bank operations.

Other experience: *Worked in these jobs in Des Moines, Cedar Rapids and Waterloo, IA, during high school and while in college in order to help finance my college education*:
DRY CLEANER CLERK. Took pride in serving customers in a cheerful manner at all times while acting as a counter clerk, operating a cash register, tagging clothes, and assisting dissatisfied customers.
SALES REPRESENTATIVE. Was commended for my "natural" sales ability while becoming the highest-volume salesperson; developed a new credit policy for the store which is still in use today after becoming skilled in calculating credit accounts and accounting for large amounts of cash.
WAITRESS. For the popular Red Lobster in Iowa City, learned to perform every job in this 150-person restaurant, and became a valuable part of the restaurant's catering business.

LANGUAGE

Proficient in speaking and understanding German.

PERSONAL

In high school, was captain of my basketball and tennis teams, and gained valuable confidence and leadership experience—including the ability to motivate others—from athletics.

Date

Exact Name of Person
Title or Position
Name of Company
Address
City, State, Zip

Dear Exact Name of Person: (or Dear Sir or Madam if answering a blind ad.)

With the enclosed resume, I would like to make you aware of my interest in exploring employment opportunities with your organization.

As you will see from my resume, I "found my way" to the property management field after excelling as a secretary and marketing representative. The owners of the 256-complex which I manage thought, when they hired me, that I would continue to experience the same problems as the previous manager. To the surprise of the owners, without previous experience in the property management field, I was able to transform a "bad reputation" into a "good name." Now a complex which was plagued with occupancy and tenant relations problems has a waiting list and is considered among the best places to live in the city.

I am a strong believer in "attention to detail" and as a personal philosophy I never leave until tomorrow what I can handle today. That concept has helped me optimize the use of my time, and I enjoy being proactive rather than reactive. I have discovered that customers who experience problems respond positively and gratefully if their dissatisfaction is addressed intelligently and resolutely right away. I try to cultivate a strong working relationship with all my customers, and they know that serving them is one of my pleasures.

I hope you will call or write soon to suggest a time convenient for us to meet and discuss your current and future needs and how I might serve them. Thank you in advance for your time.

Sincerely,

Kristen Nelson

Alternate last paragraph:
I hope you will welcome my call soon to arrange a brief meeting at your convenience to discuss your current and future needs and how I might serve them. Thank you in advance for your time.

KRISTEN NELSON

1110½ Hay Street, Fayetteville, NC 28305 • preppub@aol.com • (910) 483-6611

OBJECTIVE

To contribute to an organization that can use a well-organized young professional who is known for my attention to detail, ability to rapid master new tasks and office procedures, as well as excellent clerical and office skills.

EDUCATION

Studied bookkeeping for small businesses, Northern Michigan University, Marquette, MI, 1996-98.

Graduated from Lake Superior High School after completing extensive studies in math, bookkeeping, and typing; Marquette, MI, 1996.

EXPERIENCE

REAL ESTATE RENTALS MANAGER. Prudential Realtors, Marquette, MI (2005-present). Was promoted to increasingly responsible roles related to the leasing of rental units, including overseeing maintenance and collecting rent.

- Took over the management of a 256-unit complex where tenant relations were poor while occupancy was low. Was credited with turning around the reputation of the complex, which now has a waiting list and is considered "the place to live" among young professionals in Marquette.
- Was complimented for my poise and "common sense" in handling tenant problems.
- Gained confidence in my ability to sell *anything*!

MARKETING REPRESENTATIVE. Lake Superior Corporation, Marquette, MI (2001-04). Became skilled in speaking to large groups while demonstrating products used in the safety and quality control field. Coordinated with quality and safety experts in dozens of industries in order to identify the products which would most benefit our client list, which included military organizations and Fortune 500 companies.

- Recruited new employees for this organization, and trained them in techniques of product demonstration and sales.
- Learned how to "think on my feet" and how to remain enthusiastic, even in the process of presenting the same information over and over again to different groups.

SECRETARY. Premier Products, Marquette, MI (1999-00). As the only person in the central office of a company that sold specialized promotional products that businesses used as "giveaways" to their customers, refined my ability to juggle numerous tasks that included:

typing	bookkeeping	payroll preparation
computer inputting	greeting customers	preparing invoices
making deposits	preparing the general ledger	

- Programmed a computer without any prior experience; demonstrated my ability to rapidly master new software and hardware. Learned how to maintain calm and collected and keep a smile on my face even when the office got very hectic!

CASHIER. Wal-Mart, Marquette, MI (1996-99). Was often commended for my reliability and customer service skills while performing cashiering and bookkeeping functions.

COMPUTERS

Proficient with software including Word, PowerPoint, Excel, and Access.

PERSONAL

Have the ability to learn quickly and efficiently, and have complete confidence that there is nothing I cannot learn and eventually master. Have been told throughout my life that I am a "people person" because I have excellent communication skills and truly enjoy working with employees and customers. Pride myself on my ability to always maintain a professional attitude, no matter what the circumstances.

CAREER CHANGE

Date

Exact Name of Person
Title or Position
Name of Company
Address
City, State, Zip

REAL ESTATE SALES

This young professional has recently relocated back to his hometown to help his mom settle the estate of his deceased dad, and he is seeking a career change from store management to real estate sales. Notice that he is using the "direct approach" in his job hunt: he is approaching a select number of employers for whom he would like to work.

Dear Exact Name of Person: (or Dear Sir or Madam if answering a blind ad.)

I would appreciate an opportunity to talk with you soon about how I could contribute to your organization through my sales and management experience along with my formal education and technical training related to real estate.

As you will see from the enclosed resume, I am licensed by the North Carolina Real Estate Commission as a sales person and am currently completing Brokers Certification courses. I completed the "North Carolina Fundamentals of Real Estate Course" at The Charlotte School of Real Estate.

My resume also will show you my "track record" of achievement in sales and management. Although I was born and raised in the Charlotte area and am living here permanently, most recently I worked in Ft. Lauderdale and Jacksonville, FL, as a Store Manager for Camelot Music. I managed other employees, decreased inventory shrinkage, opened new stores, converted acquisition stores to Camelot systems and procedures, and was specially selected to manage a new "superstore" of more than 10,000 square feet.

I am sending you this resume because, after conducting extensive research of real estate companies, your company is the one I would most like to be associated with. I hope you will find some time in your schedule for us to meet at your convenience to discuss your needs and goals and how I might serve them. I shall look forward to hearing from you, and thank you in advance for your time.

Yours sincerely,

Michael Jenkins

MICHAEL JENKINS

1110½ Hay Street, Fayetteville, NC 28305   •   preppub@aol.com   •   (910) 483-6611

OBJECTIVE   To contribute to an organization that can use a resourceful and congenial sales professional with excellent customer relations skills who offers a proven "track record" of accomplishment in both sales and operations management.

REAL ESTATE
- Licensed by North Carolina Real Estate Commission.
- Currently completing Brokers Certification courses.
- Completed "North Carolina Fundamentals of Real Estate Course" at the Charlotte School of Real Estate.

EXPERIENCE SUMMARY
- Eight years of restaurant and retail management experience.
- Skilled in hiring, training, scheduling, and maintaining sales staff dedicated to superior customer relations.
- Proven commitment to meeting deadlines and serving customers.
- Exceptionally strong analytical and problem-solving skills.
- Known for my positive attitude and cheerful disposition.

EXPERIENCE   **STORE MANAGER.** Camelot Music, Jacksonville, FL, and Ft. Lauderdale, FL (1993-2005). Earned a reputation as a skilled store manager who was equally effective in starting up new retail operations, "turning around" existing stores experiencing sales and profitability problems, and managing "superstores."
- After managing three Camelot Music retail stores in Jacksonville and Ft. Lauderdale, was selected to manage a new 10,000 square foot freestanding "superstore."
- Was responsible for opening new stores and converting acquisition stores to Camelot's procedures, methods, and systems.
- Devised and implemented effective merchandising techniques.
- Specialized in maintaining superior inventory conditions.
- Achieved consistent sales increases and ranked among the chain's highest volume stores.
- Diminished shrinkage and substantially increased profits.
- Implemented effective off-site sales locations utilizing radio and television as well as popular musicians and bands at successful local events.

Other experience:
After earning my Associate of Arts degree, excelled in restaurant management and was selected for management training programs.
- Worked in Hardee's and was selected for their corporate training program; was handpicked as co-manager of a Hardee's at Myrtle Beach.
- Worked in Quincy's Restaurant as an assistant manager after completing their corporate training program.

EDUCATION   **Associate of Arts (A.A.) degree in Restaurant and Hotel Management**, Baltimore's International Culinary College, 1990.
- Completed renowned management training programs with established restaurants, Hardee's and Quincy's.

Completed high school at Hargrave Military Academy and Flora McDonald Academy.

PERSONAL   Am an accomplished guitarist and musical collector. Excellent health. Single.

CAREER CHANGE

Date

Exact Name of Person
Title or Position
Name of Company
Address
City, State, Zip

**REAL ESTATE
SALES AGENT and
INDEPENDENT
BROKER**

Dear Exact Name of Person: (or Dear Sir or Madam if answering a blind ad.)

With the enclosed resume, I would like to make you aware of my interest in exploring employment opportunities with your organization.

As you will see from my resume, I am excelling as a Real Estate Sales Agent and have won numerous awards for my sales accomplishments. In 2005, I was honored as Sales Person of the Year for selling the largest number of homes of any agent in my company. In the previous year, I was named Top Marketing Agent and Top Sales Person.

Although I enjoy my current situation, I am exploring opportunities which would allow me to diversify into the commercial real estate area. A goal setter by nature, I feel that becoming a leader in commercial sales is a goal I want to tackle. I realize that your company is the leading corporation in the U.S. in commercial property sales, and I want to "be the best" and "work for the best." I can provide outstanding references at the appropriate time.

I hope you will call or write soon to suggest a time convenient for us to meet and discuss your current and future needs and how I might serve them. Thank you in advance for your time.

Sincerely,

Priscilla Rockingham

Alternate last paragraph:
I hope you will welcome my call soon to arrange a brief meeting at your convenience to discuss your current and future needs and how I might serve them. Thank you in advance for your time.

PRISCILLA ROCKINGHAM

1110½ Hay Street, Fayetteville, NC 28305   •   preppub@aol.com   •   (910) 483-6611

OBJECTIVE To offer a blend of well-developed sales, motivational, and communication skills to an organization that can use a mature, enthusiastic, and energetic sales professional who excels in building mutual respect with others while focusing on the bottom line.

EDUCATION & TRAINING Am pursuing a **B.S. degree in Accounting and Business** after earning an **A.S.** in the same areas of concentration, University of Missouri, Kansas City, MO; degree to be awarded spring 2006.
* Have been named to the university Dean's List for my academic accomplishments.
Completed several real estate sales and broker's courses:
MO Real Estate Brokerage Course, Jefferson City, MO, 2004
Jackson County Real Estate School, Kansas City, MO, 2004
Frances Sweeney Real Estate Sales Course, St. Louis, MO, 2003
Principles of Real Estate Sales, Penn Valley Community College, Kansas City, MO, 2001
Attended additional classes in Marketing, Physiology, and Computer Operations

LICENSES Licensed by the MO Real Estate Commission as Broker-in-Charge

EXPERIENCE **REAL ESTATE SALES AGENT** and **INDEPENDENT BROKER.** Allstate Real Estate, Kansas City, MO (2001-present). Am winning numerous awards for my sales accomplishments and have been recognized each year as a million-dollar producer in the highly competitive field of residential home sales.
* Quickly built a reputation as someone who really listens to clients and takes the time to develop a warm personal relationship while helping each family find the right home at the best price. Was honored as the "Sales Person of the Year" for 2005 for selling the largest number of homes of any agent in my company.
* Accomplished a sales volume of $1.8 million in a newly established small company while overcoming the worst real estate market in many years.
* Earned recognition as the top marketing agent and top sales person of 2004 for my high level of listings, expertise in marketing each home to its greatest advantage, and volume of sales.

OWNER, GENERAL MANAGER, and **SALES REPRESENTATIVE.** Rain Tree Service, Overland Park, MO (1985-01). Prospected for new accounts and "sold" the business and its services to commercial accounts while managing as many as 15 employees and up to 15 accounts.
* Created and built this company from the ground up and made it into a profitable and successful entity which I sold in order to move into the sales field.
* Developed a reputation as a highly effective communicator who could deal with people at all levels and express my views in a convincing and effective manner to the professionals made decisions on which cleaning service their company would use.
* Was known as a good listener who would find out what prospective and existing customers needed and make a way to provide them with the services they required at a fair price.
* Established accounts with nearly every area bank including Bank of America, National Bank of Missouri, and Wells Fargo Bank as well as with medical offices and other professional firms. Sold and ensured that each customer received top-quality services.

PERSONAL Enjoy giving my time to help others and have been a American Cancer Society Volunteer as well as a Teacher's Aide. Am an outgoing and energetic person who excels in communicating my ideas and views to others in an honest, open, and fair manner.

Date

Exact Name of Person
Title or Position
Name of Company
Address
City, State, Zip

REALTOR Dear Exact Name of Person: (or Dear Sir or Madam if answering a blind ad.)

Please excuse the impersonal appearance of this letter, but my husband and I have just relocated permanently to California, are in the final stages of closing on our house, and all the equipment which I would use to personalize this letter to you is in storage until the end of July!

With the enclosed resume, I would like to introduce you to my qualifications and experience and acquaint you with the considerable skills which I have to offer. As you will see from my resume, I most recently worked in Maine as a Realtor, and I handled commercial, residential, and land transactions.

We are permanently settling in California, and I am seeking an organization where I can make a permanent, long-term contribution. My husband has been in the military, but he is on his final tour with only a two-year obligation left to serve. We are eager to "put down roots," and I am confident that I can significantly contribute to your organization.

If you can use a self-starter with unlimited initiative, excellent public relations skills, and a talent for solving stubborn problems, please call or write me at the address or phone number on my resume and I will cheerfully make myself available to you for a personal meeting at your convenience. I can provide outstanding personal and professional references.

I hope to have the pleasure of talking with you in person soon.

Sincerely,

Sally Ann Midas

SALLY ANN MIDAS

1110½ Hay Street, Fayetteville, NC 28305 • preppub@aol.com • (910) 483-6611

OBJECTIVE

To contribute through my sales experience to an organization that can use an energetic, hard-working young professional with a strong customer service orientation.

PROFESSIONAL TRAINING

Completed Real Estate School, Bangor Real Estate Academy, 2000, and am a licensed real estate agent/realtor for the state of Maine.

EXPERIENCE

REALTOR. Hearth and Home Inc., Bangor, ME (2000-05). Handled commercial, residential, and land transactions; worked extensively with VA loans.

SALES REPRESENTATIVE and **OFFICE MANAGER.** Barry's Cleaning, Inc., Fantan, NC (1998-00). Applied my communication skills in maintaining contact with potential and existing customers in order to gain new business while providing quality service to all.

- Earned a reputation as a fast learner and was soon entrusted with preparing bids for jobs with the federal government; typed and prepared support documents.
- Discovered ways to reduce costs while ordering supplies and controlling inventories.
- Gained experience in office operations including answering phones, taking care of accounts payable and receivable, and typing various kinds of paperwork.

HEAVY EQUIPMENT OPERATOR. C.R. Right Construction, Conyers, GA (1997-98). Displayed my adaptability as the "right hand" and assistant to a construction site supervisor: drove heavy equipment to as many as 20 scattered work sites.

- Became known for my dependability in consistently having equipment at the right place at the right time while always "pitching in" and doing whatever needed to be done.

SALES ASSOCIATE. Georgia's Decorating, Inc., East Point, GA (1994-96) Was cited for my ability to "upgrade" sales while providing excellent customer service helping clients choose the right colors, designs, and amounts of paint and wallpaper. Gained customer confidence which resulted in "repeat sales."

RETAIL SALES ASSOCIATE. GenCom, Inc., Atlanta, GA (1992-93). Provided excellent back-up and "service after the sale" in the highly competitive growing field of pager sales: called on prospects to make sales and saw that regular customers were informed of new products as they became available.

- Was honored as the company's "Top Sales Professional" two years consecutively.

Developed and refined leadership and supervisory skills while succeeding in roles calling for adaptability, U.S. Army National Guard, Atlanta, GA (1985-91):
SUPERVISORY INVENTORY CONTROL SPECIALIST. Supervised 12 employees; prepared paperwork in support of household goods/furniture shipments, took warehouse inventories, and processed documents for personnel being transferred.
SUPPLY TECHNICIAN and **COMPUTER OPERATOR.** Learned to use IBM computers with Lotus software while taking regular inventories and filing/maintaining records.
MEDICAL SPECIALIST. Received specialized training in advanced lifesaving, CPR, and first aid which qualified me to work as a medic. Graduated at the top of my Medical Specialist class and was given the opportunity to work in a major military medical center's labor and delivery department.

PERSONAL

Known as an extremely hard-working quick learner, enjoy the challenge of learning new things. Feel that my greatest strengths lie in sales and in contributing as part of a team.

Date

Exact Name of Person
Title or Position
Name of Company
Address
City, State, Zip

REALTOR   Dear Exact Name of Person: (or Dear Sir or Madam if answering a blind ad.)

In the interest of investigating potential career opportunities within your organization, I am submitting my resume for your review and consideration.

As my resume indicates, I have obtained two Masters Degrees, one of which is in Education and the other in Business Administration and Education/Management. These degrees will indicate to you, I hope, that I am a motivated hard worker who believes in the value of training.

You will notice that real estate sales is my second career, and I spent a distinguished first career in teaching. Although I enjoyed the challenge of educating young minds, I have found it stimulating to work with adults of all ages in my second career. My outgoing personality is well suited to the heavy public contact required of the real estate professional, and my years of teaching helped me acquire the patience to deal with all kinds of personalities.

Since I realize that a resume can neither detail all my accomplishments nor predict my potential to you and your organization, I would appreciate a personal interview to further explore employment possibilities.

Thank you for your consideration of my inquiry and resume. I look forward to meeting with you in the very near future.

Sincerely,

Bertha Cooper

BERTHA COOPER

1110½ Hay Street, Fayetteville, NC 28305   •   preppub@aol.com   •   (910) 483-6611

OBJECTIVE
To attain a challenging managerial position within a progressive organization which will utilize my leadership, organizational, decision-making, and problem-solving skills while allowing me to express my sincere desire to help others.

EDUCATION
Real Estate License, Montana Real Estate School, Butte, MT, 2004

Master's Degree in Business Administration, Education/Management, University of Montana, Billings, MT, 1995

Master of Education Degree, University of Montana, Missoula, MT, 1988

B.S. in Education, University of Montana, Billings, MT, 1983

QUALIFICATIONS
Able to offer special skills, abilities, and experience as highlighted in the following summary of expressed, proven, professionally developed career applications:

Ability to establish, develop, implement, and monitor a plan of action for completion of objective.

Ability to communicate effectively and efficiently in both verbal and written form.

Motivated to perform in a team environment that inspires professional achievements.

Excellent organizational skills in meeting deadlines and completing multiple tasks.

Strong leadership, motivational, and decision-making skills applied to serve an organization.

Possess enthusiasm and positive attitude in expanding creativity and growth within an organization.

EXPERIENCE
REALTOR. Coldwell Banker United Realty, Butte, MT (2004-present). VIP Sales Certification, Rookie of the Year, One Million in Sales.

TEACHER. *Twenty years challenged as a dedicated professional utilizing leadership, organizational, and communication skills in a creative, responsive, and stimulating classroom environment.*
2001-2003: Butte Private School, Butte, MT
1999-2001: Silverbow County School District, Butte, MT
1997-1999: Missoula County School District, Missoula, MT
1996-1997: Yellowstone County School District, Billings, MT
1988-1996: Gallatin County School District, Bozeman, MT
1983-1988: Missoula County School District, Missoula, MT

COMPUTERS
Proficient with Word, Excel, Access, and PowerPoint.

PERSONAL
Outstanding references on request. Will cheerfully travel and relocate as needed.

CAREER CHANGE

Date

Exact Name of Person
Title or Position
Name of Company
Address
City, State, Zip

REALTOR Dear Exact Name of Person: (or Dear Sir or Madam if answering a blind ad.)

With this letter and enclosed resume, I would like to make you aware of my interest in the Property Manager's position for Cornhusker Apartments in Omaha, NE. I am skilled in all aspects of sales, customer service, and accounting.

As you will see, I have recently excelled as a Realtor with Prudential Realty. Although I have been highly successful in sales in a competitive market, I have decided to transfer my experience and knowledge into property management. Through my experience in sales, marketing, and accounting, I offer a background which could be valuable to you.

I am a licensed Realtor with a B.S. degree in Business Administration and minor concentration in Marketing. While working closely with the Prudential agent who handles the rental property management area of the firm, I have gained exposure to property management operations in a large real estate company. I am very knowledgeable of the Omaha market, and I am skilled in every aspect of showing property.

With a background which has included the sale of communications services, payroll processing, as well as accounts receivable and payable, I am skilled at handling multiple administrative tasks. My computer skills are strong and include proficiency in QuickBooks Pro and Excel as well as with the Microsoft Office and software programs unique to the real estate and insurance industries.

I am confident that you would find me in person to be an articulate and adaptable professional who enjoys meeting challenges head on and finding innovative solutions to problems. If you are interested in further discussion of my reasons for believing that I am the perfect candidate to serve as Property Manager for the beautiful development you are building, please contact me. I can provide excellent professional and personal references at the appropriate time.

Sincerely,

Lauren Yanez

LAUREN YANEZ

1110½ Hay Street, Fayetteville, NC 28305 • preppub@aol.com • (910) 483-6611

OBJECTIVE

To benefit an organization through my top-notch skills related to accounting, sales, customer service, and marketing as well as my excellent organizational and time-management abilities.

EDUCATION

B.S. in Business Administration with a minor in Marketing, Creighton University, Omaha, NE, 2001; consistently made both the Dean's and Chancellor's Lists.

COMPUTERS

Proficient with Windows and with software including, but not limited to, QuickBooks Pro, Word, PowerPoint, Excel, Adobe PageMaker, and software specific to real estate.

LICENSE

Real Estate Sales License, NE, since 2002.

EXPERIENCE

REALTOR. Prudential Realty, Omaha, NE (2005-present). Apply a wide range of sales and marketing as well as human relations and administrative skills while listing, marketing, and selling properties in the Omaha area.
- Work closely with the agent who handles rentals: learned the professional standards for property management, how rent is received, and how to perform six-month inspections.
- Complete all stages of the process from producing a comparative market analysis, to showing properties, to preparing closing/settlement documents when a property sells.
- Provide administrative support by completing duties such as filing, ordering reports, preparing correspondence, and controlling inventories of supplies and forms.

SALES REPRESENTATIVE. Best Buy, Lincoln, NE (2003-05). Consistently met or exceeded sales quotas while assisting customers with cellular, paging, and long-distance needs and sold them the services and products which would fill their communications requirements.
- Carried out support and administrative functions which included completing contracts, verifying credit reports, programming phones, and maintaining daily sales logs.
- Operated cash registers while accepting payments; prepared reports of deposits made.

PAYROLL ADMINISTRATIVE ASSISTANT. Douglas County Board of Education, Omaha, NE (2002). Provided assistance to Payroll Department and Accounting Manager during the maintenance of payroll records and communication of payroll-related information to employees and outside vendors.
- Reconciled monthly insurance billings, coordinated payments to professional organizations, input data into an automated system, and maintained W-2 forms.
- Prepared various reports and word processed letters, memos, and payroll schedules.
- Resolved problems and answered questions on payroll-related issues.

ADMINISTRATIVE ASSISTANT. Century 21 Financial Group, Omaha, NE (2001). Excelled in several functional areas while working for this financial services group where my duties included an emphasis on customer service and handling correspondence.
- Gained experience with QuickBooks Pro while handling accounts payable and receivable.

CHILD SUPPORT INTERN. Superior Clerk of Court, Douglas County, NE (2000). Served a three-month internship providing financial, clerical, and administrative support to the Child Support Division. Handled a wide range of financial transactions including processing bad checks. Prepared docket sheets for use by the county's District Attorney.

PERSONAL

Am a flexible professional who enjoys challenges, problem solving, and maximizing resources. Have received numerous outstanding work performance evaluations.

Date

Exact Name of Person
Title or Position
Name of Company
Address
City, State, Zip

REALTOR/
SALES ASSOCIATE

Dear Exact Name of Person: (or Dear Sir or Madam if answering a blind ad.)

I would appreciate an opportunity to talk with you soon about how I could benefit your organization through my proven background of managerial experience.

As you will see from my resume, I built a "track record" of consistent advancement ahead of my peers while serving my country in the U.S. Army. I was involved in managing teams of as many as 44 employees in technical maintenance, inspection, and administrative operations.

During the past three years since leaving military service, I have further applied my creativity and attention to detail while gaining experience in the highly competitive field of real estate sales. Within a year after completing intensive training programs, I reached the prestigious $2 million sales level.

I am a self-motivated individual with a reputation for always achieving exceptional results. Excelling in motivating and developing others, I expect employees to meet my high performance standards.

I hope you will welcome my call soon to arrange a brief meeting at your convenience to discuss your current and future needs and how I might serve them. Thank you in advance for your time.

Sincerely yours,

Jolene Johnson

Alternate last paragraph:
I hope you will call or write soon to suggest a time convenient for us to meet and discuss your current and future needs and how I might serve them. Thank you in advance for your time.

JOLENE JOHNSON

1110½ Hay Street, Fayetteville, NC 28305   •   preppub@aol.com   •   (910) 483-6611

OBJECTIVE To contribute my management expertise to an organization that can use a professional with the proven ability to foresee problems and find solutions while applying outstanding attention to detail as well as communication and motivational skills.

EXPERIENCE *Refined my time management skills while further polishing my ability to relate to others as a REALTOR/SALES ASSOCIATE, Union, NJ:*
Re/Max Homeowners Ltd. (2005-present). Am polishing my skills in marketing and selling residential and commercial properties and land.
- Conducted the market analysis of properties to determine their true value while involved in interviewing and counseling prospective buyers and sellers.
- Collected and analyzed financial information in order to qualify prospects.
- Applied my communication skills while coordinating with other professionals including attorneys, appraisers, lenders, surveyors, and contractors.

Prudential (2004-05). Made important contributions in promoting and marketing while achieving the respected $1 million sales level in less than a year.

Coldwell Banker United Realty (2002-04). Sold commercial and residential properties worth approximately $2 million in two years with the company.
- Completed training sponsored by the NJ Association of Realtors and the Kean University as well as an intensive company-sponsored sales training course.

Earned advancement ahead of my peers while polishing my managerial, supervisory, and leadership abilities, U.S. Army, Ft. Benning, GA:
MAINTENANCE SUPERVISOR. (2000-01). Was the acting department manager for 40 employees maintaining 22 helicopters.
- Provided technical advice and guidance for employees in numerous job fields including avionics, engine repair, quality control, production control, and supply.
- Was twice selected as an evaluator for a team inspecting Kansas National Guard units.

QUALITY CONTROL SUPERVISOR. (2000). Supervised a team of 14 specialists conducting technical inspections on maintenance, safety, aircraft recovery, and job proficiency.
- Was handpicked to manage aviation maintenance inspection teams.

SUPERVISORY AIRCRAFT MAINTENANCE SPECIALIST. (1999). Refined my organizational skills overseeing 35 employees maintaining vehicles and ground support equipment. Coordinated with production control and other sections to ensure the quality of maintenance and safety of $5 million worth of aircraft, tools, equipment, and vehicles.

QUALITY CONTROL SUPERVISOR. (1998). Was selected for advanced schooling and advancement to higher managerial levels on the basis of this job which included supervising 30 administrative employees and 14 aircraft technical inspectors.

EDUCATION **Associate's degree in General Studies**, Columbus Technical Community College, Columbus, GA, 2001. Earned degree at night in my spare time.

PERSONAL Was the "distinguished graduate" of several Army leadership and technical training schools. Always strive for excellence and motivate employees to meet my high standards.

Date

Exact Name of Person
Title or Position
Name of Company
Address
City, State, Zip

**RENTAL PROPERTY
MANAGER**

Dear Exact Name of Person (or Dear Sir or Madam if answering a blind ad):

I would appreciate an opportunity to talk with you soon about how I could contribute to your organization through my experience in financial management, my skills in the areas of personnel and operations management, as well as my strong customer service orientation.

You will see from my enclosed resume that I offer an in-depth knowledge of finance and business. My most recent job was as Controller and General Manager of a real estate rental company for approximately eight years. During this time I substantially reduced the company's debt load, virtually eliminated the amount of uncollectibles, and increased occupancy rates to a consistently high 95%. Through my diplomatic but assertive managerial style, I brought this business out of debt and transformed it into a viable operation.

During a successful career in the U.S. Army, I advanced to hold increasingly more responsible managerial positions in the fields of finance, budgeting, and pay administration as well as in personnel administration. I gained skills and refined a natural aptitude for analyzing, controlling, and resolving problems while earning a reputation as a versatile and adaptable professional.

With an Associate's degree in Banking and Finance, I feel that I offer the dedication to excellence that would make me a valuable asset to an organization that can use a mature individual with the ability to get along with others in supervisory roles.

I hope you will welcome my call soon to arrange a brief meeting at your convenience to discuss your current and future needs and how I might serve them. Thank you in advance for your time.

Sincerely yours,

Lonny F. Geary

LONNY F. GEARY

1110½ Hay Street, Fayetteville, NC 28305   •   preppub@aol.com   (910) 483-6611

OBJECTIVE

To offer a track record of success in managerial roles with organizations requiring knowledge of finance, personnel, and administrative functions along with a reputation for keen analytical skills, attention to detail, and a strong customer service orientation.

EXPERIENCE

RENTAL PROPERTY MANAGER. Liberty Rentals, Sarasota, FL (1999-present). Brought about major improvements in several important functional areas while handling multiple roles as a financial manager, partner, and operations manager for a company with 160 rental units.
- Reduced the organization's debts more than $20,000 within less than a year through the application of my knowledge and prior experience in business management and finance.
- Almost totally eliminated uncollectibles while reducing them to under 1%.
- Prepared advertising materials which resulted in improved occupancy levels and consistently maintained 95% fill rates on leased units.
- Took charge of all aspects of finance and business administration ranging from maintaining books, to processing all accounting data, to accounts receivable and payable.
- Prepared and managed the budget and reconciled bank accounts.
- Diplomatically but assertively resolved a wide range of customer service as well as budget and fee problems.

GENERAL MANAGER. Fun Bingo and Novelty Co., Sarasota, FL (1992-97). Applied my knowledge of business and finance to build this company from a concept into a viable organization.
- Dealt with all aspects of establishing and successfully operating a small business: prepared and managed budgets, made bank deposits, and reconciled bank accounts as well as maintaining accounts receivable and payable ledgers.
- Controlled inventory, from ordering supplies and merchandise to setting prices.

Highlights of earlier experience: Gained and refined knowledge of personnel management and finance/pay activities during a career with the U.S. Army, locations worldwide.
- As the Manager of a program studying the need for changes to the personnel structure of the Army, processed information and contributed input used in budget preparation.
- As a Senior Personnel Management Supervisor, directed the activities of 40 specialists engaged in processing promotions, reclassifications, transfers, and performance reports.
- As a Finance Section Manager, updated personnel's finance records and verified information before entering it into computers; maintained ledgers, cash books, and all related accounting records.
- As the Chief of Military Pay and Travel, processed pay activities for personnel in 11 states and four overseas areas.
- As Manager of a Personnel Actions Section, processed military personnel and their family members who were going overseas; provided information and briefings on customs, laws, and conditions in overseas areas.
- As a Retirement Counselor, oversaw activities in a center which processed personnel upon their separation from the military service.

EDUCATION & TRAINING

A.S. degree in **Banking** and **Finance,** Franklin Technical Community College, FL, 2001.
Completed numerous courses in finance, management, and personnel administration.

PERSONAL

Am known for my high level of initiative and dedication to seeing any job through to completion.

CAREER CHANGE

Date

Exact Name of Person
Title or Position
Name of Company
Address
City, State, Zip

Dear Exact Name of Person: (or Dear Sir or Madam if answering a blind ad.)

With the enclosed resume and State of NV Application, I would like to formally make you aware of my interest in the position as Property Administrator of the Museum of the Silver State.

As you will see from my resume, I have completed 1½ years of graduate studies toward the Master of Arts degree in History/Archeology at University of Nevada. I am pursuing completion of the degree in my spare time and wish to simultaneously work full-time as a property administrator. As a graduate student, I worked as a Library Services Specialist for the Thomas Library at University of Nevada, where I functioned in a supervisory capacity while assisting in the hiring, training, and management of 14 employees for Thomas Library. I offer expert skills in conducting historical research and am knowledgeable about how to make use of information systems worldwide.

My supervisory skills were significantly refined in a job in which I managed six employees for a busy retail store while overseeing all business functions including financial control and customer service. Known for my high degree of creativity, I developed advertisements and merchandising displays which significantly boosted customer traffic and bottom-line results. I feel certain my aptitude for creating visually appealing displays would allow me to excel in developing museum exhibitions, programs, and activities which the public would find exciting.

With a reputation as an outstanding public speaker and writer, I hold an undergraduate degree in History/Government Pre-Law. I feel certain that I could contribute significantly to the museum's property management function.

I feel certain that I offer the wide range of skills and abilities you are seeking, and I hope you will give me the opportunity to meet with you in person to show you that I am the outgoing, creative, and detail-oriented professional you are seeking for this administrative role.

Yours sincerely,

Taylor Malone

TAYLOR MALONE

1110½ Hay Street, Fayetteville, NC 28305   •   preppub@aol.com   •   (910) 483-6611

OBJECTIVE   To benefit the Museum of the Silver State as its Administrator through my experience in historical research, ability to plan and supervise complex projects, outstanding written and oral communication skills, as well as my ability to establish excellent working relationships.

EDUCATION   Working towards **Master of Arts in History/Archeology**, University of Nevada Graduate School, Reno, NV; completed 1 ½ years of coursework towards the degree, and am pursuing completion in my spare time.
Completed **Bachelor of Arts degree in History/Government Pre-Law**, University of Nevada, Reno, NV, 1998.
Attended Truckee Meadows Community College, 1994-95; attended the Truckee Meadows Community College Writing Institute.
Graduated from Reno Senior High School, 1994; was active on Debate Team.

EXPERIENCE   **RESEARCHER & TITLE SPECIALIST.** Western Industries and Property Acquisitions, Inc. (PAI), Reno, NV (2004-present). Was hired on a special assignment in 2004 by PAI to research historical real estate and tax records for Sprint on properties ranging from 40 to 200 years old; when this assignment ended, I joined Western Industries.
- Research property titles for clients and negotiate selling prices and terms.
- Manage advertising, public relations, as well as accounts payable and receivable.

ACTING MANAGER. Banana Republic, Reno, NV (2002-04). Hired, trained, and managed six employees for this popular retail store; worked up to 72 hours a week while overseeing seven-day-a-week operations.
- Became known for my merchandising flair and creativity; created advertisements which boosted store traffic and sales, and also created visually appealing in-store displays.
- Supervised business functions including budgeting and forecasting, accounts payable and accounts receivable, inventory and pilferage control, and financial recordkeeping.

LIBRARY SERVICES SPECIALIST. University of Nevada, Reno, NV (1999-01). While attending graduate school full time as a candidate for the master's degree, was specially selected as a Graduate Assistant to work in conjunction with library technical services and the *Nevada History* magazine.
- Played a key role in hiring, training, and supervising 14 employees for technical services.
- Was instrumental in revising the library system at a time when technical services was experiencing tremendous growth; input data into a computer and searched records.
- Became highly skilled at conducting historical research; gained expert skills in making use of information retrieval systems worldwide to obtain hard-to-find data.

HISTORICAL WRITER. *Nevada History*, University of Nevada, Reno, NV (1999-01). Was a popular and respected contributor of articles for monthly and quarterly publications dealing with history. Meticulously researched many state matters and stories of interest, and gained insight into the unique history of the Toiyabe National Forest.

Other experience:
LEGAL ASSISTANT TRAINEE. Edward B. Anthony, Attorney, Reno, NV (1997). Worked for an attorney for six months while deciding whether I wanted to pursue a law degree; was accepted at law school but decided that I wanted to pursue a master's degree.

PERSONAL   Am a highly creative individual with outstanding skills in relating to the public.

Date

Exact Name of Person
Title or Position
Name of Company
Address
City, State, Zip

RESIDENTIAL REAL ESTATE SALES AGENT

Dear Exact Name of Person: (or Dear Sir or Madam if answering a blind ad.)

With the enclosed resume, I would like to make you aware of my interest in exploring employment opportunities with your organization.

As you will see from my resume, I have demonstrated my ability to excel in handling multiple simultaneous projects while handling both administrative and sales responsibilities. As a real estate agent, I have worked closely with government agencies, especially those offering homes that have been foreclosed. In the sale of such homes, I have worked with home owners and investors.

I offer a proven ability to establish and maintain strong working relationships, and that ability has allowed me to become quickly successful in sales.

The reason I am contacting you is that my wife and I are moving to your area, and I am seeking to join a real estate firm there. If you can use an energetic self-starter to complement your respected team of professionals, I would be interested in talking with you.

I hope you will call or write soon to suggest a time convenient for us to meet and discuss your current and future needs and how I might serve them. Thank you in advance for your time.

Sincerely,

Michael Roberts

Alternate last paragraph:
I hope you will welcome my call soon to arrange a brief meeting at your convenience to discuss your current and future needs and how I might serve them. Thank you in advance for your time.

MICHAEL ROBERTS

1110½ Hay Street, Fayetteville, NC 28305   •   preppub@aol.com   •   (910) 483-6611

OBJECTIVE

To offer my experience in office administration and operations as well as my outstanding abilities related to sales and customer service to an organization that can use a mature professional known for attention to detail and organizational skills.

**EQUIPMENT
KNOWLEDGE
&
SPECIAL
SKILLS**

- Am familiar with software programs including First Choice, CEO Write, and Word.
- Operate standard office equipment including calculators, fax machines, copiers, and postage meter.
- Type 66 wpm, and in recent testing by a temp agency made a 93 on a vocabulary test.
- Received my OR **Real Estate Sales License,** March 2005.

EXPERIENCE

Excelled in office administration and real estate sales, MacLeay Real Estate, Portland, OR:
RESIDENTIAL REAL ESTATE SALES AGENT. (2005-present). Refined my time management skills while juggling the demands of remaining the company's Administrative Assistant during my first year in residential real estate sales.

- Sold or listed 23 properties, approximately one-third of which were government owned.
- Developed tact and diplomacy while coordinating with government agencies to assist potential buyers in obtaining loans.
- Matched buyers to available properties and then assisted them in obtaining financing.

ADMINISTRATIVE ASSISTANT. (2004-present). Applied my eye for detail and capacity for accuracy while typing and collating real estate appraisals in an office which appraised, managed, and marketed property seized by U.S. Marshals in 44 eastern counties.

- Simplified the procedures for screening prospective tenants for 75 rental units of which 40 were government-subsidized housing.

Provided clerical support and office administrative services to the OR Department of Crime Control and Public Safety's Victim and Justice Services offices:
SECRETARY. Portland, OR (2002-03). Sent to provide clerical support for a facility which had been understaffed for some time, typed and filed and assisted in other areas for an office with more than 350 active cases in a program resulting from new DUI laws.

- Based on my ability to work with others and contribute to team efforts, was sent into an area where political conflicts had hampered the program's progress.

ACTING COORDINATOR. Beaverton, OR (2001). Provided clerical support in an understaffed office while managing a caseload of 175 people convicted under DUI laws.

- Honored with one of only three "Superior Service Awards" from among more than 300 employees, worked nights and weekends to handle two jobs.

ADMINISTRATIVE ASSISTANT. Beaverton, OR (1995-01). Handled day-to-day office activities including typing, filing, and answering questions by phone or in person.

- Set up the filing system, drafted form letters, and helped in efforts to inform the public and court officials of how this new program would work.

**EDUCATION
& TRAINING**

Completed approximately two years of college course work in general studies areas.
Attended programs in computer operations and assertiveness training.

PERSONAL

Have repeatedly been singled out for special assignments in organizations with heavy workloads, lots of public contact, and too few employees. Remain calm under pressure.

Date

Exact Name of Person
Title or Position
Name of Company
Address
City, State, Zip

RESIDENT MANAGER   Dear Exact Name of Person: (or Dear Sir or Madam if answering a blind ad.)

With the enclosed resume, I would like to make you aware of my interest in exploring employment opportunities with your organization.

As you will see from my resume, I offer a track record of accomplishment in property management. In my current position managing 188 units, I have increased ROI 25%. In my previous position managing 280 units, I increased occupancy 65% in six months. In my job prior to that as a Leasing Manager and Assistant Manager, I increased the leased percentage 7% in six weeks.

My management style emphasizes attention to detail. In property management, I have learned that problems do not go away. They need to be resolved immediately whether they are maintenance issues or tenant concerns.

I hope you will call or write soon to suggest a time convenient for us to meet and discuss your current and future needs and how I might serve them. Thank you in advance for your time.

Sincerely,

Sheldon Henderson

Alternate last paragraph:
I hope you will welcome my call soon to arrange a brief meeting at your convenience to discuss your current and future needs and how I might serve them. Thank you in advance for your time.

SHELDON HENDERSON

1110½ Hay Street, Fayetteville, NC 28305 • preppub@aol.com • (910) 483-6611

___

OBJECTIVE   To obtain a challenging managerial position where my experience in property management and customer relations may be effectively utilized to assist your professional needs.

EXPERIENCE   **RESIDENT MANAGER.** Roger Williams Apartments (188 units), Providence Properties, Providence, RI (2005-present).
- Manage the administrative, public affairs, and internal office responsibilities.
- Supervise and evaluate employees.
- Maintain accounts receivable and accounts payable.
- Analyze credit applications and recommend approval or denial.
- Prepare and maintain budget guidelines.
- Prepare and process statements of deposit accounts.
- Research and prepare various statistical reports of previous residents for regional manager. Inspect and schedule apartments for turnover.
- **Increased ROI 25% this year.**

RESIDENT MANAGER. Knightsville Apartments, (280 units), Providence Properties, Providence, RI (2004).
- **Increased occupancy 65% in six months.**
- Managed administrative, public affairs, and internal office responsibilities at new construction property. Inspected individual units/building upon construction completion.
- Prepared various statistical and construction update reports for the Regional Manager.
- Hired, trained, supervised, and evaluated employees.
- Analyzed credit applications and recommended approval or denial.
- Inspected and scheduled apartments for turnover.
- Prepared and processed statements of deposit accounts to previous residents.

LEASING/ASSISTANT MANAGER. King Park Apartments (356 units), Providence Properties, Providence, RI (2003-04).
- Provided assistance to the property manager in administrative and internal office areas.
- **Increased leased percentage 7% in six weeks.**
- Assisted the manager with accounts payable and accounts receivable.
- Prepared marketing reports for the manager. Scheduled apartment turnover.
- Assisted the manager in purchasing and controlling budget guidelines.

ASSISTANT MANAGER. Seekonk Bay Apartments, Providence, RI (1999-03).
- Managed the administrative, public affairs and office responsibilities in the absence of the community manager.
- Interacted with prospective and current residents.
- Maintained resident files and periodically reviewed them for accuracy.
- Scheduled apartment turnover. Handled leasing of units.
- Generated appropriate correspondence to residents who have vacated.

STRENGTHS
- Excellent organizational skills and proven problem-solving abilities.
- Work well independently as well as with a team.
- Maintain a strong background in leadership, management, and professionalism.
- Am an outgoing people-oriented person.

EDUCATION   Graduated from Greenwich Bay Senior High School, Warwick, RI, 1999.

Date

Exact Name of Person
Title or Position
Name of Company
Address
City, State, Zip

RESIDENT MANAGER   Dear Exact Name of Person: (or Dear Sir or Madam if answering a blind ad.)

I am sending this resume as my formal indication of interest in working for Pierre Residential Services. As the Resident Manager at Griffin Park Rental Condominiums in Pierre, SD, I have enjoyed a long-standing relationship with the local industry and served for three years as the secretary of the Hughes County Apartment Association.

Through my association with other apartment managers in the area, I have become familiar with the operations and personnel at Hilger Apartments. I have been very impressed with the quality of lifestyle offered at Hilger as well as the professionalism of the management personnel of Griffin Park.

In addition, I am certain that, if offered a position, I would bring with me the dedication and professionalism that has kept Griffin Park on the leading edge in the apartment industry. I have played a key role in maintaining the 104 units at Griffin Park at 98% occupancy. Prior to that, I was instrumental in maintaining 99% for the 273 units at Euclid Arms Apartments.

I would like to be considered for any upcoming vacancies, and please be assured that I possess not only the experience but also the personality to become a part of your management team. I look forward to hearing from you soon. Thank you in advance for your time.

Sincerely,

Helen Church

HELEN CHURCH

1110½ Hay Street, Fayetteville, NC 28305   •   preppub@aol.com   •   (910) 483-6611

OBJECTIVE

To contribute to an organization that can use a cheerful, hardworking, creative professional who can successfully initiate, plan, and implement new projects, tasks, and ideas.

EDUCATION

Buffalo High School, Pierre, SD, graduated June 1999.
Related Courses:
- Office Occupations I, II (II-COOP)
- Typing II, III

EXPERIENCE

RESIDENT MANAGER. Griffin Park Rental Condominiums, Pierre, SD (2005-present). Achieved 98% occupancy while managing 104 units. While managing an apartment community that normally experiences high turnover due to the fluctuation of military professionals coming in and out of town, have raised occupancy levels from 90% to 98%.
- Handle general accounting and cash handling procedures for thousands of dollars monthly, including accounts payable/receivable; initiate legal matters concerning collections and property damage.
- Have demonstrated effective communication skills while diffusing potentially difficult resident problems.
- Coordinate upkeep and maintenance among numerous vendors.
- Run credit background checks and approve lease applications.

ASSISTANT MANAGER. Euclid Arms Apartments, Pierre, SD (2004). For a complex with 273 units maintained at 99% occupancy, was fully trained to take over during any absence of the resident manager.
- Responsible for securing clientele over the telephone and in person.
- Responsible for all administrative and clerical duties.
- Handled large sums of money while collecting rents and making bank deposits.
- Prepared monthly newsletter.
- Experienced in serving court papers for delinquent rents.
- Gained experience in "Prentice-Hall On-Site Management" software system.

MERCHANDISING ASSISTANT. Sears, Pierre, SD (2001-03). Assisted in selling, merchandising, displaying, and organizing the special sizes and dress departments of the Women's Fashion division.
- Responsible for completing administrative duties in these departments.
- Handled customer complaints and managed large sums of money while operating cash register.
- Maintained close coordination with supervisor on errors and shortages.

STORE MANAGER. The Pantry, Pierre, SD (2000-01). Responsible for complete operations of 24-hour convenience store.
- Supervised staff of six.
- Completed all administrative duties on a daily basis.
- Ordered and maintained all store stock.
- Interviewed, hired, and trained employees.
- Responsible for large sums of money.

AFFILIATIONS

- Served two consecutive terms as secretary of Hughes County Apartment Association (2003-04), and was reelected in 2005.

Exact Name of Person
Title or Position
Name of Company
Address
City, State, Zip

SALES ASSOCIATE   Dear Exact Name of Person: (or Dear Sir or Madam if answering a blind ad.)

With the enclosed resume, I would like to make you aware of my interest in exploring employment opportunities with your organization.

As you will see from my resume, I have recently demonstrated my ability to excel in real estate sales, and my first-year production was $2.5 million. I got into real estate sales after my husband and I relocated to Myrtle Beach, SC. After briefly distinguishing myself in classified newspaper advertising, I was recruited by one of my customers to join her real estate firm. I feel fortunate to have "found my professional home."

I am now interested in specializing in the sale of oceanfront homes, and I realize that your real estate firm is the leading realtor in the area in oceanfront properties. I am very knowledgeable of this particular type of oceanfront property as my parents owned multiple oceanfront homes in Florida and in the northeast while I was growing up. I am confident that I could profitably impact your company's bottom-line, and I can provide outstanding references.

I hope you will call or write soon to suggest a time convenient for us to meet and discuss your current and future needs and how I might serve them. Thank you in advance for your time.

Sincerely,

Nicole Turpin

Alternate last paragraph:
I hope you will welcome my call soon to arrange a brief meeting at your convenience to discuss your current and future needs and how I might serve them. Thank you in advance for your time.

NICOLE TURPIN

1110½ Hay Street, Fayetteville, NC 28305   •   preppub@aol.com   •   (910) 483-6611

OBJECTIVE I want to contribute to an organization that can use a dynamic and highly motivated individual who offers strong interpersonal skills along with excellent problem-solving abilities.

EDUCATION **Bachelor of Science in Business Administration and Management**, The University of Texas at Dallas, TX, 1999
Associate of Arts Degree, Mountain View College, Dallas, TX, 1997

EXPERIENCE **SALES ASSOCIATE.** Myrtle Beach Real Estate, Myrtle Beach, SC (2005-present). Excelling as a Commissioned Sales Associate for leading real estate firm; first-year production $2.5 million.
- As a Corporate Present Business Developer, created and developed a corporate relationship with several hospitals, doctors' offices, major industries, and banking institutions.
- As a volunteer Ambassador to the Chamber of Commerce, was recognized for leading the last two Chamber drives in membership development.
- Elected President of Myrtle Beach Referrals, 2006.

SALES REPRESENTATIVE. Myrtle Beach Sun-Times, Myrtle Beach, SC (2004-05). Advertising Salesperson for local newspaper publication. Consistently exceeded monthly sales goals. Designed creative advertisements for clients.

SALES ASSOCIATE. Lasso & Co., Dallas, TX (2003-04) Responsible for sales and marketing of various office equipment and supplies. Extensive territory management, cold calling, product demonstrations, and group presentations.

SALES REPRESENTATIVE. Best Buy, Lincoln, NE (2002-04). Consistently met or exceeded sales quotas while assisting customers with cellular, paging, and long-distance needs. Sold the services and products which would meet communications requirements.
- Carried out support and administrative functions which included completing contracts, verifying credit reports, programming phones, and maintaining daily sales logs.
- Operated cash registers while accepting payments; prepared reports of deposits made.

PAYROLL ADMINISTRATIVE COORDINATOR. Douglas County Board of Education, Omaha, NE (2001). Provided assistance to Payroll Department and Accounting Manager during the maintenance of payroll records and communication of payroll-related information to employees and outside vendors.
- Reconciled monthly insurance billings, coordinated payments to professional organizations, input data into an automated system, and maintained W-2 forms.
- Prepared various reports and word processed letters, memos, and payroll schedules.
- Resolved problems and answered questions on payroll-related issues.

FIXED INCOME TRADER. Lone Star Securities, Dallas, TX (1999-01). Sales and marketing analysis for over 800 salesmen throughout the region. Researched retail broker requests regarding stocks and bonds. Executed trades when appropriate. Direct liaison between brokers, banks and other financial organizations. Consistently exceeded sales goals thereby maximizing bonus potential.

COMPUTERS Highly computer proficient with Word, Excel, Access, and PowerPoint.

CAREER CHANGE

Date

Exact Name of Person
Title or Position
Name of Company
Address
City, State, Zip

**SALES MANAGER,
CONDOMINIUMS**

Dear Exact Name of Person: (or Dear Sir or Madam if answering a blind ad.)

Can you use an experienced sales professional with a history of success in training others and setting sales records?

As you will see from my resume, I have excelled in a "track record" of promotion within a company which markets resort condominium ("time share") properties at Planter's Plantation ($35 million annual sales). As Recruiting and Training Manager, I use a variety of tools including running ads and recruiting top industry candidates from other resorts, and I am in charge of hiring and training 60 sales employees yearly. On my own initiative, I have instituted a predictive index which has reduced turnover from 90% to 10%. I have also made drastic changes in recruiting to eliminate the hiring of marginal employees.

I am interested in applying my strong sales skills outside the time share industry, and I am confident I can become a valuable asset to a company that would value a hard charger who is highly skilled at closing the sale.

If you can make use of my considerable talents and experience, I hope you will contact me to discuss your needs. Thank you in advance for your time.

Sincerely yours,

Matthew T. Leisure

MATTHEW T. LEISURE

1110½ Hay Street, Fayetteville, NC 28305 • preppub@aol.com • (910) 483-6611

OBJECTIVE

To benefit an organization that can use an innovative sales manager who offers a proven ability to increase bottom-line profits by applying my outstanding motivational and communication skills.

EXPERIENCE

Since 1990, have excelled in the following "track record" of promotion within a company which markets resort condominium ("time share") properties at Planter's Plantation ($35 million annual sales), Resort International, Williamsburg, VA:
SALES MANAGER. (2005-present). Using a variety of tools including running ads and recruiting top industry candidates from other resorts, am in charge of hiring and training 60 sales employees yearly.
- Instituted a predictive index which has reduced turnover from 90% to 10%.
- Have made drastic changes in recruiting to eliminate the hiring of marginal employees.

SALES MANAGER. (2000-05). Managed ten people and trained them in presenting the product and closing the sale.
- Transformed a team which had produced poor sales results and led it to be ranked consistently in the top half in sales and productivity.

IN-HOUSE SALES. (1999). Sold resort properties to previous time-share buyers.
- Ranked in top 20% of southeastern sales representatives.

FRONT-LINE SALES REPRESENTATIVE. (1996-98). Excelled in closing prospective buyers and obtaining referrals for potential resort property buyers.
- Was ranked #1 out of 60 of my colleagues in 1997!
- In 1996, was ranked #1 on the referral closing average.

Was promoted from Sales Representative to Sales Manager by Old South Food Service, Charleston, SC (1988-96).
SALES MANAGER. (1990-96). Because of my excellent sales record and management ability, was promoted to turn around this troubled office; transformed the operation into a top producer while increasing the sales team to 11 representatives.
- Increased sales figures 35% in 1996 compared to 1995.
- Became known for recruiting and training "top salesmen."
- Was an active member of the Charleston Jaycees; served as Charleston Chapter President and South Carolina District Director; was named one of the ten best chapter presidents in SC and one of the best in the nation.

SALES REPRESENTATIVE. (1988-90). Was named "Salesman of the Year" for the entire company consisting of more than 100 representatives, and put myself in the position where I acquired 95% of my sales through referrals!

Gained valuable customer-service and time-management experience working as a SALES MANAGER/REPRESENTATIVE, Trust Insurance Company, Charleston, SC; and SALES ASSOCIATE, Leland Hardware, Charleston, SC.

TRAINING

Completed three years of college course work in Business Administration, Charleston Technical Community College and Charleston State University, GA.

PERSONAL

Dynamic and highly motivated salesman known for my bold and innovative style.

CAREER CHANGE

Date

Exact Name of Person
Title or Position
Name of Company
Address
City, State, Zip

**SENIOR MORTGAGE
LOAN SPECIALIST**
interested in
pharmaceutical sales

Dear Exact Name of Person: (or Dear Sir or Madam if answering a blind ad.)

With the enclosed resume, I would like to make you aware of my interest in employment as a Pharmaceutical Healthcare Representative with Bayer. I believe you are aware that Robin Whitfield, one of your Healthcare Representatives, has recommended that I talk with you because he feels that I could excel in the position as Pharmaceutical Healthcare Representative.

As you will see from my enclosed resume, I offer proven marketing and sales skills along with a reputation as a highly motivated individual with exceptional problem-solving skills. Shortly after joining my current firm as a Mortgage Loan Specialist, I was named Outstanding Loan Officer of the month through my achievement in generating more than $20K in fees.

I believe much of my professional success so far has been due to my highly motivated nature and creative approach to my job. For example, when I began working for my current employer, I developed and implemented the concept of a postcard which communicated a message which the consumer found intriguing. The concept has been so successful that it has been one of the main sources of advertisements in our office and the concept has been imitated by other offices in the company.

In addition to my track record of excelling in the highly competitive financial services field, I gained valuable sales experience in earlier jobs selling Nikon equipment and sleep systems. I have also applied my strong leadership and sales ability in the human services field, when I worked in the adult probation services field. I am very proud of the fact that many troubled individuals with whom I worked told me that my ability to inspire and motivate them was the key to their becoming productive citizens.

If you can use a creative and motivated self starter who could enhance your goals for market share and profitability, I hope you will contact me to suggest a time when we could meet in person to discuss your needs and goals and how I could meet them. I can provide strong personal and professional references at the appropriate time.

Yours sincerely,

Diana Martin

DIANA MARTIN

1110½ Hay Street, Fayetteville, NC 28305   •   preppub@aol.com   •   (910) 483-6611

OBJECTIVE

To offer my experience in sales, marketing, and customer service to an organization that would benefit from my aggressive style of developing customer relationships and my desire to work for an organization that seeks to maximize market share and profitability.

EDUCATION

B.S. in Business Administration, University of Wisconsin, Eau Claire, WI, 1996. Previously completed two years of studies in Business Administration, Marquette University, Milwaukee, WI, 1991-93.

EXPERIENCE

SENIOR MORTGAGE LOAN SPECIALIST. Carson Park Mortgage Services, Eau Claire, WI (2005-present). Have continuously excelled in this position which requires excellent sales, customer service, decision making, and problem-solving skills.

- In March 2005 was named Outstanding Loan Officer for generating more than $20K in fees.
- Process VA, FHA, conforming, and nonconforming first and second mortgages while handling debt consolidations, refinancing, and other financial arrangements.
- Consult with attorneys, VA and FHA officials, appraisers, and other construction and lending officials on matters related to loan conveyances and loan closings.
- Research property to assess value, ensure liens, and assess credit worthiness of clients.
- Am known for my gracious style of communicating with the public and for my ability to explain technical concepts in language that is understandable to lay people.
- Have gained valuable experience in marketing services which are not well understood by the average consumer.

MORTGAGE LOAN SPECIALIST. Chippewa Mortgage, Eau Claire, WI (2003-05). Gained expertise in all aspects of mortgage loan processing while becoming an expert in handling slow payments and credit repairs.

ADULT PROBATION SERVICES OFFICER. WI Department of Corrections, Eau Claire, WI (1998-03). Because of my exceptional work performance, excellent attitude, and superior work performance, was promoted in the following track record:

2002-03: Adult Intensive Probation Parole Officer. Was promoted to a supervisory position which involved providing guidance and supervising a caseload of 50 clients.

- Earned widespread respect for my ability to establish rapport and cordial relationships with a wide variety of individuals from troubled backgrounds and with turbulent case histories.

1998-02: Adult Probation/Parole Officer. Took pride in the fact that an extremely high percentage of my caseload clients completed their probation and went on to become well adjusted and productive citizens; was frequently told that it was my leadership and motivation skills which made the difference in their lives.

- Provided supervision and guidance for up to 150 clients per month who were on court-ordered probation; completed paperwork and reports in a timely fashion.

DEPUTY CLERK. Eau Claire County Clerk of Superior Court, Eau Claire, WI (1996-98). Processed affidavits for court traffic tickets, misdemeanors, and felonies in the Criminal Division; was known for my professional style of interacting with others.

PERSONAL

Enjoy tackling, achieving, and exceeding ambitious goals through my ability to work effectively with others. Excel in prospecting for new business. Resourceful and high energy.

Date

Exact Name of Person
Title or Position
Name of Company
Address
City, State, Zip

SALES REPRESENTATIVE   Dear Exact Name of Person: (or Dear Sir or Madam if answering a blind ad.)

With the enclosed resume, I would like to make you aware of my interest in exploring employment opportunities with your organization.

As you will see from my resume, as a manufactured homes sales representative, I was awarded the prestigious **Top Gun** Award for Best Sales Performance, and I was also inducted into the **Million Dollar Club.** I have become known for my highly refined skills in developing and maintaining outstanding customer relations. I live by the philosophy that a satisfied customer is worth numerous referrals and repeat business, and I try to develop relationships with customers that will last a lifetime.

I believe that the success of the company overall must be the first goal of each salesperson, and I believe my natural sales ability combined with my genuine enthusiasm for manufactured housing as a product has been the key to my exceptional sales achievements in this job. I have learned how to balance customers' needs for quality and features with the dealer's need to maximize gross profit.

I hope you will call or write soon to suggest a time convenient for us to meet and discuss your current and future needs and how I might serve them. Thank you in advance for your time.

Sincerely,

Randall Wheaton

Alternate last paragraph:
I hope you will welcome my call soon to arrange a brief meeting at your convenience to discuss your current and future needs and how I might serve them. Thank you in advance for your time.

RANDALL WHEATON

1110½ Hay Street, Fayetteville, NC 28305　　•　　preppub@aol.com　　•　　(910) 483-6611

OBJECTIVE	To contribute to an organization that can use a dynamic sales professional who has a proven track record in achieving high levels of profitability and customer satisfaction while consistently meeting or exceeding ambitious sales targets.
EDUCATION	Completed one year of General Studies, Central Virginia Community College, Lynchburg, VA, 1991-93. Received high school diploma, Lynchburg High School, Lynchburg, 1991. Have excelled in extensive sales and sales management training sponsored by Virginia Distributing Company, Campbell Homes, and Gary Billings.
LICENSE	Became a **Registered Housing Specialist**, March 2005.
EXPERIENCE	**SALES REPRESENTATIVE.** Campbell Homes, Lynchburg, VA (2004-present). Have developed expert knowledge of the manufactured housing industry while excelling in every aspect of sales.

- Was awarded the prestigious **Top Gun** Award for Best Sales Performance.
- Was inducted into the **Million Dollar Club.**
- Have completed numerous inhouse seminars designed to refine sales and marketing skills as well as product knowledge specific to manufactured housing.
- Have become known for my highly refined skills in developing and maintaining outstanding customer relations; live by the philosophy that a satisfied customer is worth numerous referrals and repeat business, and try to develop relationships with customers that will last a lifetime.
- Am trusted and respected by my colleagues, and am known for my willingness to generously share my product knowledge and sales know-how with my associates; believe that the success of the company overall must be the first goal of each salesperson.
- Believe my natural sales ability combined with my genuine enthusiasm for manufactured housing as a product has been the key to my exceptional sales achievements in this job.
- Have learned how to balance customers' needs for quality and features with the dealer's need to maximize gross profit; am skilled at making tradeoffs that assure profitability.
- Have acquired expertise related to inventory ordering and control.

SALES REPRESENTATIVE. Virginia Distributing Company, Lynchburg, VA (1996-04). For this consumer products giant, advanced rapidly and was promoted to Sales Representative in the company's top-volume market because of my exceptional sales achievements.

- Earned a seat in the prestigious **President's Circle** of Virginia Distributing Co.
- Won numerous inhouse sales contests. Won two district sales contests in which "the best of the best" were in competition with each other.
- Worked with a wide variety of retailers while utilizing my expertise in merchandising products in a highly competitive environment.

SKILLS	Offer highly refined skills and abilities in these and other areas:

sales and sales management	inventory control
product merchandising	retail marketing
interpersonal communication	motivating myself and others

PERSONAL	Can provide exceptionally strong personal and professional references. Highly competitive by nature, in my spare time enjoy competing in martial arts tournaments, playing softball and basketball, and going hunting and fishing. Am a devoted father and husband.

Date

Exact Name of Person
Exact Title
Exact Name of Company
Address
City, State, Zip

**SUPERINTENDENT &
GENERAL MANAGER**

Dear Exact Name of Person (or Dear Sir or Madam if answering a blind ad):

With the enclosed resume, I would like to express my interest in exploring employment opportunities with your organization. A skilled construction superintendent with experience in all areas of construction including plumbing, electrical, drywall, and paint, I offer an outstanding personal reputation and can provide excellent references.

I began my career in the construction industry right after high school and became a skilled carpenter. Subsequently I worked for firms in Georgia as a Home Warranty Manager, Assistant Superintendent, Finish End Superintendent, and Superintendent. When the housing market soured due to soaring interest rates, I was laid off, and then my father and I established a construction business in Atlanta. We built custom homes and additions while performing extensive fire and flood renovation work for major insurance companies. I have earned a reputation as a resourceful problem solver for tough construction issues, and I have become skilled in managing all aspects of a construction operation. Although the company has been successful, we are in the process of closing the business because my wife and I wish to relocate to New Mexico near family, and my father will retire.

It is my desire to utilize my vast construction knowledge to benefit an established construction firm in New Mexico. I am comfortable in all aspects of the business—from dealing with customers, to working with inspectors and customers and subcontractors.

Known for my commitment to quality assurance and safety, I believe that relentless attention to detail is the key to a quality construction product. My ability to maintain effective working relationships has also been instrumental in my successful career in the construction industry. I have an unusual amount of "common sense," which someone told me once is "the least common of all the senses." I have found that common sense is the key to solving many problems in construction.

If you can use a knowledgeable and reliable professional with a strong bottom-line orientation, I hope you will contact me to suggest a time when we might meet to discuss your needs. My years as an entrepreneur taught me to "think ahead" and manage multiple tasks, and I am confident that my technical expertise and business know-how could profitably impact your company. I hope you will contact me to suggest a time when we might meet in person to discuss your needs.

Sincerely,

Everett Harrison

EVERETT HARRISON

1110½ Hay Street, Fayetteville, NC 28305   •   preppub@aol.com   •   (910) 483-6611

OBJECTIVE

To contribute to an organization that can use a knowledgeable superintendent and project manager who offers experience in all aspects of construction including business management.

LICENSE

Class A License in Georgia (the highest license conferred in the state)

EXPERIENCE

SUPERINTENDENT & GENERAL MANAGER. Georgian Builders, Inc., Atlanta, GA (2001-present). My father and I established Georgian Builders, a construction company which has developed an outstanding reputation in an area ranked 87th for growth and development in the U.S. Nearly all our business is from repeat customers and word-of-mouth referrals since we do not advertise. After a successful run, we are closing the business because my wife and I wish to relocate to New Mexico and my father is retiring.

- **Multiple management responsibilities:** Contract and work with all subcontractors; work with homeowners on custom selections; meet with inspectors and perform walk-throughs; utilize a computer for inventory control and accounting; manage accounts receivable and payable; handle collections as needed. Maintained an outstanding credit reputation and worked with the best suppliers while becoming proficient at all aspects of budgeting and business management.
- **Extensive work with insurance companies:** Performed fire and flood renovation work as we worked with major insurance companies including All State, State Farm, Nationwide, and several small insurers. On numerous occasions, devised resourceful solutions so that flooded homes could be rebuilt in the same location.
- **Custom home building:** Built new custom homes and additions. In my spare time, designed a 4,000 sq. ft. log home as a personal residence and moved into it four months earlier than the completion date predicted by the manufacturer and distributor.

SUPERINTENDENT. Southern Nation Corporation, Atlanta, GA (1990-01). Was recruited to oversee all phases of construction and was instrumental in the land development phase. Was laid off when the housing market soured due to soaring interest rates.

FINISH END SUPERINTENDENT. Custom Georgian Homes, Atlanta, GA (1988-90). Picked up custom homes priced $350,000-$650,000 at the drywall stage and followed through to completion. Settled five houses monthly. Ordered materials and scheduled subcontractors.

ASSISTANT SUPERINTENDENT. Georgia Homes, Atlanta, GA (1988). Met with inspectors and performed final inspections. Handled walk-through and settlement.

HOME WARRANTY MANAGER. Wendler Homes, Atlanta, GA (1984-87). Was placed in charge of three subdivisions—one condominium subdivision, one townhouse subdivision, and one single-family subdivision. Supervised three punch-out men and other employees.

- When I took on this job, I inherited a backlog of repair items of up to one year; after only four months on the job, eliminated the backlog and satisfied homeowners.

EDUCATION

Completed formal training in computer operations, management, and other areas. Extensive hands-on training in all aspects of construction.

Graduated from Atlanta High School, Atlanta, GA, 1983.

PERSONAL

Outstanding references. Known for my commitment to quality assurance and safety. Believe that relentless attention to detail is the key to a quality construction product. Learned the construction business as a youth since most of my family work in the industry.

Date

Exact Name of Person
Title or Position
Name of Company
Address
City, State, Zip

TITLE RESEARCHER   Dear Exact Name of Person: (or Dear Sir or Madam if answering a blind ad.)

Can you use a young professional who offers proven experience in sales and customer service, supervisory skills, and a real talent for developing employees through leadership and training?

In a "track record" of success and advancement with Miami Automotive, I was highly effective in finding innovative ways to improve my sales and customer service skills and in passing that knowledge to other employees. My ideas led to a more professional and productive operation with increased sales, more satisfied customers, and improved morale and cooperation among employees.

My experience in title research gave me opportunities to apply my detail orientation while conducting searches through masses of material. After gathering the information I had to analyze it and then compile detailed reports which were clear and concise and let the client know exactly where he stood.

I am sure that my education and experience, when combined with my personal qualities of determination and honesty, would combine to make me a valuable asset to any company that can use my sales and customer service expertise.

I hope you will welcome my call soon to arrange a brief meeting at your convenience to discuss your current and future needs and how I might serve them. Thank you in advance for your time.

Sincerely yours,

Richard Shaw

Alternate last paragraph:
I hope you will call or write soon to suggest a time convenient for us to meet and discuss your current and future needs and how I might serve them. Thank you in advance for your time.

RICHARD SHAW

1110½ Hay Street, Fayetteville, NC 28305   •   preppub@aol.com   •   (910) 483-6611

OBJECTIVE   To offer my experience in sales and customer service to an organization in need of a proven motivator and leader with a reputation for attention to detail and the ability to work and lead others under pressure and deadlines.

EDUCATION   **B.B.A., Petroleum Land Management**, Miami State University, Miami, FL, 2003.
- Specialized course work included:

business administration	computer science
production and operations management	finance and accounting
inventory and materials management	business law

COMPUTER SKILLS   Am familiar with software and operating systems including Microsoft Windows XP, Adobe PageMaker, QuickBooks Pro.

EXPERIENCE   **TITLE RESEARCHER.** Abode Realty, Inc., Miami, FL (2005-present). Search county records for data on real property ownership of mineral and surface rights, liens, or disputes to ensure clear titles are available.
- Have become known for producing clear, concise documentation which informed clients of information necessary for them to make informed decisions.
- Computerized records for faster error-free production.
- Played a key role in clearing titles related to a 3/4 million acre prospect quickly and accurately.
- Gained familiarity with the sheer volume of contracts, leases, and other types of documents needed to operate a business.

Earned rapid promotion in a "track record" of success in sales and customer service with Miami Automotive, Miami, FL (2000-04):
SALES AND CUSTOMER SERVICE SPECIALIST. (2003-04). Worked closely with customers to determine their needs, then sold them the specific parts and services required, and advised automotive technicians on what would be required to best satisfy the customer.
- Played a key role in the department's achievement of annual gross sales in excess of $1 million.
- Displayed a "knack" for selling customers on additional parts and services and was selected to train other sales associates in these techniques.

SUPERVISORY CUSTOMER SERVICE ADVISOR. (2002-03). Coordinated and directed the work flow for 15 automotive technicians servicing 75 cars a day.
- Communicated with customers to make sure they understood what work needed to be done to their vehicles. Developed a "buddy system" for technicians to allow more productive use of their time, tools, and available work space.
- Improved morale through my leadership and effective communication skills.

TITLE CONSULTANT. Cape Fear Realtors, Raeford, NC (1999-01). Gained experience in translating legal language while inspecting county land records to obtain information necessary for clients to secure clear titles.

PERSONAL   Have worked with handicapped children and find this type of volunteer work especially rewarding. Have a working knowledge of French. Will relocate.

Date

Exact Name of Person
Title or Position
Name of Company
Address
City, State, Zip

UNDERWRITER   Dear Exact Name of Person: (or Dear Sir or Madam if answering a blind ad.)

With the enclosed resume, I would like to express my interest in exploring employment opportunities with your organization.

As you will see from my resume, I am excelling in my current position and can provide outstanding references at the appropriate time. As an Underwriter, I am accustomed to producing outstanding work under tight deadlines, and I am known for my ability to establish and maintain excellent relationships with my office colleagues as well as industry professionals. Within our small office, I have earned respect for my creativity and resourcefulness in solving complex underwriting problems, and my colleagues often turn to me for help when they are solving a tough problem under tight deadlines.

In a previous position with a nonprofit organization, I was promoted rapidly from an entry-level role to the job of Assistant Program Coordinator. I was respected for my personal initiative and commitment to excellence in all areas, and I traveled throughout four states to train staff and promote humane animal activities.

My computer skills are strong, and I am proficient with software including Excel, PowerPoint, and Word. In one of my earliest jobs after high school, I learned to handle multiple simultaneous tasks as I handled a variety of accounting, bookkeeping, and customer service responsibilities.

Known for my strong personal initiative, I am continuously seeking ways to improve myself. In my spare time, I am pursuing a bachelor's degree through an online university program. While involved in the real estate industry and underwriting business, I have become a licensed title agent and hold an SC license for Property & Casualty and well as Life & Health. I offer a proven ability to excel in any type of training program.

If you can use a versatile and outgoing young professional, I hope you will contact me soon to suggest a time we might meet to discuss how I could contribute to your organization. I can provide excellent professional and personal references at the appropriate time. Thank you for your time and consideration.

Sincerely,

Carmen Dosier

CARMEN DOSIER

1110½ Hay Street, Fayetteville, NC 28305   •   preppub@aol.com   •   (910) 483-6611

OBJECTIVE

To contribute to an organization that can use a versatile professional with strong marketing skills who offers a proven ability to establish strong working relationships while utilizing my communication skills to influence and persuade others.

COMPUTERS

Highly proficient with software including Excel, PowerPoint, and Word; experienced in using the Microsoft XP operating system. Utilize specialized software such as E-Flight.

LICENSES

Licensed Title Agent; hold an SC license for Property & Casualty and well as Life & Health.

EXPERIENCE

UNDERWRITER. Title Insurance Company, Myrtle Beach, SC (2005-present). Am accustomed to producing quality work under tight deadlines: my employer has a productivity requirement that any job coming in by fax or e-mail must be underwritten in 30 minutes.
- **Solving problems:** While 70% of my work involves routine underwriting, 30% requires resourceful problem solving. I act as an investigator as I work with title attorneys and paralegals to analyze discrepancies and find missing information.
- **Building relationships:** Work with three underwriters and an office manager; enjoy the interaction with my colleagues as well as with industry professionals.
- **Maintaining high level of productivity:** Commended for my high productivity.

SALES REPRESENTATIVE & OFFICE ASSISTANT. Nationwide Insurance Company, Myrtle Beach, SC (2004-05). Was recruited by Tyler Brisson, the senior agent, to join the firm in a sales and marketing role. Performed cold calling utilizing lists of prospective clients. Played a key role in helping the office adjust to change when the senior agent left.

BANK TELLER. Wachovia Bank, Myrtle Beach, SC (2003-04). Thoroughly enjoyed the process of serving customers and achieving a high level of customer satisfaction.

ASSISTANT PROGRAM COORDINATOR. American Cancer Society, Myrtle Beach, SC (1999-02). Was promoted rapidly to increasing responsibilities within a national, nonprofit organization. Worked in an independent role as I traveled to four states—NC, SC, VA, and TN—to train staff and promote humane animal activities.
- **Database maintenance:** Maintained a national database of organizations of interest to supporters of humane animal activities.
- **Training management:** On my own initiative, assumed responsibility for organizing workshops for animal control personnel; this responsibility had never been assumed by anyone before, and my leadership was credited with improving the professionalism of staff members in four states.
- **Marketing and sales:** Was involved in support activities related to securing private donations and obtaining grants for the conduct of this nonprofit organization and eight offices nationwide.

EDUCATION

In my spare time, am pursuing a Bachelor of Arts in Marketing at the University of South Carolina; this is an online university.
Completed numerous workshops and training programs related to computer software, program management, real estate, insurance, and other subjects.

PERSONAL

Outstanding references upon request. Known for my commitment to quality results. Offer a warm and enthusiastic personality which enables me to work effectively with others.

You may already realize that applying for a federal government position requires some patience and persistence in order to complete rather tedious forms and get them in on time. Depending on what type of federal job you are seeking, you may need to prepare an application such as the SF 171 or OF 612, or you may need to use a Federal Resume, sometimes called a "Resumix," to apply for a federal job. But that may not be the only paperwork you need.

Many Position Vacancy Announcements or job bulletins for a specific job also tell you that, in order to be considered for the job you want, you must demonstrate certain knowledge, skills, or abilities. In other words, you need to also submit written narrative statements which microscopically focus on your particular knowledge, skill, or ability in a certain area. The next few pages are filled with examples of excellent KSAs. If you wish to see many other examples of KSAs, you may look for another book published by PREP: "Real KSAs--Knowledge, Skills & Abilities--for Government Jobs."

Although you will be able to use the Federal Resume you prepare in order to apply for all sorts of jobs in the federal government, the KSAs you write are particular to a specific job and you may be able to use the KSAs you write only one time. If you get into the Civil Service system, however, you will discover that many KSAs tend to appear on lots of different job announcement bulletins. For example, "Ability to communicate orally and in writing" is a frequently requested KSA. This means that you would be able to use and re-use this KSA for any job bulletin which requests you to give evidence of your ability in this area.

What does "Screen Out" mean? If you see that a KSA is requested and the words "Screen out" are mentioned beside the KSA, this means that this KSA is of vital importance in "getting you in the door." If the individuals who review your application feel that your screen-out KSA does not establish your strengths in this area, you will not be considered as a candidate for the job. You need to make sure that any screen-out KSA is especially well-written and comprehensive.

How long can a KSA be? A job vacancy announcement bulletin may specify a length for the KSAs it requests. Sometimes KSAs can be 1-2 pages long each, but sometimes you are asked to submit several KSAs within a maximum of two pages. Remember that the purpose of a KSA is to microscopically examine your level of competence in a specific area, so you need to be extremely detailed and comprehensive. Give examples and details wherever possible. For example, your written communication skills might appear more credible if you provide the details of the kinds of reports and paperwork you prepared.

KSAs are extremely important in "getting you in the door" for a federal government job. If you are working under a tight deadline in preparing your paperwork for a federal government position, don't spend all your time preparing the Federal Resume if you also have KSAs to do. Create "blockbuster" KSAs as well!

FEDERAL RESUME OR RESUMIX

OLIVER A. JERRY
SSN: 000-00-0000
Mailing Address: 1110 1/2 Hay Street, Fayetteville, NC 28305
Home Telephone: (910) 483-6611
Work Telephone: (910) 483-6611
preppub@aol.com

Highest permanent play plan or grade held: grade, month/year from ___ to month/year
Position, Title, Series, Grade: Property Technician, GS-09
Announcement Number: DN-00-000

**ACCOUNTING and
PROPERTY TECHNICIAN**

Here you will see an
example of a four-page
federal resume.

Notice the words in bold in
this federal resume (often
called a "Resumix.") We put
these words in bold to
remind you to highlight
your accomplishments in all
your jobs.

EXPERIENCE

ACCOUNTING and PROPERTY TECHNICIAN. Cherry Bekaert & Holland, LLP, 1860 Hannover Square, Warren, MI 56845, Charles Adams, Supervisor, phone: (333) 333-3333, hours worked: 45-50, (2004-present). Excelling in handling diverse responsibilities, have been credited with making changes which have significantly improved operating procedures while supervising three people including accounting clerks and office staff for a business with five separate plant locations.

- Streamline operations in the accounting department and implement changes which have reduced the time needed to complete support activities; for instance, payroll processing which had taken three days is now completed in one.
- Apply knowledge in database creation to establish a new system for tracking equipment purchases and status of computers, printers, vehicles, and other equipment.
- Prepare payroll for up to 36 Cherry Bekaert employees in the company's five plants.
- Manage Workmen's Compensation claims and yearly audits, preparation of forms for OSHA, and monthly approval of employee health insurance; prepare daily bank deposits; post payroll and accounts payable check numbers; issue and then post manual checks; prepare the petty cash sheet; process state and federal tax payments.
- Verify data between the general ledger, accounts payable, and accounts receivable.

ACCOUNTS PAYABLE AND PAYROLL TECHNICIAN. Pechmann-Ellis & Associates, 2583 Ravenhill Circle, Warren, MI 56845, Charles Adams, Supervisor, phone: (444) 444-4444, hours worked: 45-50, (2001-04). After my retirement from the U.S. Army, was recruited by this commercial construction company to handle accounts payable for multimillion-dollar projects and to process payroll for 200 employees.

- Assisted in purchasing support for large projects; prepared weekly and monthly reports for Project Managers and Supervisors.

Other experience gained in the US Army:
PROPERTY ACCOUNTING TECHNICIAN. U.S. Army, 37th Finance Division, Fort Rucker, AL, 77646. Supervisor: MAJ Edgar Nixon, (555) 555-5555, hours per week: 40, (1998-01). As a Property Book Officer and senior logistician for a logistics battalion, was commended in writing for "excellent performance in superbly

performing all assigned missions" while directing management and accountability procedures for supplies, property and equipment worth over $105 million. Worked closely with the subordinate companies to assure smooth transfers of excess equipment out of the battalion. Identified over $750,000 of excess items for turn-in with 63%+ redistributed throughout the corps. Acquired shortage items and force modernization equipment. Expertly utilized both manual and automated property accounting procedures, including VLOS and TAQlS. Exercised staff supervision of the battalion logistics low-density program. Supervised one NCO and one soldier. Ensured all M35A2 cargo trucks were turned in through supply channels. Executed the M4 carbine fielding to the battalion. Achieved "zero defects" in hand-controlled inventory. This battalion's supply and property accountability ranked among the best at Fort Rucker. **Provided the leadership for a drive to reduce excess property and became the "go-to" manager for all companies in the battalion seeking guidance in reducing excess property.**

PROPERTY BOOK OFFICER. U.S. Army, 151st Finance Division, FA Bn, Stuttgart, Germany, APO, AE 564, Supervisor: MAJ David N. Butler, (666) 666-6666, hours per week: 40, (1996-98). Supervised 11 people as Property Book Officer for a Finance Division in Stuttgart. During this time, played a key role in the operation of the Battalion's Finance office in Germany for 2 years, and maintained accountability of one Battalion fuel point, maintaining formal property book records through the use of the Standard Property Book System. Redesigned (SPBS) property valued at $2.1 billion. Provided technical expertise to the chain of command on logistical and budget policies and procedures. Ensured the battalion maintained a rating consistent with its Authorized Level of Organization. My performance was rated as "absolutely outstanding" in this position. Maintained 100% accountability of the organization's property. On my own initiative, developed training and orientation procedures which ensured smooth transition when new personnel assumed control of property. Provided leadership in fielding new modernized equipment including SINCGARS radios, data transfer devices, squad automatic weapons, and radio meters. **Was described in writing as "without a doubt the subject matter expert on property management."**

PROPERTY BOOK OFFICER. U.S. Army, 43rd Intelligence Brigade, Fort Riley, KS 46323-5442. Supervisor: SSG Larry Norris, (555) 555-5555, hours per week: 40, (1993-96). Responsible for all administrative matters pertaining to the Property Book of the Intelligence Brigade, a 1,000-man independent combat team. Maintained organizational hand receipts for eight companies and one battery, including associated shortage annexes and documents supporting files in excess of $70 million. Supervised two enlisted personnel to ensure cyclic and sensitive item inventories were properly conducted and hand receipts reassigned in a timely manner. In this position, constructed a property accounting system using the Standard Property Book System (SPBS-R). In May 1994 during Operation Mission Relief, ensured the brigade's supply requirements were met, coordinating support for two other bases in Fort Campbell, KY, Fort Myer, VA, and Fort Wainwright, AK. Yielded a zero deficit accounting record for all equipment on hand. Also oversaw the transfer of well over 100 railcars of equipment from inactivating intelligence units into the command and the fielding of new equipment. **In a formal performance evaluation, was described thusly: "his knowledge, long-range vision, and desire to conduct all property and supply transactions properly have had a significant impact on the battalion."**

PROPERTY BOOK TECHNICIAN. US Army, B-253rd Intelligence Division, Fort Hood, TX, 87646, Supervisor: SFC Scott Grenald, (666) 666-6666, hours per week: 40, (1990-93). Property Book Officer for this Intelligence Division. Once assigned to the unit, maintained organizational and installation hand receipts for five batteries to include associated shortage annexes and document supporting files in excess of $50 million. Managed excess property by coordinating and monitoring turn-in and lateral transfer directives. Monitored training programs and supervised 11 enlisted personnel. Directed and supervised the fielding of several Force Modernization items of equipment including SINCGARS radios, M40 protective masks, M16A2 rifles, and Mobile Subscriber Equipment (MSE). **Developed a plan for the turn-in or transfer of excess equipment in the battalion totaling 27 LIN items. Maintained 100% property accountability for two separate books.**

PROPERTY BOOK TECHNICIAN. HHC-535, Artillery Brigade, APO AE 13856, Supervisor: MAJ Nathan Jennings, (777) 777-7777, hours per week: 40, (1988-90). Brigade Budget Officer/Supply Technician responsible for monitoring and advising the brigade commander, battalion commanders, and the brigade S4 on the status of budget operations and expenditures. Assisted four battalion property book officers in maintaining property book accountability and providing technical advice and assistance. As the HHC Brigade Property Book Officer, responsible of the accountability of $9 million worth of equipment, property, and supplies. Ensured proper codes and fund cites were placed on unit requisitions to ensure the brigade would receive proper credit, resulting in over $585,000 of funds reimbursed. Instrumental in the development of the brigade's FY 89 budget. Monitored the budget accounts for the brigade and tracked the battalion's budget expenditures and recording procedures. Ensured excess property was identified, redistributed when possible, or disposed of in accordance with standard regulations. Communicated with outside agencies to obtain essential equipment that was critically short within the Army supply system. Ensured all classes of supply were obtained to sustain a field artillery brigade consisting of 5 battalions, 3,000 soldiers, 90 155mm howitzers, 18 rocket launchers, and over 960 wheeled vehicles for six months and during combat operations.

Excelled in a "track record" of promotions with the US Army at Fort Polk, LA:

1986-88: **DIVISION PROPERTY BOOK TEAM CHIEF.** HHC, 67th Artillery, Fort Polk, LA 76307, Supervisor: SSG James A. Hennegan, (888) 888-8888, hours per week: 40. As Property Book Team Chief for Property Book Teams One and Two, provided property accountability for the 1st and 2nd Brigades. Managed over $89 million of assets for the 82d Signal Bn, 307 Engineer Bn, and 618th Engineer Company. Ensured all authorized property was on hand or on requisition. Verified CBS-X asset reporting, unit readiness output, and ensured all records, forms, and printouts were accurate. Responsible for installation and training of a new automated cross-leveling/redistribution program which resulted in saving the Division hundreds of thousands of dollars. From Jan to Jul, served as the Government Accountable Officer (GAO) in Korea prior to being Team Chief for two Property Book teams consisting of 40 units. **As GAO, brought all measures of supply performance above DA standards.**

1984-86: **SUPPLY TECHNICIAN.** 7th Division Infantry, Supervisor: SGT Harold G. Nicholls, (999) 999-9999, hours worked: 40. Maintained organization hand receipts for 19 units, to include associated shortage annexes and supporting documentation files. Provided an audit trail for all supply transaction, and ensured that cyclic and sensitive item inventories were properly conducted and hand receipts signed. Verified CBS-X asset reporting; established and monitored training programs and supervised four enlisted personnel. Utilized state-of-the art equipment to manage $4.6 million worth of deployable equipment of the 1/504th Parachute Infantry Regiment and the 73d Signal Battalion. **Personally cited by GAO auditors and given praiseworthy comment by the Brigade Commander for the timely support and management of supplies and equipment.**

1982-84: **SUPPLY TECHNICIAN.** HHS, 321st Logistics, Supervisor: SGT Wesley K. Combs, phone unknown. hours worked: 40. Was team chief in charge of maintaining organization and installation of hand receipts for 23 units, including associated shortage annexes and supporting documentation files. Managed excess property by coordinating and monitoring turn-in and lateral transfer directives. Verified equipment on-hand asset reporting, unit readiness output, and ensured all cards, form, and printouts were accurate. Established and monitored training programs and supervised team operations consisting of three enlisted personnel.

EDUCATION	**Bachelor of Science Degree in Accounting,** Detroit College of Business, Dearborn, MI, 2000.
	Associate of Science degree in Business Administration, Central Texas College, Killeen, TX, 1993.
SPECIALIZED TRAINING, LICENSES, & CERTIFICATES	Military courses include: Unit Level Logistics System Operator Course, 2001; Property Accounting Technician, 1999; Depot Inventory Reconciliation, 1998; Physical Inventory Management, 1998; Standard Property Book System, 1998; General Supply Technician, 1997; Warrant Officer Entry Course, 1997; NCO Officer Logistics Course, 1996; Supply NCO Advanced Course, 1996; Division Logistics Course, 1995; Unit and Organizational Supply, 1995, and Organizational Maintenance of Radio Field Equipment, 1994.
AWARDS	Humanitarian Service Medal, Noncommissioned Officer's Professional Development Ribbon, Army Service Medal, Overseas Service Ribbon (2nd award), Germany Liberation Medal, Legion of Merit, Bronze Star Medal, Meritorious Service Medal, Army Commendation Medal (2nd award), Army Achievement Medal (3rd award), Army Good Conduct Medal (4th award), National Defense Service Medal (2nd award), European Service Medal with 3 bronze Service Star.

FEDERAL RESUME OR RESUMIX

LAURA C. BRYANT

Address: 1110 1/2 Hay Street, Fayetteville, NC 28305
Home number: (910) 483-6611
SSN: 000-00-0000
E-mail: PREPpub@aol.com

Position, Title, Series, Grade: Human Resources Coordinator, GS-8888-88
Announcement Number: DN-00-000

ADMINISTRATIVE ASSISTANT

Here you see a resumix of a woman who is seeking a position in the property management field.

Notice the words in bold in this federal resume (often called a "Resumix.") We put these words in bold to remind you to highlight your accomplishments in all your jobs.

EDUCATION

Currently pursuing a **Bachelor of Arts degree in Human Resources**, Essex County College, Trenton, NJ.
• Am only one Economics course short of completing my degree.
Completed two-year program at Mercer County Community College, Trenton, NJ 1996.
Graduated from E.A. Burnes High School, Trenton NJ, 1994.

EXPERIENCE

ADMINISTRATIVE ASSISTANT. Maxwell Properties, 698 Wallace Trail, Trenton, NJ 22678 (07/2005-present). Supervisor: Thomas Deaver, Executive Manager: (222) 222-2222. Provide administrative support to four top-selling real estate executives.
• Manage finances for more than 25 staff members.
• Act as the Human Resources representative for personnel pay, travel, and recruitment issues.
• Manage a $100,000 travel budget for real estate executives traveling to company property in various national locations.
• Manage financial, administrative, and travel records while also coordinating efforts with our home office in New York.
• **On formal performance evaluations, was evaluated as "a hard charger who is willing to do whatever it takes to get the job done;" and "an individual with unique ability to coordinate group efforts toward common goal in any given situation" and as "an individual whose advice and technical knowledge is regularly sought by subordinates, peers, and superiors alike."**
• Routinely write and deliver press releases which have been praised for their articulate and concise style; communicate via e-mail and the Internet while also communicating extensively through telephone, meetings, and written correspondence.
• Utilize computers regularly, and develop specialized expertise with Excel while using that program to manage the monthly supplies budget. Am skilled in database management.
• Maintain daily statistical records for annual reports.
• Continuously seek new methods of improving internal efficiency while maintaining administrative and personnel files.

ADMINISTRATIVE ASSISTANT. Wachovia Bank, 6644 Garner Road, Baltimore, MD 29845 (04/2001-07/2005) Supervisor: Allison Malone, Bank Manager (333) 333-3333. In this administrative position, performed numerous human resource duties.
• Reviewed and corrected evaluation reports.
• Prepared reports related to personnel strength, promotions, branch transfers, staff actions, evaluation reports, and various banking personnel assignments.

- Assisted in preparing, coordinating, and monitoring personnel accountability actions.

ADMINISTRATIVE ASSISTANT. Department of Defense, 1548 Faxton Avenue, Baltimore, MD 29887 (05/1999-04/2001). Supervisor: Carlton M. Busch: (444) 444-4444. Assisted three managers supporting 45 staff members; was involved in managing the full range of personnel administration activities.
- Typed military and non-military correspondence. Used notes, drafts, verbal instructions, and other tools to prepare documents.
- Prepared suspense control documents and maintained suspense files.
- In an ongoing process once a month, acted as supervisor in charge of training and managing soldiers in administrative and combat duties; developed lesson plans and gave formal classes; counseled soldiers about personal and career matters.
- Researched, prepared, and processed retirement packets, reclassification packets, "early out" request packets, and other specialty actions.
- Acted as Customer Service Representative for the battalion.
- Analyzed and resolved any problems soldiers and civilians were experiencing related to their promotions, awards, personnel records, and financial matters.
- Handled duties which included filing, writing, and preparing reports and documents.
- Utilized computers for word processing and statistical analysis, and became skilled in database management. Played a key role in providing humanitarian aid and disaster relief for hurricane victims, and received the Humanitarian Service Award.

CLERK TYPIST. Jones & Martin Law, 1168 Cool Springs St., Baltimore, MD 13546 (11/1996-05/1999). Supervisor: Carolyn Heyward: (555) 555-5555. Processed legal documents; performed transcription and dictation duties for memoranda and managed records of oral briefings and conversational notes.
- Maintained database of client evidence, court records, and hearing documentation; distributed copies to lawyers, clients and court attendees. Conducted briefings which included question-and-answer sessions which refined my ability to "think on my feet."
- Used computer databases, files, typed, prepared training reports and documents, and maintained statistical information and records used to compile annual reports.
- Nominated for Employee of the Month for September 1997.

PHOTO-LAYOUT SPECIALIST. Photo Design, 346 Second Street, Trenton, NJ 22877, (7/1995-11/1996). Supervisor: Michael Rowan: (666) 666-6666. Produced photographs, processed and developed film, opaque, and revised maps.

COMPUTERS

Highly proficient in utilizing a variety of software and operating systems.
- Used Microsoft Office including Word, Excel, Access, and PowerPoint.
- Have used Adobe Acrobat when dealing with Internet and HTML software.
- Have automated thousands of files; produced numerous graphics for briefing presentations; produced and maintained administrative files and databases; wrote and produced hundreds of written reports of oral briefings and conversational notes.

TRAINING

Administrative Specialist Course, September 2003
Management Development and Leadership Course, April 2002
Business Management Course Phase I, February 2002
Business Finance Course Phase II, July 2001

CLEARANCE

Held Top Secret security clearance; SCI in progress

HONORS & AWARDS

Achievement Awards (2); Humanitarian Award; Good Conduct Medal; Joint Meritorious Unit Award, Certificate of Appreciation.

FEDERAL RESUME OR RESUMIX

MILDRED R. BROOKHART

1110 1/2 Hay Street

Fayetteville, NC 28305

Home: (910) 483-6611

Work: (910) 483-6611

SSN: 000-00-0000

Position Title/Series/Grade: Housing Manager, GS-0000-00

Announcement Number: DN-00-000

HOUSING MANAGER   **Veteran's Preference:**

EDUCATION & TRAINING

Completed extensive training and continuing education which has included:

Computers: Microsoft Excel for Windows, MS Word 6.0, Microsoft Office 2000, PowerPoint and Systems Administration

Leadership and Professional Development: programs emphasizing human relations, interacting and communicating with the public, Managing for the 21st Century, problems and trends in local government administration

Housing Management and Real Estate: professional housing management seminars, fundamentals of real estate, (licensed real estate salesperson), fair housing workshops, and seminars on Evictions and Landlord/Tenant Law

Personnel Administration: personnel actions, recognizing the legal problems of migrant workers, preventive techniques in employment, sexual harassment, management development and coaching supervision, diversity in the workplace

EXPERIENCE

HOUSING MANAGER. Department of Housing and Urban Development, 2638 McCormick Blvd, Lake Charles, LA 77210 (2001-present). Starting salary: $17,860, ending salary: $38,900. Supervisor: Malcolm Bloomfield, (333) 333-3333, ext. 444. Provide referral services, housing information, and assistance to low-income family members who are authorized to live in the supplemental housing community; assist with management of special projects.

- Receive, investigate, mediate, and resolve landlord/tenant complaints; represent the Department of Housing at Community Development meetings; communicate on a daily basis with realtors and landlords; gather data and prepare documentation for discrimination complaints; inspect property for adequacy.
- Communicate with legal professionals such as magistrates, the State Attorney General's Office, the Staff Judge Advocate (SJA), and with clients of various governmental agencies including state and federal agencies.
- Receive and investigate tenant complaints and coordinate actions with the appropriate housing staff and /or installation officials to include preparing eviction letters; conducting sanitation inspections; and clearing of abandoned quarters.
- Process applicants and manage Section 8 waiting lists; maintain a wide range of records/reports; prepare letters, and memoranda.
- Develop and present awareness and informational briefings to Public Housing organizations nationwide.

- Maintain working knowledge of Section 8 and other related regulations, policies, and procedures pertaining to maintenance/repairs, inspections, eligibility, assignments, occupancy, and terminations.
- Work closely with Housing Authority of Lake Charles on renovation projects, maintenance and repairs, and related issues.
- Operate a data access terminal on-line in order to enter, retrieve, and modify data in the Public and Supplemental Housing Programs (PSHP).
- From Jun 01-Oct 03, handled additional duties as the monitor for mobile home park inspections; provided clerical support using MS Excel to maintain statistics, attended the Housing and Urban Development Control Board Meeting.
- From Jun 02-Feb 03, administered the Utility Deposit Waiver Program to include establishing and administering records and weekly reports, processing applications and coordinating with the Lake Charles Public Works and five other utility companies, acting as liaison for bad debt collections, and identifying trends and making recommendations.
- From Jul 01-Mar 02, was detailed as Customer Service Representative with a focus on receiving, investigating, and resolving complaints on personnel housed in government quarters referred by staff, department directors, and customers. Represented Louisiana State Housing Division at meetings and socials which included City Council Meetings and staff meetings. Researched, set up, and monitored employee customer care and image training. Initiated improvements to customer service and employee morale and comfort. Processed exceptions to policy, prepared eviction letters, conducted sanitation inspections, and responded to client inquiries, coordinating actions with appropriate with government and state officials. Was Project Officer/Editor for a bimonthly housing occupant bulletin which included preparing monthly reports. Evaluated customer feedback and recommended changes/solutions. Developed public awareness information articles, bulletins, and news releases for publication and presentation, coordinating with the Public Affairs Office when appropriate. Responded to Community Mayors and sponsoring unit representatives. Accompanied the Director of Public Housing and Advisor of the Urban Development on community inspection tours and prepared correspondence for the Director's signature mandating corrections of deficiencies noted. Attended Family Symposiums and prepared follow-up responses.
- Serve as Housing Representative on Housing and Urban Development Control Board.
- Member, Professional Urban Development Association (PUDA); served as Vice-President, Treasurer, Secretary and Committee Chairs.

DIRECTOR, JEFFERSON-DAVIS COUNTY HUMAN RELATIONS DEPARTMENT. Jefferson-Davis County, Lake Charles, LA 77212 (1997-01). Salary: $16,000. Supervisor: Eugene Paige, the present County Manager. Position with the county was equivalent to a GS-9/10 in the federal grade structure. Served as an advisor to county officials and local businesses on equal opportunity, human relations, and community issues, reducing conflict and tension among citizens and promoting equal rights; reported directly to the County Manager.
- Managed two employees and worked closely with a 14-person Advisory Commission and the Board of County Commissioners as the liaison for resolving problems.
- Applied analytical skills while mediating and sitting in on meetings to discuss disciplinary actions to be taken against county and local business employees.
- Evaluated and counseled employees; maintained time sheets/personnel records.
- Prepared/administered the departmental budget; developed department objectives.
- Interviewed and counseled individuals and groups with complaints and investigated each situation to find solutions to problems relating to housing, employment, and credit problems; workmen's compensation, employee-employer disputes, and discrimination issues; as well as maintenance, repair, contaminated water supply, poor drainage, and road repair problems.

HOUSING MANAGER

- Prepared and delivered presentations at schools, churches, civic clubs, seminars and on radio and TV talk shows; prepared news releases and articles on human relations issues and programs and publicized noteworthy endeavors.
- Represented the County Manager at statewide and local meetings and served as liaison with other state, county, and federal agencies as well as with the local businesses and the general population to include the Governor's Office, Department of Social Services, Jefferson-Davis Metropolitan Housing Authority, the Lake Charles Health Department, and other organizations involved in human relations/equal opportunity matters.
- Conducted surveys and compiled and analyzed statistics on human relations issues.
- Developed a personnel polices handbook for one local manufacturing company which was having serious personnel problems with disgruntled employees; as a result, management adopted benefit enhancements and less stringent requirements and was rewarded with higher production and lowered turnover and complaints.
- Developed and implemented community awareness workshops and training for local businesses and the local population; member of state and national Human Relations Associations, Lake Charles-Jefferson-Davis County Housing Task Force, Jefferson-Davis County Youth Needs, Legal Aid, and Law Enforcement Relations Committees.
- Developed contests held in county schools to include judging/awards criteria.

EDUCATION & HONORS

Associate of Arts degree in Business Management, McNeese State University, Lake Charles, LA, 1999.
Received numerous certificates of appreciation and achievement including:
Jefferson-Davis County Public Service Award, for work "above and beyond," 2002
Professional Customer Service Award, for exceptional customer service, 2002
Vice President's Certificate of Achievement for "commendable service," 2001
PUDA William P. Fenton Award, 2001
Plaque from Department of Housing and Urban Development for "unselfish and dedicated services," 1999-01
Exceptional Performance Appraisals, 1997-1998, and 1998-99, with monetary awards
Certificate from Governor Carlton E. McDaniels for "outstanding citizen involvement," 1997
Profiled in the March 1997 issue of the Louisiana Human Relations Council newsletter
Certificate, St. Peters Baptist Church for "meritorious human relations service," 1999

PERSONAL

Offer a keen eye for detail and excellent organizational and interpersonal skills.

EXAMPLE OF A KSA

PAIGE L. FORBES

SSN: 000-00-0000

ACCOUNTING CLERK, GS-05 ANNOUNCEMENT #XYZ123

KSA #1: Ability to communicate in writing.

Overview of my work experience: In the jobs described below, I have received a **Certificate of Outstanding Performance** each and every year from 2003-present and have been cited each year for **performing all duties in an outstanding manner.** I have been commended on numerous occasions for my ability to communicate in writing in a concise, articulate, and effective manner. I have earned a reputation as an excellent writer.

In my current position as Accounting Clerk, NF-2, I communicate extensively in writing in the process of reviewing, analyzing, and preparing a wide variety of documentation and paperwork while assuring that paperwork is always within guidelines established by regulatory authorities and other authorities. In creating documents for written communication and transmission, I maintain, update, and utilize a variety of data systems and using personal computers. I operate a computer with Time Management Labor System software and Microsoft Office software to include Word, Excel, PowerPoint, and Access. I communicate in writing by composing and typing all correspondence for Supply and Warehouse Section. While communicating in writing, I demonstrate my outstanding knowledge of English grammar and my mastery of spelling. One of my responsibilities is to communicate in writing as I present my analysis of the supply budget on Excel software and as I prepare flyers for the MWR Auction on PowerPoint. Furthermore, I maintain and prepare all NAF time cards using the Time Management Labor System software. In addition, I maintain the annual budget for Supply & Warehouse and the Recycling Section and I use the internal software (NAF Financial Management Budget System). My writing skills combined with my knowledge of computer programs enables me to write and edit all performance appraisals for all employees within the section; to type memoranda for the Chief, Technical Services Branch; to maintain and print all NAF time cards, and to maintain written correspondence related to the annual budget for Supply and Warehouse and Recycling Section and Forward to Budget Office.

Knowledge and Training related to this KSA:

- In 2005 I took a Microsoft Office course at Galveston Technical Community College. This course enabled me to use Word, Excel, PowerPoint, and Access to type a variety of material and documents for the Supply and Warehouse Section.
- In 2001 I took 116 hours of IBM Operations at Western Texas Technical College. This refined my knowledge, skills, and abilities in operating a computer.
- In 2000 I took a NAF Financial Management Budget System Course at Fort Hood, TX. This course gave me the knowledge, skills and ability to maintain the NAF budget for Supply and Warehouse, and the Recycling Section.
- In 1999 I took 33 hours of word processing with Word at Galveston Technical Community College. This enabled me to type documents and material using Word.

EXAMPLE OF A KSA

SEAN V. TIMMONS

SSN: 000-00-0000

BUILDING MANAGER, GS-07 ANNOUNCEMENT #XYZ123

BUILDING MANAGER, GS-07 Announcement #XYZ123 KSA #1

KSA #1: Knowledge of government building practices, regulations, and policies.

Through my military career, which I began as an enlisted soldier and finished as a CW4, I have been placed in charge of multimillion-dollar assets and in charge of government buildings.

From 2001-05, while serving as a Property Manager at Ft. Bragg, handled a wide range of responsibilities in addition to my job as an instructor pilot.

Property Management and Maintenance Management Responsibilities:

- Played a key role in determining maintenance needs of the fifteen UH-60A helicopters in this organization's fleet.
- Was responsible for the development and implementation of an annual and long-range maintenance program with emphasis on preventive maintenance. Coordinated and scheduled critical repairs and maintenance/cleaning and conducted installation or cleaning in the facility and grounds. Monitored all maintenance and equipment installation projects for timeliness, correctness, and completion. Oversaw replacement and/or repair of fixtures and devices of buildings which housed the organization's aviation fleet. Exercised control and responsibility over the facility ensuring that all necessary maintenance, repair, alternations or modifications were accomplished.

This KSA relates to a Property Management position.

From 1998-01 as Property Officer for the 419th Special Operations Aviation Detachment (Airborne) at Yuma Proving Ground, was in charge of $70 million in equipment including four buildings and a hangar. In that same job I also functioned as Executive Officer so it was my responsibility to oversee the management of maintenance building, dining facilities, medical facility barracks, and administrative buildings. Since this organization was in a "start-up" phase, it was my responsibility to establish the organization's first annual and long-range maintenance program with emphasis on preventive maintenance. Coordinated schedules for critical repairs and maintenance/cleaning and conducted installation or cleaning in the facility and grounds. Since it was my responsibility to purchase all equipment and fixtures within the structures which I managed, I exercised control of the equipment installation projects for timeliness and correctness. Exercised control and responsibility over a $10 million budget.

My training and education related to this KSA includes:

Basic Noncommissioned Officer Course, 1996; Advanced NCO Course, 1997
Warrant Officer Basic Course, 2000; Warrant Officer Advanced Course, 2002

My formal education has helped me acquire knowledge of effective property management techniques. I hold a B.S. in Professional Aeronautics with a Minor in Safety. I am completing a Master of Science in Aerospace Technology and hold an A.S. in Criminal Justice.

KSA #2: Ability to communicate effectively, both orally and in writing.

I believe my outstanding communication skills, both oral and written, have been the key to my highly successful military career which began as an enlisted soldier. Progressed rapidly into the NCO ranks, and then into the warrant officer career field. In all of my jobs since 2001, I have worn the hat of Instructor Pilot and/or Flight Examiner, which put me in the position of training, evaluating, and communicating with other pilots. In the formal performance evaluation for my most recent job during the period 2002-05, was cited as the "key element in the successful formation and train-up of Mike Company." Trained 10 pilots from RL3 to RL1 status in day, night, and night vision goggles in a three-month period in a new organization recently formed under the Aviation Restructuring Initiative. Was described in writing as "a spectacular role model for all the young warrant officers in the company" and was praised for leading by example and making myself available at all times to provide advice or guidance. **Cited as "an unequaled source of learning for aviators of all experience levels" and "a trainer who radiates self confidence and enthusiasm that is infectious to all."**

Also proved my ability to communicate effectively, orally and in writing, in activities other than pilot training and evaluation. For example, I was DA-selected and personally requested by the commanding officer of a newly started organization in 1998-01 at Yuma Proving Ground, AZ. It was my responsibility to act as Property Officer and Information Management Officer for this special operations aviation unit. As one of my first management actions, I literally got on the phone and secured $300,000 in funds which allowed me to get the organization into a mission-ready posture. While managing the organization's $1.4 million budget and making all purchasing decisions related to equipment and property needed by this organization, I communicated extensively with vendors to obtain assets.

My communication skills were evident in my career as an enlisted soldier, too. For example, as Senior Drill Sergeant from 1997-98, I trained and supervised six other drill sergeants at a correctional facility which received up to 60 new soldiers every nine weeks who had committed criminal offenses of some type. Earned widespread respect for my communication skills and was praised in a formal enlisted evaluation report:

- **"Has developed innovative motivational training which instilled a high degree of team work among the trainee personnel."**
- **"His efforts have constantly resulted in higher motivated teams with superior personal standards and a higher degree of morale than other teams in the Activity."**

My training and education related to this KSA includes:
Basic Noncommissioned Officer Course, 1996; Advanced NCO Course, 1997
Warrant Officer Basic Course, 2000; Warrant Officer Advanced Course, 2002
B.S. in Professional Aeronautics with a Minor in Safety

BUILDING MANAGER, GS-07 Announcement #XYZ123 KSA #2

You'll see the communication KSAs very frequently!

MORE EXAMPLES OF KSAs

GWENDOLYN McLEOD

SSN: 000-00-0000

CONTRACT ADMINISTRATOR, GS-09 ANNOUNCEMENT #XYZ123

KSA #2: Ability to meet and deal effectively with others.

In my most recent job as a contract specialist from 2/15/03 to present, excelled in administering the contract with Konica for 32 copiers and was the author of the training manual used to teach local personnel to use this new equipment. In this capacity I met regularly with and dealt effectively with a wide variety of people including civilian vendors. I was the point of contact in charge of arranging for these vendors to teach classes in which local personnel learned to use the copiers correctly. I also dealt with others while involved in most aspects of contract administration which included making recommendations during contract disputes, small purchase actions, and contract termination actions as well as during the negotiation of rates and charges, modifications, small purchase actions, and the issuance of contract modifications and change orders. Applied my ability to deal with others effectively while conducing complex negotiations in order to acquire equipment and services for the computing center. While using my purchasing expertise and research skills to reduce contract costs, was the point of contact for maintenance and repair calls as well as for checking the machines, escorting the service technician and explaining the problem, monitoring their work on the machines, handling the paperwork for payment, and tracking funds. In general, was counted on to solve many problems in the contracting area and streamlined the renewal process.

Applied my effective "people" skills during a functional reorganization from resources management to support services and personally underwent a radical redefinition of my responsibilities and program areas. One of my major new responsibilities was in the area of helping coach and train new analysts who assumed my old responsibilities. Trained and provided mentoring and guidance in the areas of procedures for running the copy center, processing print requests, administering a cost-per-copy program, and monitoring contract renewals for FY 05. Displayed my time management skills and willingness to assist other employees while working continuously under a heavy workload and extremely tight deadlines. Refined the ability to prioritize simultaneous high-priority jobs and worked closely in cooperation with my supervisor to ensure needs and expectations were met. Was cited for my availability to other workers and willingness to help them meet their goals during peak periods.

From 2/00 to 3/03 as a contract specialist, became a trusted advisor to higher level management personnel and a respected colleague who was often called on by others to provide technical advice regarding all aspects of contracting. In the capacity of technical advisor to other purchasing agents and new contracting specialists, provided on-the-job training, dealt with personnel from outside the organization while acting as point of contact for the acquisition of complex technical equipment, supplies, and services through the use of invitations for bids and requests for proposals. As the bid opening officer, conducted contract negotiations and managed the procurement process for specialized ADP equipment as well as for accompanying maintenance, repair, and technical services. Demonstrated the ability to communicate clearly, tactfully, and effectively and deal with a wide range of people from employees, to vendors, to managers, to HTB representatives. Became recognized as the chief problem solver for any type of contract administration problems and became the individual in charge of training new employees in the proper procedures for contract preparation and administration. These skills were also applied during dispute resolution activities when I worked with contractors and government personnel to handle disputes and was the one who issued the final decision. Processed protests to the agency, FGP, or FTCDB according to applicable regulations. Stayed aware and anticipated possible problems so disputes could be avoided.

From 11/97 to 2/00 as a purchasing agent with the Internal Revenue Service, applied my skills in dealing with others in an effective manner while providing guidance to contractors, reviewing and analyzing any problems which occurred, investigating problems, and processing disputes. Was sought out for my positive attitude, cheerful manner, and reputation as a fast worker and asked to help out in the administrative area during an extremely busy period with a heavy backlog of work.

From 8/96 to 11/97 as a homemaker and mother, applied my ability to deal with others effectively in numerous community volunteer roles and held leadership roles in numerous organizations. Volunteered more than 150 hours in an elementary school reading and remediation program and more than 216 hours as a kindergarten instructor and classroom assistant. Was elected to the executive board of a PTA and served on numerous scholarship and arts committees.

From 7/94 to 8/96 as a purchasing agent, demonstrated strong analytical skills and a record of excellent performance and was selected to receive special training in construction contract administration. In this job I was required to deal with people effectively while developing and refining skills in negotiating terms and prices with contractors. Was often called on to clarify issues such as billing procedures and equipment and material substitutions.

Education and training related to this KSA

Hold a Bachelor of Science Degree in Political Science from the Seattle Pacific University. In addition to my extensive hands-on, on-the-job education and training in every aspect of the contracting process, have taken advantage of every opportunity to increase my knowledge of contracting through formal courses, seminars, and workshops including:

- Analysis Review of Management (4/05)
- Law and Government Contracts (11/05)
- Defense Purchases Training (9/02)
- Techniques of Contracting (6/02)
- Technical Officer/Contract Representative (TOCR)/Quality Assurance Evaluator (QAE) Competition Advocate's Training - Competition in Contracting (3/01)
- Justification for Other than Full and Open Competition (10/01)
- Preparing Statements of Work and Purchasing Descriptions (5/00)
- ADP Contracting (4/00)
- Procurement Techniques (1/00)
- Contracting by Negotiations (12/00)
- Contracting by Sealed Bid (8/99)
- Small Purchase/Scheduled Contracts (8/99)
- Cost/Price Analysis and Negotiation Techniques (11/99)
- Contract Administration (2/98)

ABOUT THE EDITOR

Anne McKinney holds an MBA from the Harvard Business School and a BA in English from the University of North Carolina at Chapel Hill. A noted public speaker, writer, and teacher, she is the senior editor for PREP's business and career imprint, which bears her name. Early titles in the Anne McKinney Career Series (now called the Real-Resumes Series) published by PREP include: *Resumes and Cover Letters That Have Worked, Resumes and Cover Letters That Have Worked for Military Professionals, Government Job Applications and Federal Resumes, Cover Letters That Blow Doors Open,* and *Letters for Special Situations.* Her career titles and how-to resume-and-cover-letter books are based on the expertise she has acquired in 25 years of working with job hunters. Her valuable career insights have appeared in publications of the "Wall Street Journal" and other prominent newspapers and magazines.

PREP Publishing Order Form

You may purchase our titles from your favorite bookseller! Or send a check, money order or your credit card number for the total amount, plus $4.00 for postage and handling, to PREP, 1110 1/2 Hay Street, Suite C, Fayetteville, NC 28305. You may also order our titles on our website at www.prep-pub.com and feel free to e-mail us at preppub@aol.com or call 910-483-6611 with your questions or concerns.

Name: _____

Address: _____

E-mail address: _____

Payment Type: ☐ Check/Money Order ☐ Visa ☐ MasterCard

Credit Card Number: _____ Expiration Date: _____

Put a check beside the items you are ordering:

☐ $16.95—REAL-RESUMES FOR RESTAURANT, FOOD SERVICE & HOTEL JOBS. Anne McKinney, Editor

☐ $16.95—REAL-RESUMES FOR MEDIA, NEWSPAPER, BROADCASTING & PUBLIC AFFAIRS JOBS. Anne McKinney, Editor

☐ $16.95—REAL-RESUMES FOR RETAILING, MODELING, FASHION & BEAUTY JOBS. Anne McKinney, Editor

☐ $16.95—REAL-RESUMES FOR HUMAN RESOURCES & PERSONNEL JOBS. Anne McKinney, Editor

☐ $16.95—REAL-RESUMES FOR MANUFACTURING JOBS. Anne McKinney, Editor

☐ $16.95—REAL-RESUMES FOR AVIATION & TRAVEL JOBS. Anne McKinney, Editor

☐ $16.95—REAL-RESUMES FOR POLICE, LAW ENFORCEMENT & SECURITY JOBS. Anne McKinney, Editor

☐ $16.95—REAL-RESUMES FOR SOCIAL WORK & COUNSELING JOBS. Anne McKinney, Editor

☐ $16.95—REAL-RESUMES FOR CONSTRUCTION JOBS. Anne McKinney, Editor

☐ $16.95—REAL-RESUMES FOR FINANCIAL JOBS. Anne McKinney, Editor

☐ $16.95—REAL-RESUMES FOR COMPUTER JOBS. Anne McKinney, Editor

☐ $16.95—REAL-RESUMES FOR MEDICAL JOBS. Anne McKinney, Editor

☐ $16.95—REAL-RESUMES FOR TEACHERS. Anne McKinney, Editor

☐ $16.95—REAL-RESUMES FOR CAREER CHANGERS. Anne McKinney, Editor

☐ $16.95—REAL-RESUMES FOR STUDENTS. Anne McKinney, Editor

☐ $16.95—REAL-RESUMES FOR SALES. Anne McKinney, Editor

☐ $16.95—REAL ESSAYS FOR COLLEGE AND GRAD SCHOOL. Anne McKinney, Editor

☐ $25.00—RESUMES AND COVER LETTERS THAT HAVE WORKED. McKinney, Editor

☐ $25.00—RESUMES AND COVER LETTERS THAT HAVE WORKED FOR MILITARY PROFESSIONALS. McKinney, Editor

☐ $25.00—RESUMES AND COVER LETTERS FOR MANAGERS. McKinney, Editor

☐ $25.00—GOVERNMENT JOB APPLICATIONS AND FEDERAL RESUMES: Federal Resumes, KSAs, Forms 171 and 612, and Postal Applications. McKinney, Editor

☐ $25.00—COVER LETTERS THAT BLOW DOORS OPEN. McKinney, Editor

☐ $25.00—LETTERS FOR SPECIAL SITUATIONS. McKinney, Editor

☐ $16.95—REAL-RESUMES FOR NURSING JOBS. McKinney, Editor

☐ $16.95—REAL-RESUMES FOR AUTO INDUSTRY JOBS. McKinney, Editor

☐ $24.95—REAL KSAs--KNOWLEDGE, SKILLS & ABILITIES--FOR GOVERNMENT JOBS. McKinney, Editor

☐ $24.95—REAL RESUMIX AND OTHER RESUMES FOR FEDERAL GOVERNMENT JOBS. McKinney, Editor

☐ $24.95—REAL BUSINESS PLANS AND MARKETING TOOLS ... Samples to use in your business. McKinney, Editor

☐ $16.95—REAL-RESUMES FOR ADMINISTRATIVE SUPPORT, OFFICE & SECRETARIAL JOBS. Anne McKinney, Editor

☐ $16.95—REAL-RESUMES FOR FIREFIGHTING JOBS. Anne McKinney, Editor

☐ $16.95—REAL-RESUMES FOR JOBS IN NONPROFIT ORGANIZATIONS. Anne McKinney, Editor

☐ $16.95—REAL-RESUMES FOR SPORTS INDUSTRY JOBS. Anne McKinney, Editor

☐ $16.95—REAL-RESUMES FOR LEGAL & PARALEGAL JOBS. Anne McKinney, Editor

☐ $16.95—REAL-RESUMES FOR ENGINEERING JOBS. Anne McKinney, Editor

☐ $22.95—REAL-RESUMES FOR U.S. POSTAL SERVICE JOBS. Anne McKinney, Editor

☐ $16.95—REAL-RESUMES FOR REAL ESTATE & PROPERTY MANAGEMENT JOBS. Anne McKinney, Editor

☐ $16.95—REAL-RESUMES FOR SUPPLY & LOGISTICS JOBS. Anne McKinney, Editor

_____ **TOTAL ORDERED (add $4.00 for shipping and handling)**

Would you like to explore the possibility of having PREP's writing
team create a resume for you similar to the ones in this book?

For a brief free consultation, call 910-483-6611
or send $4.00 to receive our Job Change Packet to
PREP, 1110 1/2 Hay Street, Fayetteville, NC 28305. Visit our
website to find valuable career resources: www.prep-pub.com!

QUESTIONS OR COMMENTS? E-MAIL US AT PREPPUB@AOL.COM